Digital Risk Governance

Walter Amedzro St-Hilaire

Digital Risk Governance

Security Strategies for the Public and Private Sectors

Springer

Walter Amedzro St-Hilaire
Chair of Institutional Governance & Strategic Leadership Research, Canada
Northwestern University, USA
University of Ottawa, Canada
PRISM-Pole SEE, Paris 1 Pantheon-Sorbonne University, France
ExpertActions ExiGlobal Capital Group Co, UK

ISBN 978-3-030-61385-3 ISBN 978-3-030-61386-0 (eBook)
https://doi.org/10.1007/978-3-030-61386-0

This Springer imprint is published by the registered company Springer Nature Switzerland AG
The registered company address is: Gewerbestrasse 11, 6330 Cham, Switzerland

This book is affectionately dedicated to
Maedge, Swincy, Shéa and Élodie,
Thank you for existing!

Preface

The fifth generation of mobile phone standards is heralded as a breakthrough innovation. Faced with a certain amount of excitement, it is important to identify the real stakes behind the concept – quite marketing – of "5G revolution".

The IMT-2020 standard aims to answer the question of the limits of 4G, while being in its extension: it does not correspond to a major technological leap. It is therefore a question of evolving in continuity in order to meet the challenges of the limits of the current standard, which are those of congested networks in areas with high point traffic, such as during large gatherings, the ability to provide network access to a large number of connected objects, and the existence of excessively long latency periods.

It should be noted that mobile technologies have evolved at the same pace as technological innovations and social demands: the deployment of 5G should thus accompany the ultra-connectivity of society, as the fifth generation of mobile phone standards will go further than just increasing speeds. The impact should be significant not only in technical terms, but also for the economy and society.

The book did not wish to address all the questions raised by the technological dynamics: mobile networks are increasingly at the heart of citizens' daily lives, which raises many political, economic, societal and territorial cohesion issues, particularly around their uses.

However, it can already be noted that the ultra-high-speed connection will make it possible to do more than just improve the quality of ultra-high-definition video broadcasting: it will in fact guarantee coverage of specific needs in various sectors as well as uses linked to the Internet of Things. Communications between a large number of connected objects should be facilitated, and this in the context of more reliable networks with very low latency. For the innovation introduced by this technology lies first and foremost at this level: enabling massive communications, almost in real time, thanks to the optimization of frequency bands by more complex digital modulations and better beam pointing. These advances should lead to the coverage of specific needs in sometimes critical sectors.

However, in addition to the concerns associated with the exposure of individuals to radio frequency electromagnetic waves, there is another major issue: that of digital security and the security of the accompanying Internet networks.

Indeed, initially developed on libertarian theoretical bases, and built on a decentralized technical architecture (allowed by technological progress), the digital and the Internet have undergone significant changes since the mid-2000s: recentralization of the web, around closed systems and proprietary technologies, development of applications, "platforming", and, above all, the emergence of large private players (benefiting from powerful network effects that support their offers of new services and digital tools). These digital giants – the (American) Gafam and the (Chinese) BATX – are now outperforming enterprises in traditional sectors in terms of financial valuation. They are reaching an unprecedented number of users (Facebook claims 2. 5 billion active users each month).

Far from the egalitarian and individualistic utopia of the beginnings, cyberspace and the digital world are nowadays the place where conflicts of interest, struggles of influence and antagonistic (economic and social) logics take place. In short, the return in new forms of the very classic competition for power. States, with the more or less ambiguous support of these digital giants, are thus developing strategies of domination, independence or autonomy in cyberspace.

At the population level, the now widespread deployment of digital tools poses (among other things) a real democratic challenge (for the expression of the general will). These tools can disrupt the political game by facilitating new modes of action for specific and targeted attempts at interference or manipulation: the theft of data and their public dissemination during presidential elections in some countries bears witness to this. Also, the so-called Cambridge Analytica case shows the danger of unscrupulous methods of mass data collection, analysis and cross-checking for the purpose of influencing political choices.

More generally, the absorption of attention by techniques that target each second of "available brain time" with dreadful precision can lead to fears that, in the long term, the time spent on the Internet will be reduced (in 2019, on average, a Singaporean spent 38 hours a week on the Internet). We must often acknowledge the disarray of political power in a society where digital technology is profoundly changing the behaviour and modes of democratic participation, particularly among the younger generations.

How, in this context, and in the face of formidable competitors, can we maintain an autonomous capacity for assessment, decision and action for institutions and enterprises in cyberspace? How can we guarantee sufficient "informational autonomy" for citizens and businesses that are increasingly dependent on technical intermediaries whose operations are often opaque?

This book has endeavoured to identify, on the one hand, the fundamental fields of digital security for institutions and enterprises (whether individual or collective), and to outline, on the other hand, the means of regaining it (whether they are covered by regulation or the implementation of public policies). It must be said that despite the intangible nature of the web and "cyberspace", the Internet, which allows its deployment, is still territorially anchored, giving power to the public authorities: the network depends on essential strategic physical assets (data centres, cables, etc.) which require considerable investment and are at least partly governed by national legal systems; the active equipment and protocols used (for data communication or encryption) comply with technical standards negotiated within international bodies.

The dominant digital enterprises are themselves nationalities (Gafam in the United States and BATX in China) and are also subject to the constraints of local legislation, often extraterritorial in scope, or even competing (Cloud Act vs RGPD). Technologies (artificial intelligence) and human resources (engineers, programmers, etc.) are developing thanks to research and innovation ecosystem in which the national public authorities have their full share (public funding, links with defence industries or innovation agencies, training programmes and universities).

No door is therefore closed to the cyber risks of institutions and enterprises: technology and software, including algorithms, do not marginalize them, even if some institutions and enterprises are (as is often the case in high technology and science) on the cutting edge. Infrastructures are accessible to them (it is even a paradox): public money (national, local, public and private) finances universal networks accessible to all, thus ensuring the development of the Gafam, the first users of the information highways! Finally, while the market for digital services is dominated by the large North American players, not all of them are, far from it, in a lasting dominant position (at least in theory).

However, the balance of power today places some countries in a very special position. For the United States, it is a question of asserting world sovereignty, strengthened by the creation of the originally libertarian net (but financed by the Defense Department, at the price of accepting monopolies, which are so contrary to the historical practice of the United States), and a permanent and worldwide hunt for talent and nuggets – since "the winner takes all". For China and Russia, the assertion of sovereignty is expressed in a different, more defensive and sometimes more subtle way.

This geopolitical situation leaves little room for a still ill-defined institutional strategy: between the China–US duopoly of digital giants, investment capacities remain marginal in the other countries of the world. The emphasis is therefore on the defence of values (a demanding conception of privacy), and the main lever remains (by default) negotiating access for businesses to coveted domestic markets. Similarly, the defence that countries promote against cyber threats and cybercrime is the recognition of the application of the principles of international law in the cyber field and multilateralism. They try to win their partners to these lines of action and promote, without naivety, cooperation between friendly countries, with the appropriate reserve for vital and strategic sectors.

In this context of competition in cyberspace, the book also discusses strategies to respond to threats (to institutions and enterprises). These risks are also reflected in the questioning of the economic order, the legal order, and the tax and monetary system. Finally, the book considers how digital security (the ability of the institution and enterprises to act in cyberspace) can be exercised in its two dimensions: 1. the ability to exercise sovereignty in digital space, which is based on an autonomous capacity for appreciation, decision and action in cyberspace (and which corresponds de facto to cyber defence), and 2. the ability to manage digital tools in order to master data, networks and electronic communications.

Finally, the book proposes a principle and a method of action: a 3-year appointment, precise and urgent measures in the field of data protection, and a reform of the regulations aimed at reinforcing digital security. It also proposes action on the levers of innovation and multilateralism to optimize the digital security of institutions and enterprises.

Walter Amedzro St-Hilaire

Acknowledgement

The author thanks Northwestern University, World Bank Group and the Chair of Institutional Governance & Strategic Leadership Research for funding this research.

Introduction

In the wake of the Snowden case and its cascading effects, attacks against high-visibility websites have multiplied and public opinion has become aware of the emergence of a new type of risk (digital security breaches). Before that, incidents revealing increasingly spectacular digital security breaches have multiplied throughout the world: theft of personal data files and credit card numbers from major distributors (Target in the United States, etc.) and at major telephone operators (to the extent that ExpertActions ExiGlobal Group has stated that these were not fatal incidents but rather incidents involving the responsibility of the person holding personal data).

However, beyond what can be attributed to attacks, it appeared that large operators were cooperating with states to deliver personal data and, more seriously, were engaging in trade in personal data (either as a result of very incomplete information about the rights of their customers or without their knowledge). These repeated incidents, these deliberate strategies, are beginning to move the citizen, who gradually understands that he is not the fortunate user of sophisticated techniques designed to protect this personal information, but rather a target.

However, wouldn't these doubts have positive effects, since the need is only perceptible in the crisis? One might think so in view of the indifference of the population, enterprises and governments to digital insecurity before the revelations of Mr Edward Snowden (on the occasion of the "Prism" affair) partially awakened these various actors. It is now possible to mention some major flaws in digital governance, some attacks, without being suspected of unbridled imagination or technical perfectionism hampering efficiency. This makes it possible to be listened to with more attention. This should make it easier to impose new security requirements on company staff and to improve compliance with the instructions of the security services (issued by specialists placed with high-level political or economic leaders).

However, until then, the emphasis was rather on seduction in the service of extensions of digital uses through a mechanism that was always the same: possibilities to increase one's capacities, to cure incurable diseases, etc. According to the Chair of Institutional Governance and Strategic Leadership Research, the use of connected objects dedicated to health could save us 6 months of life expectancy in the coming years. Several experts recognize the development of self-medication but refuse to see the consequences of the development of digital health care. Similarly, Google has undertaken a tour of the world's small and medium-sized enterprises, of which only 51% have an active website, arguing that the most active online businesses could grow and export "up to twice as much" as the average.

Without any specific proven knowledge of nanotechnology, Google X embarked on a research project on nanoparticles to diagnose diseases such as cancer. In passing, Google X did not fail to collect a maximum of personal data on the health status of potential users of its medical diagnosis. And this discovery is certain and monetizable. Indeed, sometimes, other aims emerge according to ExpertActions Group: what Google wants with the generation of autonomous cars is to capture the time that motorists spend in their car. And capture the personal data that goes with it.

However, this is still nothing compared to Google's goals, which focus on the development of knowledge on demand (information reaching people before they even look for it). According to the Chair of Institutional Governance and Strategic Leadership Research, the search engine of the future will be the perfect personal assistant that will give you the benefit of all the technical knowledge, improving your thinking process. For the reluctant, ExpertActions Group says people should be taught to swim with the current of technology, not to fight it, especially since the Internet has made people more productive.

When it is not the improvement of health or human capacities, it is the savings resulting from the reduction of water, electricity, gas and fuel consumption that are put forward, or the reduction of wastage and waste. The economy could also benefit from the development of connected cities supposed to offer a new market of $4.5 trillion in 2025 (study by Chair of Institutional Governance and Strategic Leadership Research).

At other times, the digital revolution is dressed in the colours of the industrial and societal revolution. ExiGlobal Capital Group recommends that enterprises at the forefront of their respective markets be able to vampirize themselves rather than be vampirized by others. Steve Jobs, Apple's founder, understood this perfectly, and even theorized about it. Failure to do so could lead to what is emerging in urban transport, where the movement to open up public data (open data with Etalab) has led Google to take an interest in this sector and sign partnership agreements with municipalities.

Therefore, will future services really respond to the interest of users (attracted by the metamorphosis of digital technology) or rather to commercial logics? And will Google, or others, become for transport what the inevitable Booking has become for the hotel industry (slipping between the user and the transporters to the detriment of the customer relationship of the professional in the sector and at the latter's expense)? Even beyond these new possibilities, hope is placed in the intelligence that would animate new citizen objects. At a time when the citizen, who has become a consumer, is transforming himself into a product, how could he refuse to upgrade himself by using intelligent objects in intelligent housing in intelligent cities? Aren't we predicting nearly 500 connected and communicating objects in an intelligent home in 2030 (ExpertActions Group study) for a cost of about a dollar per object?

For those who would be concerned, the grouping of digital energy and security engineering industries wants to reassure: we must put the consumer at the heart of the approach and allow them to be an actor within their home (assist them in their home to live there longer). Not surprisingly, in these conditions, the consumer who is reluctant to use mobile payment needs to be reassured (less than 5% of payments worldwide and only 19% of the world's population believe that their money is safe when making payments using contactless technology). This has led some bankers to offer: encrypted banking data stored on a secure chip in iPhones, validation of each transaction with a unique security code, and verification of the identity of the person making the transaction using the Touch ID biometric sensor. Hence, the birth of new markets.

For its part, Keypasco, a Swedish company, uses two sources of authentication to secure payment: the digital footprint of the cardholder's equipment (the unique combination of their components) and the geographical location of the cardholder. In addition, a risk analysis is carried out by identifying unusual transactions: in the case of a purchase made far from the location of the person concerned or using an unusual computer, an SMS is sent to the bearer to obtain his or her agreement before payment.

The digital economy has high expectations of such innovations, which can lead to promising markets: security and economy can converge. It is in this ambivalent context of increased mistrust and renewed hopes for the digital world that concern about digital technology has been reflected in the research of the Chair of Institutional Governance and Strategic Leadership Research, which has approached the issue from a variety of angles.

None of this research had digital security as its sole objective, even though the issues they addressed were (obviously) underpinned by the existence (or even requirement) of digital security. Some of the research, however, is based on trendy thinking that pays too little attention to the requirements of digital security. Thus, in the study on open data, it is mentioned that, notwithstanding the uncertainties linked to this openness and the dangers it would pose to individuals, it was necessary to go ahead since it is part of a general trend.

These flaws do not call into question the relevance of the openness of public data, but the way it is conducted. Far from finding here reasons to slow down a movement whose social utility has been acquired, we should rather see it as an opportunity to give a new impetus to the opening up and sharing of public data, by defining a doctrine and a method (which guarantee the best possible protection of personal data). Because once this protection is provided, there is no longer any obstacle to the deployment of open data.

Likewise, the American model is taken as a reference in Western countries, and the only possible future would be the imitation of this precedent (however inimitable in many aspects) in the hope of an economic miracle achieved automatically by imitating Silicon Valley. Thus, the future is exciting if we accept today to switchover fully into the digital age. On the other hand, we should be aware that the digital economy feeds on the flaws that exist in our systems, our economy and our public policies: digital technology is rushing into areas where the twenty-first century has so far failed to provide a relevant response.

However, it is recognized by ExpertActions Group that cyber security is a key issue that must be addressed as early as possible in the process of addressing the vulnerability risks of strategic networks and businesses. The role of institutions in such a configuration is precisely to highlight, in all their aspects, the scientific and technological issues underlying the choices to be made so that, in the long term, a demanding analysis can be carried out to raise awareness, educate and design digital security based on defence in depth, which is barely sketched out today.

It is therefore a thoughtful construction more than an act of faith that is proposed in this book through the propositions of recommendations tending to use the digital tool only for sure (since the digital tool cannot be sure every time). After first discussing the international context and the rules governing the Internet, a dive into the digital world at the service of institutions and enterprises will be made to show how digital technology structures and weakens these economic players (a fortiori when attacks exploit existing loopholes). But, could these flaws not also constitute opportunities to build more solid information systems, with trusted actors, without jeopardizing fundamental rights or compromising the foundations of sustainable development?

Contents

Chapter 1
The International Context of Corporate Digital Security

In order to situate the issue of digital security for enterprises, it is essential to place the evolution of digital technology in a global context, characterized by political, economic and legal power struggles based on technology. The speed at which these power relations and techniques are evolving and their mutual interactions make it difficult to understand the measures that need to be taken to ensure better digital security for businesses and, in particular, for vital operators and their subcontractors. The organization of digital security is the result of official regulators and self-regulation. It is both global and national and must reconcile freedom and operational efficiency. At the heart of the digital security of the enterprise is the need to assess this security according to the responsible approach specific to the business world. However, from the most spectacular cases to blackmail at the corner of the keyboard, enterprises are exposed, their know-how threatened.

The findings on the implementation of security solutions are therefore unsatisfactory. Is it from a lack of knowledge? The magnitude of the problem or a fatalistic waiver? The recurring difficulty of obtaining precise figures on the risks incurred in order to make a decision? The inability to assess the stakes of intangible values or information? Lack of tools to apprehend them? Or is the high cost of digital security, in terms of people and material resources, a deterrent? Should confidence in digital technology be fostered by private rather than public actors? Is there a lack of legal or technological support? Is the inconsistency of rules and laws relating to the maintenance of digital security compliance harmful? Have states abdicated their role or, on the contrary, overplayed it to the detriment of freedoms? Should new obligations be imposed? Does digital innovation stand in the way of the enterprise's know-how?

Depending on the enterprises and incidents considered, these factors combine to make digital security a key issue. In this context, the organization that the enterprise puts in place to ensure or facilitate the protection of businesses against digital risk plays an essential role, the consistency of which can be assessed on the basis of the analysis of incidents, data collected by specialized observatories and the articulation

W. Amedzro St-Hilaire, *Digital Risk Governance*,
https://doi.org/10.1007/978-3-030-61386-0_1

between technical and legal standards. The Internet has crept into everyone's life, little by little or very quickly, without the question of its governance coming to mind as a priority. The Internet was first perceived as a space of freedom, of access to knowledge – intellectual or social. And yet, because the Internet presupposed an organization, this organization, though not very visible, was bound to be in some hands.

Given the considerable size of the Internet, when two geographically distant interlocutors in distant countries wish to exchange information, it has been necessary to define routing and addressing zones. With more than 620,000 routes according to ExpertActions Group, routing zones have been defined and prioritized to form relay zones. The gigantic size of such a complex raised the question of its management, hence the decision to propose technical governance on a global scale. At present, the allocation of IP addressing areas is organized by continent. Internet management is essential for allocating IP addresses, DNS domain names and other elements that contribute to the functioning of the Internet Protocol. At present, the organization of this governance is not the result of any international text. In resolution 65/41, the United Nations expressed its concern that information technology and information resources could be used for purposes inconsistent with the maintenance of international stability and security and could undermine the integrity of the infrastructure of states, thus affecting their security in both civilian and military fields.

Today, the question of the global management of the Internet has been raised and the need for its reform acknowledged, but neither the objectives nor the timetable is self-evident, since important issues are at stake. The spider's web that encircles the world, the Net, the Internet, the web, is in contact with all domains. The discreet rules of its establishment and organization benefited commercial enterprises and their home states, while the world's population was eagerly and recklessly lending itself to this global stranglehold on minds and objects alike. The weaving of the global spider's web was done by a few unknown actors such as:

- IAB, the Internet Architecture Board, appointed by the Internet Society, the committee responsible for monitoring and developing the Internet.
- ICANN, the Internet Corporation for Assigned Names and Numbers, which manages the root file of the domain name system, ensuring the correspondence between domain names and IP addresses; under California law, this association is supervised by the US Department of Commerce.
- IETF, the Internet Engineering Task Force, responsible for Internet engineering, which participates in the development of standards for the Internet.
- ISOC, the Internet Society.
- W3C, the World Wide Web Consortium, which is the organization for the global network.

The current management of the Internet is the result of the combined action of all these players, all American, whose governing bodies include American digital giants. It is only in the last 10 years or so that a reflection has been initiated on this curious structure through the creation, in 2005, of the Internet Governance Forum

(IGF), a space for multi-stakeholder but not interstate dialogue. It took the Snowden affair in 2013, the public revelation of the identity of the spider waiting at the heart of its web, the National Security Agency, to lead to a global conference on Internet governance in Brazil in April 2014, whose final declaration condemned online surveillance and affirmed founding principles for a free and democratic Internet. In order to retain as much of its current prerogatives as possible, the United States has proposed to start privatizing the management of the Internet, probably in order to avoid the creation of an intergovernmental organization or the influence of any other state.

Faced with this situation, the experts on the democratization of Internet and digital management proposed a new architecture based on:

- The drafting of an international treaty enshrining the founding principles of the São Paulo World Net and leading to the globalization of Internet management
- The creation of a World Internet Council (resulting from the transformation of the Internet Governance Forum or IGF)
- The transformation of ICANN into a WICANN (WorldICANN) under international or Swiss law while organizing international supervision of the root file of domain names
- The establishment of an independent and accessible appeal mechanism allowing the review of a decision of WICANN
- The establishment of a functional separation between WICANN and the operational functions of allocating top-level domain names (the root), IP addresses and Autonomous System Numbers (ASNs) to the regional Internet registries and the definition of Internet protocol parameters (list of port numbers, etc.)
- The definition of independence criteria for WICANN board members to eliminate conflicts of interest

The new architecture of Internet management proposed by the senatorial fact-finding mission obviously does not meet with the enthusiasm of ICANN, which intends to reform itself in its own way. Several regional structures have presented several papers on this topic calling for more transparent, accountable and inclusive Internet governance, but they are far from being all on the same line. In fact, the alignment with the United States still appeals to many countries, not including Germany, despite the proven spying of the Chancellor's private communications by the United States. However, in São Paulo, some countries affirmed their support for a single, open, free, secure, reliable and unfragmented Internet. Some countries wish to take a stand for freedom of expression, freedom of association, freedom of information, the right to privacy, accessibility, open architecture of the Internet, multi-stakeholder governance, openness, transparency, accountability and a system that is inclusive and fair and promotes open standards.

Faced with the United States, suddenly in favour of privatizing Internet management, some countries are moving towards a moralization that includes the right of states – and not just one – to control Internet management. If the desirable evolution of Internet management is mentioned here, it is to show that the challenges of digital network security are situated in a framework that is itself constructed as a place of insecurity. Therefore, placing one's information and interests in a spider's web implies the acceptance of being a prey. Awareness of this reality by individuals and enterprises alike can only stimulate their thinking. One only surfs the Net if the spider is willing, momentarily, to grant this closely guarded freedom.

With respect to global management of digital security incidents, it should be noted that for many years, institution-wide monitoring services have been offered; most of these services are the result of North American initiatives. The National Institute of Standards and Technology (NIST) is part of the US Department of Commerce and is now the organizational and operational entity responsible for promoting the competitiveness of enterprises confronted with the use of complex technologies. Originally a physical science laboratory in 1901, NIST has expanded its scope since the late 1980s to include information technology standardization. NIST is mandated by the North American government to host and manage the National Vulnerability Database. NIST is a powerful institute behind the use or development of most standards for security monitoring purposes (OVAL, CVE, CVSS bulletins). As a result, all the knowledge of the majority of vulnerabilities is now concentrated and federated on the Security Content Automation Protocol (SCAP), the NIST platform born from the idea of networking security knowledge between scientific and industrial research.

Through the SCAP platform, NIST centralizes and disseminates security events considered to be hazardous in order to foster cooperative efforts at the national and international levels. SCAP also provides a unique and common knowledge of vulnerabilities. In its standard, NIST SP800-126, NIST proposes a standardization of vulnerabilities in order to express them in the same format. Following a vulnerability that affected more than 10% of Internet resources, the North American state also set up a computer incident processing centre, the CERT/CC (Computer Emergency Response Team Coordination Center). CERT/CC was created by the SEI, under the impetus of the Defense Advanced Research Projects Agency (DARPA) and the United States Department of Defense (DoD), located in the heart of Carnegie Mellon University. After this founding incident, CERT/CC's mission was to federate mixed industrial and scientific teams to curb the multiplication of system failures. This strategy had to preserve the competitiveness of software-using enterprises by setting a major player against the publishers at the origin of the ever-increasing number of security breaches.

That is why one of CERT/CC's missions has been to disseminate these vulnerabilities to the general public in the form of "bugtraq" bulletins, in a way putting software publishers on notice to correct their flaws. Since that date, 60,000 vulnerabilities have been the subject of a detailed CERT analysis on more than 27,000 software products, most of which have been patched. The CERT/CC has become a reference, publishing a free daily list of vulnerabilities with a detailed analysis. SCAP and US-CERT are among these North American community-based initiatives supported by the Department of Homeland Security (DHS). Thus, DHS announced the creation of US-CERT, a joint effort with the CERT Coordination Center. US-CERT relies on CERT/CC capabilities to help prevent cyber attacks, protect systems and respond to them.

The success of CERT/CC has led to the development of a global network to federate scientific and industrial safety knowledge and provide a service to users worldwide. CERT/CC has set up a certification mechanism; any state or entity wishing to be an actor in its security can join this network. CERT/CC issues certification to all CERTs. In Western countries, on average, about 20 CERTs are in operation; some are state CERTs such as ANSSI, and others depend on professional sectors. The operational value of all these CERTs is to be linked together at different levels, national and international, in order to exchange information on the discovery of new vulnerabilities. All of these are centralized by CERT/CC and identified by SCAP, whose role, like ICANN, is to establish a globally unique identification. In a context where digital technology is a strategic issue, we can question the neutrality and sustainability of SCAP.

On the state side, the situation is also worrying: institutions are exposed to attacks on a national scale, and attackers in the pay of states are organizing themselves into real armies. Some countries have adopted a communication to improve the protection of critical infrastructure against terrorism, as the disruption of such infrastructure could lead to loss of life and property and the collapse of public confidence. A package of measures has been initiated. The North Atlantic Treaty Organization (NATO) is also involved in the fight against terrorism. It has not remained inactive in the area of cybersecurity since, following the cyber attack that paralyzed Estonia in 2007, a centre of analysis and expertise on cybersecurity was set up in Tallinn. This centre is regularly the target of violent denial of service attacks. Also in 2008, NATO created the Cyber Defense Management Authority (CDMA), a political authority with the mission to initiate and coordinate immediate and effective cyber defence measures whenever circumstances require and also to organize large-scale cyber attack simulation exercises.

One element of the Atlantic Alliance's approach has been to encourage greater cooperation among nations in dealing with cyber attacks. Many rich countries have become involved in the implementation of trust in electronic exchange systems. Awareness of the dangerousness of threats on the Internet and via modern electronic modes of exchange is the challenge of the next decade. The most advanced steps seem to have been taken in Denmark, where, in order to build confidence in electronic payment systems, a state-secured payment infrastructure has been deployed. Similarly, in response to the need for citizen safety, a campaign was conducted in the form of 333 different initiatives across the country under the name NetSafe Now (a major step forward). What was once covered up in words or as hypotheses for reflection on possible developments in cybernetic clashes between states is now openly evoked, especially when the hacking of the Sony Pictures studio, attributed to North Korea in retaliation for the announcement of the release of a film entitled "The Interview" or "The Interview that Kills," which shows the assassination of North Korean head of state Kim Jong-un by journalists recruited by the CIA, came to light.

What's more, Sony Pictures employees have been the direct target of pirate threats. Then there were threats of attacks against the theatres that would screen the film, which led Sony Pictures to abandon the release of the film the next day, as thousands of exhibitors wanted to avoid any risk. The Federal Bureau of Investigation (FBI) directly pointed to North Korea as the driver of the attack, and the North American president promised a "proportionate and timely" response and called Sony Pictures' waiver a mistake. This is the first time that the United States has named a foreign nation as the target of a cyber attack. In the end, more than 300 cinemas decided, in the name of freedom of expression, to screen the film, which was also made available on the Internet. Technically, the FBI revealed that the North Korean signature would be expressed by lines of computer code, encryption algorithms and data expression methods similar to those used by the North Korean regime in an attack on South Korean banks and media. In addition, IP addresses associated with North Korean infrastructures are said to have communicated with those identified as responsible for the hacking.

It should be noted that North Korea had called the making of "The Interview" an "act of war" and threatened "strong and ruthless" reprisals. Senator John McCain, a Republican senator, called the hacking of Sony Pictures "an act of war." At the same time, Russia and North Korea have multiplied signs of their rapprochement, notably with the invitation to the North Korean leader to visit Moscow. At the same time, for almost nine hours, the Internet connection between North Korea and the world – which passes through China – was interrupted. Was this the work of China, the United States, or North Korea itself to prevent the effects of a North American cyber attack? Or of South Korea as a victim of the hacking of the plans of certain nuclear reactors and their cooling systems, as well as the personal data of nearly 11,000 employees – a cyber attack attributed by South Korea to North Korea?

At the same time, although it went more unnoticed, a giant breakdown affected Microsoft's Xbox live and Sony's PlayStation live servers, threatened in early December with a cyber attack by a group aiming to take these two networks offline permanently. These events show that, from cybersecurity to cyber-warfare, the borders separating civil risks from military risks, and those separating risks from dangers, are increasingly impossible to discern and that the search for a high level of digital security for businesses must be, more than ever and as soon as possible, a real priority for states and their civil security actors, including every digital user.

In such a context, what is the balance of power between Internet giants, states, enterprises and citizens? It must be said that, where the law should set out the applicable rules, it is currently a question of power relationships that prevail. While the law is slow to develop, de facto situations are being created that may limit the creative margins of legislators. The example of Google in some countries illustrates these contradictions. Firstly, while these countries are questioning the existence of the abuse of a dominant position of which the search engine Google would be guilty according to some 30 complainants, the legislator voted a motion calling for the dismantling of Google and a Google tax was voted, to protect the intellectual property of the tools of press publishers used free of charge by Google Noticias.

With regard to these initiatives, it should first be noted that prosecuting Google for these abuses of a dominant position, because of the use of its 90% market share to promote all its services to the detriment of those of its competitors, involves notifying Google of the objections against it and initiating proceedings which will last for years, during which the alleged abuse will continue or worsen, hence the preference for conciliation in most cases. As for the motions voted by the various Parliaments, apart from their media coverage, which is moreover rather limited despite the audacity of these texts, one may wonder whether their scope is not more symbolic than real.

Finally, the mere announcement of the Spanish Google tax led Google to announce the closure of its news service, resulting in the immediate retreat of newspaper publishers who were to be protected by the tax from Google's free loans. Faced with this situation, a global reaction does not seem possible, if only because some countries have obtained funding from Google for the Digital Press Enhancement Fund.

Secondly, no country seemed to be in a position to introduce a tax obliging Google to make any payment proportionate to the profits made in each country. At most, a directive should allow value-added tax to be paid in the country where a cinematographic work or a song is bought on Apple or Google.

Thirdly, Google's implementation of the right to oblivion, following the decision of the European Court of Justice, leaves Google alone to judge the relevance of the 200,000 or so requests for deletion of links made. In addition, the European Union has had to adopt a regulation on personal data in order to subject such data to the law of the country where the data subject is located, regardless of the location of the servers hosting such data. Finally, the regulators are in dispute with Google, which they accuse of unilaterally changing its privacy policy for messaging, search and storage. Judging by the test to be imposed on – Booking – three national regulatory authorities, acting in concert against the clauses imposed by this online booking site on hoteliers, this type of concerted action could be a quicker and more effective route than institutional solutions. However, the image of a face-to-face meeting between Google and the states must be complemented by the possibility of cooperation between them.

For years, Google has been responding to requests from governments to obtain the private data of Internet users held by this operator. As of 2010, www.google.com/governmentrequests/ allows you to see, state by state, the number of government requests made to Google, either for private data or to remove content. This means that Google owns the locations of connections, the configuration of connected computers, browsing history, the content of searches performed, the content of email messages, etc. Businesses are not exempt from this system. As a result, Google holds far more information about individuals and businesses than most states and has financial clout that surpasses that of many states as well. At this level, this makes this North American private company – like all those at its level – a political player. On this basis, would a draft free trade agreement between regional areas be viable?

It must be said that, for several years now, negotiations have been underway on the conclusion of a comprehensive transatlantic agreement on trade and investment between the United States and the European Union, among others. Several rounds of discussions have been concluded, reflecting the will of both sides to move forward at an extremely rapid pace towards the creation of a large deregulated transatlantic market in which the will and economic interests would be substituted for laws passed by national parliaments. It is envisaged that once this agreement is adopted, its scope can be extended without the need to reopen negotiations in the light of the new areas of convergence identified. Since then, it has been publicly established that the United States has been spying on a large scale on the telecommunications and computer networks of all the states responsible for negotiating this international agreement.

This is why it is desirable (for two reasons) to mention the negotiation of this agreement insofar as it may concern digital technology (the security of which is nevertheless a digital security issue) and where the insecurity of digital technology is interfering with its negotiation or even demonstrating the danger of its conclusion. Will the countries concerned demand that their rights to privacy and personal data protection be respected in the final text of this agreement? Will they demand the exclusion of personal data protection from these trade negotiations? Are they going to demand that their citizens enjoy the same level of protection as North American citizens?

In referring to these negotiations, it should be stressed that there are four parallel chronologies concerning the future of digital technology: the establishment of international Internet governance, the negotiation of the transatlantic free trade agreement, the drafting of a new European regulation on digital technology and, finally, the drafting of a new French law on digital technology. It is essential that international guarantees are needed in the protection of personal data and the management of the Internet before the digital clauses of the free trade agreement are adopted.

Furthermore, digital should not be included in the trade agreement because digital includes commercial and not the other way around. Digital should therefore be considered as justifying a digital exception in the same way as the cultural exception. As a result, this sector would be excluded from trade negotiations. This is all the more so since the arbitration procedures envisaged in the free trade agreement subject the signatory states to the will of the dominant enterprises in the market through recourse to a private supranational tribunal called an "arbitration panel." Even in the absence of this agreement, this situation is already that observed in the digital field; it is urgent to modify it by avoiding transforming this situation of momentary de facto inferiority of these states in the digital field into a situation of definitive law.

It is therefore true that the ability to protect against, detect and identify the perpetrators of computer attacks has become one of the elements of digital security. To achieve this, governments and businesses must support high-performance scientific and technological skills. Also, most of the world is underdeveloped in the digital world and is threatened with global underdevelopment tomorrow, as digital gradually takes control of all activity. It is interesting to clearly identify the threats to countries' control over data, calling into question their independence and freedom. To address this, it is proposed that states be given effective control over citizen data in the face of cloud computing, communicating objects and multiple US jurisdictions that, in the name of counter-terrorism, continue to expand their collection of data on non-US citizens outside North America on a large scale.

In this area, non-American citizens are granted fewer rights than American citizens, while other countries apply texts of universal scope (right to privacy, respect for correspondence, protection of personal data) to all individuals. It would obviously be desirable for each country to emphasize respect for these rights in the development of cloud computing, but the various hesitations expressed during the preparation of the proposal for a regulation give rise to fears of a strong North American influence from this stage. How then can we guarantee the protection of privacy and personal data by digital cloud service providers that fall, or may fall from one day to the next, under North American law as the identity of the owners of their assets changes?

Once this drift has occurred, what protection can be afforded to the development of the Internet of objects whose rules should be designed today; all the more so as many of these connected objects will concern the quantification of self, the chosen domain of privacy. To the abandonment of their digital security (by the States), may respond the abandonment by the States of the protection of the rights of their citizens threatened by the digital controlled from abroad. It is in this changing and fragile context that it is important to secure digital networks that are subject to attack. Faced with the possible scale of the damage caused by such attacks, states must conceive of the protection of society's critical infrastructures, that of the operators of vital importance (OIV) as well as critically connected citizens. The notions of vulnerability and resilience, in the face of and following digital attacks, will then take on their full meaning.

That is why some countries have set up National Security and Information Systems Agencies to prevent computer attacks and help vital operators to respond to crises. As it may be essential to extend this prevention and assistance to subcontractors, customers and the staff of these operators, it soon becomes clear that it is the national rather than the European level that can weave this preventive and curative network. This requires the use of reliable equipment (locally manufactured or internationally labelled), systematic controls, legal rules that place the imperatives of digital security very high and responsible behaviour in the face of digital risks.

At the regional level, this requires states to recognize the need for regional preference for security markets for highly strategic digital equipment. This concept must take precedence over the freedom of competition in sectors of vital importance. What lessons have been learned from the situation? Following Edward Snowden's disclosures, a commission of inquiry charged with reforming the National Security Agency (NSA) surveillance system developed 46 proposals based on the idea that free nations must protect themselves and nations that protect themselves must remain free in order to balance the needs of national security, economic interests and the privacy guaranteed by the US Constitution.

In this context, the NSA would cease to systematically store all telephone metadata (dates and times of calls, origins, recipients, etc.); it could only obtain them from telecommunications operators on a case-by-case basis and by decision of a judge. In addition, these experts also proposed that US hardware and software manufacturers should no longer systematically incorporate backdoors. The experts also recommended granting the same protection to non-Americans as to North American citizens. Under the 1974 Privacy Art, Americans have the right to access personal data about themselves collected by government agencies or publicly disclosed. Finally, the oversight of political figures should be controlled by Parliament and not by intelligence leaders. What will be the fate of these proposals? Are they, like the changes in ICANN's management, just a new false nose designed to hide the face of the crook?

Chapter 2
National Frameworks for the Implementation of Digital Security

In addition to technical standards, legal standards continue to play a major role in imposing evolving frameworks that respect freedoms. Faced with the consequences of digital technology for freedoms and its imperfections, the need to legislate is often mentioned. But does the improvement of all the components of digital security require the adoption of new legal rules?

The technologies of the Internet and the digital spaces that they have created do not only invite lawyers to explore and conquer a new terra incognita; they transform from within, or even disrupt, the conditions for the exercise of fundamental rights and the traditional mechanisms for their conciliation. The right to oblivion and dereferencing, very often cited as significant advances, are not real guarantees of security. Digital technology allows the development of certain freedoms (of expression, association or entrepreneurship, for example) while at the same time threatening privacy and security in general, given the rapid development of cybercrime.

A number of specific features of the digital environment make it difficult for it to be governed by the rule of law in several states. Thus, the management of the Internet is not governed by an international text but by negotiation reports that do not even result from a confrontation between states but from a balance of power within an American private law foundation, ICANN (Internet Corporation for Assigned Names and Numbers) (where states are poorly represented – even if a rebalancing of this governance has been envisaged). The rule of law, which is characterized first and foremost by the territoriality of the standard, seems to have no control over the digital that is (de facto) governed by North American law. It should also be noted that while the circulation of data is a regional competence, national security is governed by the law of the Member States. However, it should be stressed that in this area, hard law should be broadly associated with soft law in order to allow the organization of transitions leading to good practice.

They also recalled the fundamental role of national regulators, who have been able to promote fundamental principles such as the framework for data collection (which must have a specific purpose and be proportionate to it) and the idea that an

W. Amedzro St-Hilaire, *Digital Risk Governance*,
https://doi.org/10.1007/978-3-030-61386-0_2

independent authority should monitor the implementation of legislation. It should be noted, however, that the issue of massive data storage and processing is difficult to reconcile with the principles of specified purpose (and proportionality). Hence the interest in recognizing a great freedom to reuse data for statistical purposes (but without compromising respect for the data of private individuals). Among the possible strategies, those relating to the reduction of numerical risk are important. On the one hand, it consists of promoting the democratization of regulatory services by creating a general assembly bringing together all stakeholders and which can call into question the responsibility of the board of directors (strengthening internal recourse mechanisms, for example, by giving a binding scope to the Independent Review Panel mechanism allowing the committee representing governments to adopt binding resolutions). It calls for, on the other hand, the composition of Internet governance bodies to be diversified, through selection criteria that impose real linguistic and geographical diversity (and the implementation of influence strategies including, in particular, the obligation of simultaneous translation during the work of these bodies).

Indeed, part of the digital risk comes from the control of the Internet by a foreign state. A profound transformation of data protection instruments is also called for, for example, by using technologies to make data less accessible to third parties and to strengthen the ability of individuals to control the use of their data. To this end, all cryptology technologies or the use of the TOR network, which allows anonymous exchanges on the Internet, could be optimized. There is already the possibility to block the recording of files or cookies on a terminal, to express preferences regarding the tracing of one's data, or to allow an individual to use a platform to access all personal data held by a set of partners.

Therefore, it would be advisable to implement a general display of the personal data use policies followed by each site by including on the computer screen, in a simple and readable format, appropriate signage (including the one recommended by the Mozilla Foundation indicating the length of the data retention period, the possibility of their use by a third party, the sharing of the advertisement and the transparency of the process). In conclusion, it should be universally recognized that there is also a need: the definition of a legal category of platforms respecting the principle of loyalty to their users; a right to dereferencing on search engines with a single dereferencing decision; the definition of a right to predictive algorithms; the reform of the concentration regime for the news media; the reconciliation of the protection of privacy; and the preservation of metadata for the purpose of preventing breaches of national security.

All these aspects would require appropriate legislation in the states. It is important to note that the digital is not a docile tool in the hands of its master. Because it carries within itself consequences that are beyond the control of its users. It would therefore not be a tool that is neither good nor bad in itself, but a tool that is both good and bad at the same time. It is worth attaching great importance to the development of a soft law, as opposed to a hard law, to provide workable legal solutions (i.e. a law that is adjustable and reversible according to usage). But the challenge is not only economic because digital technology must take into account "the challenges of knowledge, education and culture" to counterbalance Internet practices.

How did we get here? In response to the freedom, of the Internet's beginnings, the multiplication of communication tools and the creativity of software, there has been increased surveillance of freedoms through its digital expressions (after September 2001): the Patriot Act, the Foreign Intelligence Surveillance Act (FISA) and the activism of the NSA are all illustrations of this. From then on, the fragmentation of the Internet into Internets accelerated and a strange game of hide-and-seek in the networks took place. The most inattentive were reminded that the net meant the web and that the spider was less and less anonymous as it sought out individual, commercial or cultural information. Bulimic spider, ant-like ascendant, demands more and more data and even stores the data it cannot decipher yet to analyse it one day with even more powerful algorithms.

Opening an account on Gmail means agreeing to have your information delivered to the US administration if you request it. In some states, mechanisms set up (very early on) as a gendarme vigilant of freedoms with regard to files exist. But the acceleration of technological change has created threats beyond the control of files alone. In general, when it comes to the security of information systems, the focus is on the risks to the enterprise, while when it comes to data protection, the focus is on the risks to individuals. The technical measures to be put in place in each of these cases are often similar. For example, data encryption guarantees the confidentiality of exchanges, which will protect both the individual and the enterprise.

In fact, in several countries, there are recommendations for businesses: such as those on data storage in the cloud, the guide for small- and medium-sized enterprises (SMEs), the advanced risk management guide developed and, finally, compliance pacts enabling businesses to integrate privacy concerns from the design stage of products. In concrete terms, a "network security" response was needed. Indeed, no single actor has all the keys to control the security of this universe. On the other hand, if we address all the actors concerned, and each of them has an action, a particular responsibility in terms of security, then collectively, it is possible to keep this universe under control (at least as far as its security is concerned).

What does it mean to have "network security"? The first axis is business. This is the heart of today's concerns. The objective is to make professional actors and enterprises responsible so that they integrate in their own functioning the objective of guaranteeing the security of networks and the security of personal data. It has to be said that regulators have to adapt constantly. The action taken by certain countries towards Google led to the conclusion that Google's privacy policy did not comply with the rules of several states. The information given to individuals when using these services was insufficient. Also, users do not have sufficient control over the combinations of data. Finally, Google did not specify the retention period as required by the data protection laws of several states.

Faced with the speed and ever-changing technical aspects of digital attacks, it is often proposed to significantly increase the number of staff in the ever-increasing demands on regulatory agencies. The use of antivirus software is becoming the norm. Since antivirus software does not cover all the risks of digital technology, the protection provided by antivirus software must be complemented by the important defence in depth. It is the stacking of safety bricks that allows a certain level of safety to be given to the tools and the uses to which they are put. The IT tool includes security updates of the hardware and software bricks (because the components are not developed in a sufficiently secure way and have security flaws). An entire ecosystem lives from the detection, production and sale of these security breaches.

In such a context, what operational security implementation do states have at their disposal? For some countries, the Directorate General of Armaments, which is the leading player in defence research, is the technical defence expert for information and communication systems, digital security, electronic warfare and tactical and strategic missile systems. This technical expertise ranges from electronic components to systems of systems, from the design of components or cryptographic algorithms to the evaluation of secure architectures of complete systems.

Within this framework, the institution develops and evaluates digital security products. It cooperates both with the Analysis Centres for Defensive IT Fighting and with the National Agencies for the Security of Information Systems to analyse the most complex digital attacks detected on networks and the most dangerous potential threats. The acute perception of the requirements of cyber defence has led to plans for the increased recruitment of experts, i.e. very high-level engineers specializing in the analysis and prevention of computer attacks and substantial support for upstream studies carried out by research laboratories on small- and medium-sized enterprises. These agencies are, for example, working on encryption systems for IP networks capable of handling information classified as "confidential defence" or "secret defence." In addition, in their own countries, they constitute a bridge between the armed forces and industry, including beyond national defence.

They develop government encryption algorithms, increasingly carry out numerical simulation and monitor export equipment for compliance with the licences issued. The foreseeable growth of cyber defence will lead to the recruitment of more and more engineers, who will make up nearly 70% of the staff. The growing convergence between civil and military technologies in the digital field is leading to the use of identical components worldwide but on very different systems, or even systems of systems (such as on a combat ship), hence the risk of penetration infiltrating everything.

In this context, barriers between systems are no longer sufficient, and interconnection can, in itself, introduce risks, hence the need for attack sensors in weapon systems, information and communication systems and industrial systems. Digital security results from the addition of cyber-protection with cyber defence – which is the equivalent of posting sentries in an information system. These agencies intervene at three levels: the design of elements which presupposes mastery of the critical part and therefore control of the components; the evaluation of components, equipment and systems over time and anticipation of the threat, which leads to putting oneself in the shoes of the attacker to test the systems. Given the many possible digital security vulnerabilities, investing in digital security should not be an extra cost, even if it may seem so in the short term.

High-security laboratories (in other countries) provide a unique academic platform for digital security research. Their activities include security expertise, proactive defence against malware and training to ensure the confidentiality of data or its local processing for sensitive research. These laboratories are part of the network of high-security laboratories but have no real equivalent worldwide. The labs analyse network traffic on a large scale to identify threats, communication channels between zombie machines and those controlling them and phishing attempts through fake trusted sites. The challenge is to secure the Internet in real time by developing a supervisory structure in cooperation with law enforcement agencies, for example, in the fight against paedophilia (40% of cartoon search files are polluted). A firewall has been developed that also works on the early search for tomorrow's hacker networks.

As far as enterprises are concerned, these laboratories are studying ways of detecting intrusions on systems, some of which may be accessible via the Internet, allowing the attacker to take control of valves, doors – including prisons when guards have gone to play on the Internet. Hence the need to protect the control-command network by means of intrusion detection all year round, day and night. These laboratories have designed a test platform for this purpose. They also study the security of environments, for example, through vulnerable configurations of devices such as Android, which is widely used in particular in mobile phones, facilitating malicious behaviour by attackers engaged in the same quest for vulnerability. These laboratories are also carrying out significant research in cryptography – particularly the so-called public-key cryptography – whose level of security must be constantly upgraded. This activity also extends to the security of protocols – or description of behaviour to be adopted – for example, cryptographic protocols for securing communications on open networks (blue cards, telephones, electronic voting, etc.). They are committed to identifying the authentication process(es) adapted to each use and study the fragility of each one. For example, the use of fingerprints or iris appears to be unsafe because it is impossible to change them once stolen – which is not very difficult; moreover, soft fingers could be manufactured. Note that once authentication has been subtly used, access to all applications is possible.

As for electronic voting, which is prohibited for political elections in several countries, it is difficult to guarantee the reliability of the voting machines as well as the secrecy of the vote, which opens the way to its purchase; moreover, verification by citizens is impossible. The analysis of the military digital security experience should make it possible to gain years in civil digital security and, conversely, that the research of the Security Laboratories could irrigate the defence sector – the two being inseparable – and that increased cooperation between military and civil actors was essential for the protection of vital operators and the infrastructure for which they are responsible. However, no effort in this direction is possible without a perception of digital vulnerabilities to their proper degree.

The mission of the national agency for information systems security in some ten countries is to advise administrations and operators of vital importance and inform businesses and the general public about computer threats and ways of protecting themselves against them – in particular through the publication of newsletters. It is also responsible for concrete threat prevention by developing a range of trusted products and services (for administrations and economic actors) and (as a matter of urgency) for early response to cyber attacks against the most sensitive networks of the administration (detected through a reinforced cyber defence operational centre operating 24 hours a day).

Beyond these initial missions, it is also concerned with the security of connected objects, whose number could approach fifty billion before 2050. He is also interested in the place of digital technology in the economy. In this respect, it reveals that every year, IT insecurity is responsible for the loss of tens of thousands of jobs on average per country because digital attacks penalize competitiveness. Hence the importance of developing tools to detect sovereign attacks through the Future Investment Program. This may also concern enterprises with scientific and technological potential, including innovative enterprises – thus beyond a list of enterprises to be protected as a matter of priority. For the future, an offensive capability is envisaged.

Other states have opted for a National Gendarmerie that observes the risks of cyberspace and takes up its challenges. This approach is part of the national digital security doctrine. For the Gendarmerie in these countries, it has long been obvious that digital technologies have the effect of weakening society, whether in the areas of transport, air or rail, energy or medical equipment. Connectivity to the Internet only accentuates this fragility. This is why the Gendarmerie is trying to speed up the collective awareness of all players, public and private, who believe that in order to deal with current threats and risks, everyone must become an actor in their own digital security, whether they are an individual, an entrepreneur, or a private or public organization.

The Information Technology Fraud Investigation Brigade, a department of the Economic and Financial Affairs Sub-Directorate of the Criminal Investigation Police Directorate in these countries, includes in its mission's awareness information and training on cybercrime for public or private actors, including the general public. In particular, this makes it possible to provide a reactive response to victims so that they acquire a cyber attitude, a cyber-secure behaviour. It tries to disseminate digital literacy to children, teenagers and their parents and grandparents. It also turns to administrations, enterprises and associations by providing preventive or legal advice in response to an attack. It focuses on hacking by enterprises, which are increasingly reporting their claims to the judicial authorities because they know that rapid support and expertise on the attack depend on this reporting. This is important in view of the limited period of time for which connection data are kept and when it is necessary to identify the attacker, who has more or less managed to make himself anonymous, and to measure the extent of the information that he has been able to extract from the attacked company.

Finally, there remains the important question of who local authorities, small- and medium-sized enterprises and individuals should turn to in the event of an incident. Today, nothing is definite. So, they turn to friends, to an after-sales service for the equipment, but they do not necessarily find answers about safety. It would be advisable to develop local actors, repairers in response to security incidents; these people should be able to restore a computer, check for viruses that have affected it, understand what has happened and explain to the victim what he or she has done wrong. Today, however, this type of person is being formed on the job or even does not exist. This type of service or training does not exist. In addition, information on these incidents does not go back up. The computer is back up and running, but the loss of important or confidential data may be regrettable. It is therefore necessary to develop training to remedy this and to create this chain including repairers.

As for industrialists, they were the first to understand the need to put in place digital security commensurate with the risk and even the threat involved. But not all industrialists do, and that is a long way off. Following the revelation of a major Internet security breach in 2008, the five largest enterprises in the computer and network industry (Cisco Systems, IBM, Intel, Juniper Networks and Microsoft) created a non-profit association called the Industry Consortium for Advancement of Security on the Internet (ICASI) to demonstrate the security risks associated with motherboards, software, processors, networks, operating systems, etc. The ICASI is a non-profit organization dedicated to the development of security solutions for the Internet.

At the local level, it must be said that many areas are today faced with the management of crisis situations arising from the threat to their digital security. The need for institutional measures is then felt concerning the specialized agencies, their role and access, standards, legal arsenal, certifications and financial aid. The role of the specialized agencies is to provide assistance within an ecosystem. To be effective, these institutions should be multi-scale, addressing individuals, enterprises, communities, countries, continents and the world, with the aim of facilitating the flow of information from the context, adjusting corrective actions and, finally, measuring changes in cybercrime. Moreover, their role (which includes both prevention and control) well deserves the name governance. This hierarchical system promotes the flow of control information despite conflicts of interest. It should be noted that the mode of access to institutions reflects their ability to provide the service expected of them (this characteristic is therefore essential).

In addition to the assessment of digital crime already mentioned, the notion of attack and its measurement would benefit from being clarified. It is with his or her usual societal references that the Internet user engages in the exchange. Among the remarkable harms resulting from acts that interact between the societal and technological spheres is identity theft, which, according to statistics from the Quebec government (one of the few to communicate on this subject), affects nearly 15% of the population of Internet users. Obtaining such statistics is hampered by the difficulty of agreeing on a technical and legal definition of such theft, hence the fact that not all countries count the same forms of theft. Moreover, only a minority of victims (21. 8% in Quebec) would report this type of harm. Finally, the lack of a monitoring methodology is linked to the low rates observed for this offense and the limited damage it causes, due in particular to the systematic compensation policy conducted by financial institutions.

On average (per country and per year), 236 million euros of petty cyber crime was committed through malicious technological and social exchanges. The dangerousness does not stem from the consequences of such theft (estimated at less than $100 per victim) but from its extent in time (repetition and recidivism) and space (lack of boundaries) as well as the insidious ease of its modus operandi. In addition to the number of victims, the scope is reflected in the very varied nature of its use, ranging from bank fraud (obtaining credit) to service fraud, whether immigration, terrorism, or justice.

In addition to the fraudulent use of credit cards or Vitale cards, identity theft also involves the offender stealing or obtaining "personal identification information" or "personal identification documents" such as a driver's license, birth certificate, social security card and employee badge or distributing or selling "personal identification information," such as a utility bill, to an organized crime group.

In addition to these concerns undermining confidence in a technological system, there is also a lack of understanding resulting from contradictory statistical results according to the various private or public security observatories consulted. For example, the incident statistics published by ExpertActions Group estimate the risk of intrusion in developed countries to be around 8%. The challenge of publishing consistent statistics is extremely high since it is through relevant and useful information tools that users will regain their confidence in the Internet.

The study of the dangerousness of behaviour is a matter for the criminal sciences and is embodied in the offense of breaking the law (an action or omission likely to disturb social harmony). The offense is punished according to a scale of value shared between society and the victim. This measure is approximate because it is based on the infringement of pre-established societal rules. In order for a crime or offense to be proven and a penalty applied, evidence must be provided. On this notion of proof, which is fundamental in law, depends the legal existence of a crime through the joint presence of the author's intention to harm, a prejudice and a complaint. In order to thwart the most dangerous forms of attack and to identify the perpetrators of crimes and offenses, modern societies have developed a scientific discipline. It is the role of forensic science, more commonly known as forensics, to study modus operandi based on tools and methods.

The foundation of forensic science is based on Locard's Principle, which concerns the use of traces as evidence. Indeed, in application of the "principle of trace transfer" which cannot fail to be observed during a crime, the identification of traces of an individual at a crime scene and/or the trace of a crime scene on an individual are sought (the "principle of individuality" then makes it possible, by comparison, to confuse a criminal. All of which are made possible by the isolation of the crime scene). However, it seems that Locard's Principle meets technical impossibilities to be applied in the field of cybercrime. The big problem with cybercrime is that there is no link between the place of the crime and the perpetrator. Indeed, the Locard exchange principle does not apply to cybercrime. It is a big change for law enforcement in general. The striker is not necessarily local; he may have bounced off a site in Venezuela or Vietnam. Or it could be an attack between two people on the same street. The loss of this geographical link necessarily calls for cooperation between international police forces.

Depending on the IT security risk analysis for an entire company previously carried out, including that of weak signals, indispensable but difficult to carry out, the causes of damage, whether observed or not, the transfer of responsibility and the possibility of insuring the damage should be analysed. As with all damages that a company may suffer, it is the duty of its managers to try to reduce their impact and to take out insurance to cover the amount of the damage suffered. In terms of digital risk, the insurance offer is very poorly developed.

Indeed, insurers are accustomed to assessing risks on the basis of reliable and independent statistics, but in this case, since numerical risks are very diverse and incidents are probably very poorly identified, particularly in terms of their cost, past numerical risks do not make it possible to predict future risks, hence a certain reluctance on the part of insurers and, a fortiori, reinsurers to take over the numerical risk market. Moreover, since it is very difficult if not impossible for the insurer to know whether its client has implemented all possible digital security measures to prevent a claim from occurring, the calculation of the insurance premium is almost impossible. If insurers were to become more interested in this area, it is likely that they would then manifest protection requirements that would sooner or later become new security standards.

What about life-threatening operations? On average, there are more than 200 vital operators, half of them in the private sector, in developed countries. However, it is obvious that digital security for these operations, which are enterprises of various sizes, should not be limited to them but should also extend to enterprises with large staffs or dealing with technological or industrial secrets, not to mention that any company can be used as a relay in large-scale attacks. The digital security of vital operators is part of an overall plan that includes security standards set by the states for critical information systems. It aims to improve the detection of cyber attacks through systems operated on national territory by qualified service providers and to notify all cyber attacks to the competent regulatory authorities in their area.

In addition, critical information systems must be controlled. Finally, in the event of a major attack, these operators will have to implement any computer defence measures decided by the authorities. These major computer attacks are considered with as much attention as a state of war, terrorism, or espionage. It should be noted that the application of these rules may encounter difficulties insofar as the list of operations is classified as "defence confidential" (some managers and, a fortiori, their staff are not always aware of the status of their company and can therefore have only a limited awareness of the national security issues related to its activity).

As the enterprise has to organize itself in view of the digital crisis states envisaged, it must start by clearly indicating to the authorities the people who are the entry points to the enterprise so that the management of the attack is not deficient from the very first minutes. Indeed, it is essential that the enterprise's management immediately understands the vital nature of the threat against them. Until then, in the event of a digital crisis, enterprises did not tend to turn to the state because there were no partnerships or, a fortiori, crisis exercises between them and government agencies. From now on, enterprises will have to study more closely the existing interdependencies between themselves and their subcontractors and suppliers.

Moreover, it is not always easy to determine the type of attacks that will have the greatest impact on a given company.

It is important that these operations set up qualified detection systems, but since the current detection systems are mostly North American, there is a sovereignty problem. It is to be hoped that from this problem, an opportunity may arise, since the possession of confidence detection probes should be able to create a market of sovereign tools. Some intelligence agencies could also help enterprises to train to test their equipment based on the detection of past incidents not officially recorded. Finally, large enterprises may be considered as vital operations (and also, or not, abroad), which may complicate the rules to be applied to them depending on the territory under consideration.

The perception of the strategic importance of vitally important operators is quite recent, and it is a decree that often lists the sectors of activity of vital importance (i.e. those related to the possibility of exercising digital security). All 11 sectors identified are digitally based. Some are very directly related to digital technology, such as equipment for intercepting correspondence, remote detection of conversations, cryptology and cryptography, and the evaluation of the security of products and information systems. Foreign investment in these sectors must be authorized by the Minister in charge of the economy. In several countries, national safety guidelines have clarified what is meant by vitally important operators and the rights and obligations attached to this status.

It should be noted that too much rigidity in this area would risk not being adapted to the speed of change. For example, in the United States of America, the president may at any time place a business sector, organization, or company under the protection of vital operators. This responsiveness can help to prevent untimely foreign investment in time. It is true that it was as early as 1998 that President William Clinton issued Presidential Executive Order No. 63 to put in place "protection of the basic infrastructure of the United States" through, among other things, coordination by the National Infrastructure Protection Center (NIPC).

The attacks of 11 September 2001, led to the reinforcement of this concern through a series of new organizations and programs, including an offensive digital security capability and the regular organization, starting in 2006, of large-scale digital attack simulations against the country, including foreign enterprises and governments such as those of Canada, the United Kingdom and New Zealand. As always in the United States of America, these initiatives were accompanied, as early as 2003, by the enactment of standards, this time relating to the security of federal government computer equipment and strategic communication systems.

To take the example of telecoms, telecom operators combine several roles: they are both operators of infrastructure and Internet and telephony services. They provide, for example, data centres that allow vital operators to outsource the hosting of their data. Faced with digital risk, telecommunications operators place the ability to react at the forefront, based on an agile organization with short decision cycles and committed, pragmatic managers and employees. As for the protection, it is designed in depth. Some telecommunications enterprises are considered to be vitally important and are therefore subject to particular constraints: for example, their IT administrators only have workstations that are not connected to messaging or the Internet and must use other stations to intervene on a remote system.

So-called "confidential defence" projects require the delimitation of areas reserved for their treatment within which, for example, the precaution of leaving one's mobile phone at the entrance and where no Internet connection is possible. Some operators have decided to limit or even exclude any outsourcing and to store their sensitive data internally. They bought their equipment but control their networks. However, for routers and mobile solutions, OEMs are subject to specific security obligations. As a result, third- and fourth-generation networks have achieved a higher level of security than the standards set by the Third Generation Partnership Project (3GPP). It should be noted that despite strong commercial competition between telecommunications operators, the high degree of interdependence between them leads them to share information rapidly in the event of crises in which the ability to react is more important than anything else.

If we take the example of the energy sector, it is clear that in the light of the attacks on Saudi Aramco and RasGas in 2012, energy operators have found that the advantage is always on the attackers' side in terms of digital risk. Hence the need for methodical anticipation, including the development of a digital risk map accompanied by an information systems security plan updated each year. For Shell, this plan is based on the following four pillars: securing the management information system, including shared services infrastructures (telecommunications, etc.) for Shell's thousand sites around the world linked to group entities (industrial information security, application security and, finally, user awareness to change their behaviour).

This plan provides for special care to be taken with control systems, within industrial information, insofar as the vulnerability of these systems is based on traditional computer components. More than a logic of prevention, Shell is moving towards a logic of detection and rapid reaction, thanks to a security operations centre. In this respect, sharing information with other energy operators or state agencies is a guarantee of increased efficiency. However, these functions are all better ensured when strategic equipment is designed by enterprises and when staff understand the need to change behaviour.

Note the reluctance of the industry to use cloud computing, which is currently insufficiently secure and needs to be accompanied by an authentication and encryption system. Some store 90% of their data in private centres (only those with no special characteristics are stored in a public cloud). Shell believed that only data of low confidentiality could be stored in the public cloud, so it was necessary to distinguish between various categories of data, some of which were prohibited from storage in a public cloud. Ultimately, Shell prefers to rent its own data storage centres. Generally speaking, Shell complies with the rules of IT hygiene and chooses its equipment and suppliers on the basis of state referencing.

Although only a small part of Shell's business (refineries, some depots, pipe lines, etc.) is considered to be under the responsibility of a vitally important operator, the global safety plan is applied to all of its activities, and the safety standard is also extended to subsidiaries and subcontractors for whom a safety assurance plan is mandatory. It must be said that vital operators have several titles. Certain data must not be attacked. In this context, any information processed by computer means is presumed to be of a professional nature. The Atomic Energy Commission, for example, has set up its own Information Systems Security Laboratory, located in the Central Security Directorate. Telephones and business subscriptions to its staff can be deactivated in case of difficulty.

These devices have an access code and do not allow the encrypted contents of the mailbox to be displayed. As for laptops, two encryption systems – anti-theft and data – ensure their security. Faced with cloud computing and outsourcing, to maintain control of its information system, it must not use cloud computing and only resort to outsourcing if it hosts subcontractors on its premises.

For others, preference is given to the integration of digital security at the design stage. In the same vein, the degree of confidentiality of the data is assessed, which then gives rise to different conditions under which the applications operate and the data are made available. Personal data are those with the best protection within the information system; 90% of the data are stored in private centres, but those without any particular characteristics are kept in a public cloud.

Chapter 3
The Complexity of Digital Technology Makes It Difficult for Enterprises to Conceive of Its Security

It is in the complex and extremely changing context described in the foreword that enterprises are all using digital technology without always having had the opportunity (and the capacity) to fully measure its potential (nor all the shortcomings). To be able to understand the current situation of enterprises faced with digital risk, it is essential to analyse the complexity of digital, the nature of a message and the place of information in the enterprise.

This chapter is limited to an overview. To design digital, which has multiple facets (components, computers, telephones, connected objects, software, networks, Intranets, Internets, etc.) which are so closely linked to daily life (that they are not even perceptible anymore), everything happens as if, to draw an elephant, each person could only see one part of its body: who is its head, who is its back, who is its trunk, who is its tail and so on. One of the ways of thinking about the complexity of digital is, for example, to talk not about the Internet but about the Internets (because there are borders separating the digital from the rest of reality). It also has its own specific borders, which are very different.

Digital usage is a relationship between the user, the owner of the resource or data and the provider. No single contract regulates the whole economy. The Internet and more generally the digital world are today at the heart of all exchanges (from the individual to the enterprise, from the enterprise to society, from society to governments). The question of the role it plays in exchanges is central: Is the Internet a tool for these exchanges or more than that? As a tool, does it carry the basic principles to protect trade? To what extent can this tool guarantee that it will not alter, in any form whatsoever, the terms of trade between the various actors in the enterprise, from the employee, customer, or supplier to the enterprise or institutions?

In order to answer these questions, it is necessary to better identify the issues and the goals sought through the exchange. In an attempt to approach the complexity of digital technology, there is a great temptation to truncate and freeze it, thinking that each piece of the puzzle can then be considered as a whole, but in reality, separating what cannot be separated. For example, digital for military use is often distinguished

W. Amedzro St-Hilaire, *Digital Risk Governance*,
https://doi.org/10.1007/978-3-030-61386-0_3

from digital for civilian use, or digital for professional use is distinguished from digital for personal use, even though these two distinctions are deceptive, since digital security is cross-cutting and mixes military and civilian, professional and personal use.

However, it has been chosen by some states not to adopt exclusively this "technophobic" and false approach – because computing obviously implies the use of a computer – and to identify possible activities with a computer. For example, the simple act of sending an e-mail and wondering how it reaches its destination opens up a wide range of questions, leading to questions about how computers are networked together across continents, how information is conveyed over these networks, etc. Failure to take this cross-cutting view of digital security would lead to a failure to understand that failure to protect the system could be the cause of a major disaster. These interrelationships must be taken into account to ensure the digital security of businesses.

However, digital technology does not have a finite form; it is protean. The difficulty in representing the digital world lies in the fact that this network of networks – including all the objects and tools linked to it – is immense, dynamic and omnipresent involved in all exchanges, whether human or technological. Thus, digital technology presents itself to everyone as one or even several fascinating "black boxes," increasing our capacity for exchange and cooperation while reducing distance, absence, or even ignorance. Nevertheless, in terms of safety, the representation of the system is an essential condition for responsible use. Indeed, if its physical characteristics (shape, weight, etc.) and the effects produced are unknown, the proper use of the tool escapes the user: every technique is neither good nor bad in itself (a hammer is used to build one's house but also to murder one's neighbour).

Thus, the Internet and digital technology more generally are only tools for carrying out exchanges. However, the abyss of the Internet is used to express the fact that the Internet is beyond the comprehension of its users, and therefore, if it is misused, it may jeopardize not only their security but also that of their interlocutors, ranging from simple users to critical infrastructure operators. To improve this understanding, it is desirable to describe the exchange in both human and digital communications because it is important to improve knowledge to build trust.

Exchange is the activity at the origin of the evolution of every living being. For man, exchange represents the means by which each person progresses towards an end that he shares with another, a community or a society. The purpose represents what everyone expects from the exchange, a project in which everyone implements a process of improving his or her existing situation by consuming or producing the object that will be useful to him or her. The object can be material (exchanging a good), informational (exchanging a message), or even knowledge (exchanging know-how). Thus, the exchange is above all accompanied by an object, material or immaterial, which determines what is at stake in the exchange; it is what calls in the exchange the reciprocal behaviour between the author and his interlocutor, where each in turn becomes the subject and the recipient.

Between finality and reciprocity, exchange represents a two-dimensional process: the so-called vertical or internal exchange led by each interlocutor within himself and the so-called horizontal exchange rather turned towards the external interlocutor to form together a "global system" that connects humans. This raises the question of the "vertical" or internal process of producing messages for exchange. The "vertical" or internal process of the exchange includes all the means to move from the project of exchanging, for example, buying or selling a car, to a series of exchange actions guided by the purpose of the exchange.

This process prepares in particular the exchanged object for its transfer with favourable conditions. During the "vertical" process, the object of the exchange will undergo three transformations: (1) materialization to define the object in the real world – it is the purchase or sale of an automobile; (2) virtualization to define the object in a system of value and reference, both individual and societal – rules must be respected and documents must be gathered that have certain characteristics when an automobile is sold; and (3) packaging to define the object in the transport system of the messages linked to this sale.

These three levels are illustrated below using the example of an exchange between two individuals whose purpose is the sale of a motor vehicle. What about the process of materializing the message? The process of materialization defines the existence of the object, here the automobile, its reality, which, unlike a virtual world or an imaginary world, translates into the existence of properties evaluated in a tangible way through our senses and our knowledge. The car is characterized by the material of which it is made and its actual properties such as its shape, colour and technical performance, all of which will affect his sale. In order to understand the difference between the imaginary, the virtual and the real, the example of the tree emphasizes that the imaginary cannot be confused with the virtual, whereas these two notions are very often confused when it comes to the digital.

The virtualization process places the object, in this case the car for sale, in a system of reference and values. The virtual framework allows everyone to represent the object in this system with the help of rules and institutions (commercial law, chosen currency, etc.). This framework makes it possible to provide the elements of decision that will guide the actions that each one envisages. This is why it is often necessary to explain that the virtual is not opposed to the real but to the actual. In the pursuit of their objective, the interlocutors agree beforehand on an individual or societal value system, regulated by a trusted third party in order to guarantee the successful completion of the exchange. This may be, for example, civil law, commercial law in force in a particular country, a bank or a trusted institution to guarantee the value of the currency of exchange. This level is described as virtual because the organization's actions only manifest themselves later in their effects.

The packaging process defines the properties that the object of the exchange will have to respect for its transport through its communication system, which also has the role of connecting the interlocutors of the exchange in the same place or as if they were in the same place. The place of exchange is the place of pacts and negotiations. This process ensures the transformation of the object for its transport, especially when the place of exchange is remote. In the case of the exchange of human messages, the conditioning process transforms the message with the help of a language and then adapts it as a signal through an adapter: the voice organ that an interlocutor will pick up with the help of his or her auditory sensory organ.

To achieve their purpose in the exchange, each one uses several communication channels, each in charge of a particular role. The social sciences and humanities describe this mode of communication, whether at the individual or group level, as "multi-channel." There are logical, physical and control channels. The logical channel represents the medium for transporting messages encoded using a language or code with the aim of making them transportable and then intelligible to its recipient(s) while preserving the original meaning and organization of the information transported. For example, a sentence in Chinese will not be understood by an Englishman who does not master Chinese. The physical channel allows the transport of the object; its characteristics will be directly related to the constraints jointly imposed by the transported object, the medium of its deployment and then the target to which it is directed and the source that emits it. This implies adaptability at each of these levels: the object, the environment, the sources and the recipients. For example, an oral message will be transmitted by voice as a signal, a car will be delivered by road. The control channel equips each individual with a regulation and control mechanism to assess a situation according to the objectives to be achieved. Using specific signs or words, this channel supervises the exchange, detects anomalies and issues alerts in case of deviation. For example, one nods in response to a caller who wants to be understood.

Exchange is above all one of the phenomena at the origin of all individual and group life; it is through their exchanges that societies of men have organized themselves for their equilibrium and against their imbalances. Since the beginning of the twentieth century, societal exchange has been a subject of study for anthropology, but also for the human and social sciences. The exchange can be reduced to a set of actions and reactions that follow one another between an individual and his interlocutor, each driven by the obligation of reciprocity. Multiple forms of exchange exist, whose manifestations can be verbal and/or non-verbal so that each can situate himself in relation to the other and decide to exchange with him according to what he observes of him and what he believes about him. Each individual exchanges with the knowledge of the functioning of the sphere(s) within which he or she exchanges and with the knowledge of the other. Hence the need for digital technology to make this knowledge available to as many people as possible, which is far from being the case at present.

Each individual prepares his or her exchange as a consumer and/or supplier. The role of the "virtual" level of each individual is to promote the chances of achieving his or her purpose in the exchange by taking into account the inter- and intra-sphere factors potentially capable of influencing the situation of the exchange. A certain type of structure of modern societies emerges which dominates where three main spheres of exchange can be distinguished: the state, the market and the individual. They are independent; each one offers circulations, shown in green on the diagram below, but capable of interacting with each other. Within each of these spheres, trade is defined as the mode of circulation of goods and services involving an assessment to reach an agreement between two parties, the producer and the consumer. It should also be noted that the mode of circulation depends on the object and purpose of the exchange; it characterizes each sphere regulated by a global and superior authority.

Modes of circulation of goods and services are treated differently according to the distance of the interlocutors, all the more so as the object of the exchange crosses the public and private spheres. In the different modes of traffic for exchange represented in the diagram below (road, postal, banking and then digital), the circulation of goods and services is supervised by regulatory bodies because it must be optimized between all users. The exchange cannot be reduced to a simple communication channel between a sender and a receiver. Thus, the role of infrastructures will be to pool societal services and, on the other hand, to organize their transport and distribution. When exchange infrastructures connect two distant interlocutors by means of public and private networks, several properties appear to be essential:

- The use that determines the purpose that the user and the service provider pursue through the provision of the network (a trip, sending a letter, buying a car, multiple uses for digital, etc.). The shape and performance of the tool will be the key elements.
- The terminal systems that are the vectors of the user's vertical (internal) journey in order to produce the object of the exchange in a form compatible with the transport medium (using a car, pen and paper, credit card, multiple terminal systems for digital, etc.).
- Education which places the user in the Community system by teaching him the concepts of use, rights, obligations and rules of prudence linked to the mutualization of the network at public level (which presupposes respect for the highway code, spelling, technical advice and still too much self-learning for digital, etc.).
- The services that determine the applications from which the user can benefit and for which he or she has been trained (taking into account the realities of road traffic, data routing times, exchange rates, countless digital services and applications, etc.).
- The expected performance of the service which determines the objective between the user and the service provider and, by the same token, the choice of tools (toll lanes, service stations, stamps, post offices, agios, bank branch, multiple tools for digital, etc.).
- Intermediate systems (relaying or routing) which make it possible to overcome the disadvantages due to distance (road interchanges, postal routing, clearing houses, multiform relays for digital, etc.).
- The density and coverage of the networks that determine the proximity of the service to the user and the equity of its distribution (road, postal, banking, national and international networks and borderless networks for digital, whereas the notion of border exists in all exchanges except for digital exchange); access to the networks that determine the flexibility offered to the user to benefit from the service.
- The security of users, networks and transported objects, which determines the risks to which they are exposed and provides for their education as well as the provision of tools so that they can control the effects of their actions (driving

license and speedometer, acknowledgment of receipt, balance of account, encryption and authentication for digital).
- Overall surveillance generally under the responsibility of the institution that manages and regulates it (state regulation except for digital exchange).

It appears that the infrastructures underlying digital exchange are clearly distinct from those underlying traditional exchanges. Their characteristics are those of the digital world: anonymity, globalization and absence of borders, multiplicity of uses and regulations.

As explained above, human exchange establishes multi-channel communication with its interlocutor by means of logical, physical and control channels. In a digital exchange, this complexity is further increased by the network made up of a multitude of interconnected intermediate systems forming a multitude of infrastructures: it is a system of systems. It is these interweaves that often lead some specialists to evoke the Internet to evoke different subsets: the Internet as a communication system composed of physical and logical channels; the Internet as a service between digital clients and servers in order to offer shared digital services such as the circulation of user data or their storage; and the Internet as an application in order to offer intelligence (communities of experience: Facebook, Doctissimo, etc.) for human and societal uses.

Digital is both an individual and a societal exchange based on a complex infrastructure. From their origins, machines have made it possible to automate the complex activities of human communication. But digital technology today seems to have raised this relationship between individuals to the level of an exchange of unprecedented complexity. In order to understand the complexity of digital technology and to enlighten those people for whom digital technology constitutes a "black box" - located beyond the familiar interface (computer, mobile phone, etc.) - through which everyone accesses the Internet, it is necessary to open it in order to offer a simplified representation. The diagram below shows the different environments of an e-mail message.

To grasp the complexity of digital and to enlighten those for whom digital is a "black box" beyond the familiar interface (computer, mobile phone, etc.) through which everyone accesses the Internet, it is necessary to open it, and to propose a simplified representation of it. The following diagram shows the different environments of an e-mail message.

In an electronic exchange, the subject of the exchange is an information message from a source to a recipient. The last few decades have shown a meteoric evolution of what is exchanged in the digital world: in the 1980s, messages were simply symbolized by signals (represented by A in the diagram below); since the 1990s, messages have been enriched with information to describe the object being sold, which may also include an image (B). But in recent years, with the advent of 3D printers, it is knowledge such as experience and now know-how (C) that is exchanged via the network, operating procedures for the manufacture of objects. Information has become a raw material from which we can achieve what we want. Like any raw material, it can be protected, sold, refined, etc. Moreover, the economic actors who use this raw material do so in a totally deregulated manner. This is not the case for all raw materials. The same principles as for human exchange, described above, are present in digital exchange: a "vertical" or internal and "horizontal" or external process.

As already seen for human exchange, the "vertical" or internal process produces an object in a form adapted to the mode of transport; for digital exchange, it is a matter of transforming the message into a digital signal. When this message is received, the "vertical" route, which is the reverse of the one made by the sender, will be followed by the recipient, who will be able to find the original message from the digital signal by applying precisely the same operations. These particular operations are generally referred to as protocols. A protocol ensures interoperability between the different processes necessary for the exchange.

The stage of the materialization of the message defines the existence of the message by giving the meaning of the message; the latter gives the message its reality and expresses the finality of the exchange: "to sell a car" which corresponds above all, for each interlocutor, to the highlighting of a need to exchange. This process of materialization also implies a shared definition of the objective and modes of exchange. During a digital exchange, several questions will arise as to the choice of virtualization process, which must also be known in advance by the parties involved. Virtualization is based on one or more reference systems in relation to the purpose to be achieved. This process starts from the materialized message and adapts it to the reference system. This is the role of applications (email, web service, etc.) or digital services or even a physical medium (Wi-Fi or 3G). Virtualization also defines protocols using languages that must be understandable by everyone. For example, a word processing software is an application for writing a text, understandable by other word processing software and recipients. Similarly, to "sell a car," the "sale" application or software allows to virtualize and translate each action contributing to the sale. Virtualization must also be compatible with the constraints of the physical medium so that the message can follow the packaging process.

The packaging process defines the properties that the message will have to respect for its transport due to the constraints of the communication system. This step produces a message that can be transmitted through the physical channel. The transition from natural language to digital language is accomplished through the process of codification. Firstly, the message initially described in natural language is transformed into binary language, i.e. a numerical code (0,1), also called signal (0 = no signal, 1 = signal), the only format understandable by computers and telecommunications equipment. In order to be transported, the message cannot retain its original integrity; it must be cut into packets and subdivided into fragments. In order to optimize its passage through digital networks, each fragment will evolve through a mesh of switch nodes. Just like postal mail, so that packages are not lost and can be reunited by the recipient, each package is placed in an envelope with the sender's and recipient's addresses and an identification number.

Secondly, the message fragmentation mechanisms must not damage the message, allow for its recompositing and allow each packet or packet fragment to be conveyed independently to the appropriate addressee while grouping together other packets belonging to other sources and/or addressees. Since its inception, the Internet has offered a multitude of protocols to adapt to the different characteristics of media and/or applications. The history of the Internet explains its complexity as a result of a succession of technological convergences ranging from the convergence of virtual operating systems (Java) or network protocols (IP and DNS) to the convergence of voice and data, copper and fibre optic cabling, etc. The Internet is a complex system, with a wide range of different technologies.

Like the multi-channel mode of human exchange, the "horizontal" process of the Internet distinguishes between the logical channel (access, transport and distribution networks to convey information); the physical channel (cables to convey the signal in order to annihilate the effect of distance); and the control channel, which allows each interlocutor to control his or her exchange has, to date, been only very weakly structured within the digital environment. As a result, the security of messages during their transport is based on the choices of the sender and the recipient, who, in the best case, establish conventions or uses with little means to control them.

The Internet infrastructure is not a "point-to-point" network because if a connection were to be established to everyone's home with everyone else, the resulting mesh would be too complex and too costly in view of the almost three billion Internet users today. Nevertheless, two interlocutors may wish, if only to preserve their privacy, to establish a dedicated point-to-point channel for their electronic communication space. Based on the concept that it is possible to create several logical channels on the same physical link, the principle of multiplexing at the signal level is then applied, for example, by reserving temporal or spatial frequencies. The use of multiplexing techniques allows this optimization.

On each side of the media is a multiplexer/demultiplexer. Such equipment hosts a large number of terminal systems at the entrance to the multiplexer. The overall transmission capacity is thus divided into sub-channels, the capacity of which depends on the technique used. These are of different kinds.

Mutualization through multiplexers raises the question of how packets are conveyed within a large network. The connection between a user and a server via an Internet network forms a chain in which the terminal systems (DTEs) are connected by communication nodes (DCEs).

The nature of the sections that make it up may be heterogeneous depending on the operator providing the service. In order to make the distance between source and destination transparent, i.e. not perceptible, messages are relayed through different devices called relays. In this way, both source and recipient feel that the messages they exchange have not undergone any transformation. This exchange is represented using sequential diagrams. A switch provides the switching function which allows the selection of a path from node to node. A switched network consists of logical channels for data transit and switches. Its role is to send the information, which arrives on an input channel, to the output channel. The most well-known types of switching are the following:

Circuit switching: terminals establish a virtual point-to-point circuit; they are in connected mode, whereby all exchanges follow the same path; the telephone network is an example. During transmission between the two terminals, the virtual circuit is blocked.

Message switching: a message is associated with the recipient's address and transmitted to the proximity switch, which waits for the entire message to be received before relaying it. In case of error and delay, the transmission is blocked.

Packet switching: a message is divided into units, each one associated with an address to enable it to be routed through the WAN and a number to enable it to be reconstructed. The units are transmitted via independent paths via switches. Packets can get lost. The IP protocol follows this principle.

Frame switching: Frame switching takes over packet switching on virtual circuits but does not provide error control. Frame relay uses this mode by offering a service of fast virtual links (similar to virtual circuit), permanent or switched.

Cell switching: a cell is a small unit of fixed size (53 bytes) which has the advantage of removing all control over the data and only exploiting the cell header. The functions of the network switches are reduced to connection establishment and routing. ATM (Asynchronous Transfer Mode) is an asynchronous transfer mode for cell switching. Their exceptional performance has enabled the implementation of multimedia applications.

Label switching: born out of IP routing and packet switching to improve switching speed while incorporating additional network services such as flow prioritization. The principle is to insert a label placed at the header of the message so that, very quickly, the router can read it and apply routing rules. These assets currently make it the most widely deployed core network architecture by the majority of telecom operators.

To cover all points of the planet, states have mobilized by deploying cable networks on their territory. The areas not covered, or white areas, have been covered in less than 10 years, providing every citizen with access to the network. But, in doing so, the states have entrusted their infrastructures to specialized operators, sometimes foreign, and have built this network by segment to spread out the sometimes-considerable budgets (3) Advanced techniques for the exchange of messages. Across a geographically extended world, the logical channel combines several functions: addressing for packet distribution, global infrastructure for end-to-end distribution and routing for selecting routes based on addresses.

Each packet is associated with a source IP address to identify the source from which the packet originated and a destination address to enable intermediary systems to transport the packets through the network to their recipients. This assumes that there is a unique way to identify each entity that may send or receive a packet. Like postal mail, the most efficient global system for assigning an address while ensuring uniqueness had to be hierarchical. Moreover, this addressing system had to be codified in order to allow its transformation into binary on the Internet media. This hierarchical system was therefore deployed in the following way with a parent addressing domain to identify a network number as a city name in a country and a child addressing domain to designate a node in the network number as a street in the city.

The principle below indicates that the number of available network numbers worldwide may become saturated. Calculating the maximum number of possible 24-bit networks (0 or 1), we reach 16,777,216 networks. When you bring this figure closer to the three billion Internet users, the need for the new IPv6 addressing, which allows addresses on 256 bits and on an additional hierarchical level, becomes obvious. However, two other techniques can be used to expand the number of network addresses: the CIDR (Classless Inter-Domain Routing) technique, which is considered a prefix that would specify the "country" of the IP address, and the subnet mask technique, which is considered a suffix that would specify the "building" on the street.

To simplify the notation, an IP address is commonly represented by four digits separated by a dot: "1.2.3.4." Packaging allows the message to be prepared for transport by cutting it up and labelling it with an IP address, both of which play a major role in the horizontal or external journey. The Internet is based on a global infrastructure made up of interchanges (like a road network) linked together by roads (links). Each house, neighbourhood, city, country, or continent is associated with an IP address. In order to ensure the uniqueness of the address of each site, a hierarchical breakdown is proposed at the global level. For example, the blue and pink zones in the diagram below contain billions of networks; three networks are represented per zone; in the blue zone, three addresses are mentioned: "company 1 – 23.168.0.0"; "user – 50.172.0.0"; and "company 2 – 23.172.1.0."

It is from the destination address that the relays or intermediary systems will decide the route the packet will take. Each exchanger has an automatic mechanism capable of reading, for each packet, the destination addresses and then putting it on the right route according to this address; this is why these devices are called routers. As soon as the process of coding the message through the logical channel into an electrical signal is completed, it is transported in this form on the physical channel. The objective of global interconnection networks such as the Internet or mobile telephony is to enable access and distribution to every citizen. In the majority of countries, distribution is carried out according to a principle of equity. As already mentioned, since the Internet infrastructure is not a "point-to-point" network, the principle for connecting the whole planet has therefore been to provide two types of network corresponding to two modes of distribution: one, rather robust, to cover large distances (the core network) and the other, more branched, to ensure the network connection to the home of any subscriber.

The extent of a network is measured by the nature of the medium and the distance between the furthest points it connects. Networks linking two remote nodes can be distinguished according to their global scale (Wide Area Network) and regional scale (Metropolitan Area Network), or at the level of a company (Local Area Network) or an individual (Personal Area Network). The connection between a user and a server via an Internet network forms a chain where Data Terminal Equipment (DTE) terminal systems are connected by Data Communication Equipment (DCE) communication nodes. The nature of the sections that make up these networks can be heterogeneous depending on the operator providing the service.

The core network is based on a reticular structure of nodes and links. The first constraint of this structure is the physical coverage of the territories, and the second constraint is the capacity to pool a very large number of communications on the same link. The physical networks are of a wired or aerial nature.

Their deployment ensures the transmission of binary elements between two equipment in point-to-point mode or between several equipment in multipoint mode where the terminals are connected on the same physical link. The structure of physical networks imposes a limitation of the rates which is measured in bit/s (signal/s); the term bandwidth is then used. Network speeds are at the heart of the problems since, for a long time, the physical limitations of media have hindered the development of applications requiring large amounts of bandwidth such as video or image in general.

The physical medium can be a physically defined cable, such as copper, coaxial and fibre optic, but can also be air, such as radio and satellite. Currently, fibre optics is the most widely used technique because of its performance, both for core and access networks. The optical transport networks of the operators' core networks deploy transponders with a capacity of around 20 terabits/s per fibre. Wireless or mobile network technologies are the result of a history in which choices of architectures have been made according to countries, expected services, or available technologies.

Currently, the convergence of these different architectures is accelerating in order to facilitate access to resources (VoIP, ToIP, Internet, etc.) but also their management. 3G and, more recently, 4G networks offer services that make mobile terminals as well connected as laptops and desktop computers. Efforts to achieve this result have focused on the core network.

A mobile network is a network in architecture 2/3 composed of an access network and a core network. In order to provide users with fluid and agile means of communication, their end network is made up of a multitude of wireless networks. The access network offers an access base called BTS at its end point, to transmit or receive the radio signal between the terminal and it. The BTSs in the same geographical area depend on a controller (BSC) authorizing access to the MSC/SGSN gateway. Its role will be to allow interconnection with users' databases in order to manage their authorizations and authentication via their identity (their SIM card). There are two types of databases: one that holds the identifiers of users on their home network (Home LR) and one that holds the identifiers of users on their visiting networks (Visited LR).

The core network not only allows messages to be relayed but also provides interconnection gateways with the public switched telephone network (PSTN) in order to contact analogue telephone sets and with the Internet network in order to contact other GPRS or ToIP/VoIP terminals. The access network, also known as the local loop, refers to all the links and equipment that connect subscriber facilities to the transmission network. The access network allows the collection and distribution of subscriber traffic. The copper pair can be used to support voice and data traffic using digital techniques. Other media can be used or combined together (optical fibre, radio, coaxial, etc.) to serve businesses or residential homes with digital speeds under varying economic conditions.

During an electronic communication, the protocols will allow each system to initiate, maintain and terminate its relationship with its interlocutor. A control loop similar to the feedback loop of systems is established between them. When a source emits information, even binary, it controls the emission action it has formulated. There are two control mechanisms: either on the message itself or on the channel.

In this second case, the log sets up messages assigned to control the other messages. Maintaining the TCP/IP connection is a fundamental principle of WANs. It is an application of the previous principle where two interlocutors (a client and a digital server) establish a logical channel. The connection is initialized, maintained and then broken in near real time during the communication between a source and its recipient. This connection provides a solid foundation for applications to run on a homogeneous channel with full transparency of the granularity of the physical network, core or access.

What digital infrastructures are in place? Like the virtual level of human exchanges, digital exchange has a global structure. It is the increasing evolution of systems to be configured and then maintained that has led to the provision of a centralized service, the DNS. The DNS infrastructure is quasi-public, federated for Internet users by institutions or governments. The overall infrastructure is based on a digital client/server architecture in which the servers are organized hierarchically.

Naming consists of juxtaposing the resource name representing each level of the hierarchy, the lowest in the hierarchy. The general principle is that the client sends a request to a proximity server to obtain the domain name resulting from the resolution, from the child servers to the root or root servers. These are the backbone of the global DNS, and there are about 13 of them, hosted in the United States of America and under the control of the Internet Assigned Numbers Authority (IANA).

From an operational point of view, the DNS allows both a technical function to communicate between domains and interconnected servers via queries and an indirect commercial function through the search and prioritization functions of a site on the domain name. The Domain Name System (DNS) allows the conversion of an IP address into a name or domain and vice versa. Since it is easier to enter name addresses than number addresses such as an IP address "1.2.3.4," the first step was to configure an IP/domain name association on each workstation. The DNS has become a business model for some players who, with the aim of speculative resale, have begun to acquire domain names from enterprises with a high reputation.

Electronic messaging enables mail to be sent from shared and/or private services by providing a number of functions derived from those offered by postal mail: acknowledgment of receipt, etc. The advantages are the acceleration in communication modes and, therefore, in decision cycles. The messaging infrastructure is a digital client/server architecture consisting of an access network on the one hand and an infrastructure for routing messages on the other. The information principle is the fundamental principle of the Internet where the essential tool for the user is the search and classification of information. The infrastructure of the web is based on three elements: the robot, also called crawler or spider, which collects all the pages; the index which contains all the words of all the pages collected by the robot, then links it to the URLs of the pages from which they come, identified using DNS domain names; and the interface for sending the request and receiving the results.

The infrastructure of the web is based on a client/server architecture where the web browser is a client and the web servers are of two types: the content server that holds the information and makes it available and the search server that holds the general index with the response ranking algorithm. The process of a digital search consists of seven steps: the user launches a query; the search engine queries the index using the words of the query; the index points to pages that contain the keywords; the index ranks the pages in an order determined by a specific algorithm: Search Engine Results Pages (SERP); the index prepares the list of responses (title, extract, URL) and transmits it to the user using HTTP and HTTPS protocols; the user clicks on the "title" of the page and connects to the site concerned; the index learns the link between the initial query and the response chosen in step 6, above, to improve the relevance of the next search.

To describe knowledge, the Hypertext Markup Language (HTML) breaks down distributed knowledge into content pages; the HTML page is the elementary entity located and uniquely identified by its URL; it links HTML pages together: a bit like the "breadcrumb trail" principle, knowledge is structured in a network. Once the information is found on a main page, the index and the links followed will lead the user to more and more precise information. Hypertext Transfer Protocol (HTTP) and Hypertext Transfer Protocol Secure (HTTPS) are the protocols for transporting links and pages within the web architecture. This capacity is based on the documentary organization of the web servers and in particular of the webmaster. Each website has a list head, often called an "index," which guides the visitor from page to page. The interest of this model is the very small size of an HTML page which allows to consider mass access.

During a visit to a website (during phase 6 of the research), the servers incorporate several capabilities into their protocol:

- Read the information transported in the HTTP protocol that makes the source of the request unique: this user. It is also possible to note its IP address, connection domain name, etc.
- Link this information to the information requested from the user: his login name, password and other information given when registering on its website.
- The server may also include in the protocol the request for a connection file called a cookie in which the servers incorporate information such as session identifiers (temporary), connection times and other information.

This small, harmless file would remain so if it were not used many times: by site managers to build so-called "user experience" profiles; by attackers to obtain session numbers and to insinuate themselves into the legitimate flow; and for any other use. Since the industrial revolution at the beginning of the nineteenth century, the search for the pooling of services which are too costly at individual level but which can be envisaged at community level has been the major societal concern, leading to the deployment of the railway, etc. In the digital world, this approach has led successively to the creation of:

- In the 1950s–1980s: "IBM mainframe" applications centralized and shared between enterprises
- In the 1980s–1990s: expert services in leased telephony (IBM, etc.) such as fax and telecom links for small businesses

- In the 1990s: mutualization of applications through application service providers (ASP, the ancestor of SaaS).

Cloud computing is now the natural evolution of the mutualized distribution of all-in-one IT services, combining in particular productivity, competitiveness, agility and organization of the enterprise's security. The failure to secure information systems, the complexity and number of standards and laws that must be respected, and the considerable costs that these obligations generate lead the enterprise to ask itself the question of outsourcing the security function as well as many others, such as that of telecom links to expensive software development applications.

Digital Cloud Computing is a new way of providing resources and services since the objective is to assemble technologies (protocols, standards, etc.) and computer components (servers, network equipment, etc.) existing and well-proven. It is a paradigm based on the principle of an "on-demand" service totally adapted to the client's one-off or ongoing needs. But what seems most original is that the resources are servers, programs and telecom links grouped together in a single service offer. After 2 years of work, the National Institute of Standards and Technology (NIST) has summarized cloud computing in five key points:

- On-demand self-service: services and resources are offered and delivered from a portal-type architecture according to the client's needs.
- Accessibility of the service offered from anywhere on the network and via various platforms (laptops, mobile phones, etc.).
- Pooling of resources: physical or especially virtual, these resources can be parameterized and brought together to be duplicated, allocated dynamically to serve several customers through a multi-tenant model.
- Elasticity in relation to need: the IT provided adapts quickly to a variation in need, measurable service. The expected results are evaluated through mechanisms capable of measuring consumption parameters, etc.

Contrary to popular belief, outsourcing is not part of the definition of cloud computing. The service models offered by the digital cloud concern three types of services:

- IaaS (Infrastructure as a Service): infrastructures are provided as a service in client/provider mode almost instantaneously without investment or installation of hardware, while retaining the possibility of changing their capacity according to their needs.
- PaaS (Platform as a Service): platforms are aimed at software developers wishing to adapt their software and put it into production without delay on powerful platforms according to their clients' demand.
- SaaS (Software as a Service): a new form of distribution, purchase and use of software, configured and activated on the SaaS provider's servers, which differs from software installed on the client's servers or workstations.

The deployment model specifies the location and organization responsible for managing the cloud infrastructure. Four models can be distinguished according to the circle of diffusion, their manager and the person responsible for them:

- Public Digital Cloud: accessible to the general public and private groups but owned and managed by a cloud provider.
- Private Digital Cloud: accessible to the external organization that manages it or entrusts it to a third party; the resources will be hosted on the premises of the organization or third party.
- Community Digital Cloud: accessible to different organizations with common interests: policies, security rules, activities, specific needs, etc., managed by one or more of these bodies or by a third party and which may be located on the premises of one of these bodies or of the third party.

The Hybrid Cloud combines several of these models. Ninety percent of our data is stored in private data centres, but data that does not have any particular characteristics is kept in a cloud, public cloud. The prospects for the digital cloud are now well established, but there are still reservations about its deployment. One of the key principles is to offer services on demand on a large scale, which implies a multi-tenant, complex and open infrastructure that may present new vulnerabilities. In particular, a public cloud model relies on the (unreliable) Internet and involves applications, sometimes business applications, which opens them up to the risk of cyber attacks.

Performance also comes into play depending on the quality of the network to access these applications. Nevertheless, these infrastructures have proven, modelled configurations from the physical layer to the application layer, which provides models, simplifies them and allows testing and verification for closer monitoring. Furthermore, data has a value that many enterprises do not measure properly. A company like Facebook invests $1. 2 billion in a data centre without charging the customer, so the resources come from the exploitation of customer data and advertising. Nothing is free on the Internet. Client concerns will be multifaceted:

- Network availability: performance being the key to a company's competitiveness; losing availability calls into question the choice of managed and shared IT; loss of physical control of data which is now only partially owned; losing control threatens the principle of confidentiality.
- Supplier viability: the multi-tenant supplier depends on several third parties; the lack of maturity of these suppliers can lead a customer to question their reliability.

As far as cloud computing is concerned, it is to be trusted to a limited extent as the geolocation of data and the degree of application of IT hygiene measures are not guaranteed. It is difficult to ensure that the provider, subject to financial profitability objectives, is able to apply the required security measures. In addition, there is a reversibility issue: once data is put in the cloud, is there a robust enough way to recover it? The support of government security agencies is crucial, given the asymmetry of means and the complexity of the issues at stake.

Chapter 4
Intense Interstate Competition in Cyberspace

The mastery of data has profound economic repercussions and has enabled the emergence of economic actors capable of competing with states. It is also a geopolitical issue, and the national strategies deployed by the states themselves compete with each other. According to ExpertActions Group, data should no longer be understood only as a legal and commercial subject but as an international policy issue in its own right. Cyberspace is unique in that it is the only strategic space created by human hands. This immaterial world appears as a world to be conquered or, at the very least, in which to exercise power, in the same way as the material world, first on land, then at sea and finally in the air, has for centuries been the site of confrontations for supremacy. The locus of these confrontations is now largely immaterial and located outside the physical borders of states, in a space without territory, but not without materiality.

Cyberspace is in fact composed of a hardware layer which corresponds to all the devices, servers, routers and computers which allow the interconnection of machines and a logical or software layer which covers the communication elements between the machines themselves, i.e. the protocols, or between humans and machines, i.e. the software. These first two layers form the technical organization of cyberspace and define the way networks work. The third layer, known as the semantic or informational layer, corresponds to all the information that passes through the first two. This segmentation into three layers justifies a difference in national approaches depending on which cyberspace culture one chooses to favour.

The United States has thought about the development of cyberspace at the same time as its positioning as a leader in this new strategic space. The ultra-liberal American model, carried by its private players, the new colonial enterprises of the digital world, is sovereign, dominating key sectors, imposing its standards and favouring its economic players to the detriment of users. This is opposed by authoritarian Chinese and Russian models, which segment the digital space in order to have perfect control over it within the country's physical borders. Is this model really sovereign? Finally, in the face of these strategies, those of other states sometimes

W. Amedzro St-Hilaire, *Digital Risk Governance*,
https://doi.org/10.1007/978-3-030-61386-0_4

appear idealistic and not very pragmatic. These states are often presented as the challenge of cyberspace, with a large consumer market. Are they really actors in these states? What is the nature of American policy in the search for undisputed leadership?

The United States has structured its strategic and geopolitical vision of cyberspace on its technical architecture, defined by its first two layers, with 90% of communications in cyberspace flowing underwater via cables, and the use of root servers to run the Internet. This is a liberal view, with fixed segments owned by the Department of Defense on the root servers, such as the server owned by the US Army research lab, or the server owned by the National Aeronautics and Space Administration (NASA). The American State thus exercises very strong material control, with private action being exerted mainly on the software and semantic layers.

Data control is the priority axis of both American economic redevelopments, structured around economic giants such as Gafam, and the American security strategy, supported by the very important powers entrusted to the National Security Agency (NSA). This priority builds on Washington's long tradition of open-door policy, or the free flow of data, which aims to open markets in order to maintain American pre-eminence, both military and economic. However, this strategy no longer seems as simple to implement as it once was. It must be said that there are complex relations between the Gafam and the American state.

No country other than the United States has so closely integrated the use or even capture of data as part of its economic strategy and security policy. This policy has been very conducive to the development of an ecosystem of innovation and economic development in the digital sector, which has led to the emergence of the American digital giants. The support of the Defense Advanced Research Projects Agency (DARPA) to the digital sector has been instrumental in the emergence of this ecosystem. The combined effects of the 2008 crisis, leading to the disappearance of the most fragile enterprises and leaving the others without competitors, and of an economic model based on the network effect have favoured the creation of monopolies, or even conglomerates.

The United States is committed to the principle of free competition and has been able on several occasions in its history to dismember the economic monopolies that had formed in the field of oil exploitation and later in telecommunications. In the case of digital, however, it is only recently that criticisms have emerged about the concentration of players in cyberspace, and even then, they are not unanimously shared by the American political class. However, legal action has been taken against Facebook and Google. In fact, the relationship of American power with Gafam and other digital enterprises is ambiguous.

Under Obama, the authorities claim ownership of the Internet in an assumed and almost messianic digital nationalism when Secretary of State Hillary Clinton promised in 2010 to bring down the digital Iron Curtain in reference to the vast Chinese online censorship system that was being deployed. By failing to support them internationally, by agitating threats of retaliation after the digital giants' adoption of taxation, or by presenting the DPMR as anticompetitive, the current US President does not presume the support of these enterprises. The Gafams are traditionally identified as supporters of the Democratic Party, within which the debate on their dismantling is taking place.

But, in fact, the border between the Gafam and the American State is particularly porous; the inter-organizational and interpersonal links that unite these two worlds contribute to the structuring of a complexes' techno-state, technocratic, even, in the almost etymological sense of the term. To take the example of Google, between 2005 and 2016, the enterprise hired nearly 200 members of the US government, a majority of whom were lobbyists, and, at the same time, some 60 of its employees joined the White House, government agencies, or Congress.

Between 2015 and 2018, Alphabet spent nearly $70 million on lobbying in Washington: 82% of its registered lobbyists for the period 2017–2018 previously worked either in the White House, government agencies, or Congress. In the end, this phenomenon is more a result of the merger than of competition between the state and the Gafams.

Basically, the data policy is based on aggressive legal extraterritoriality. Beyond the supposed or real link between the political authorities and these enterprises, the conflict between Apple and the American government is symptomatic of a battle for digital security between the American state and American digital enterprises: in 2015, Apple refused to hand over to the FBI the keys to the encryption of the iPhone of the author of the San Bernardino shooting. In 2016, it was Microsoft that refused to deliver to the FBI the emails of a drug trafficker, hosted on servers in Ireland. The direct requisition, without international judicial cooperation, seemed illegal to Microsoft and likely to further damage the trust of its customers, already begun by the Patriot Act and the Snowden revelations.

The CLOUD Act (Clarifying Lawful Overseas Use of Data Act) was the US government's legal response to the reluctance of digital enterprises. This law makes it easier for the US government to obtain data stored or transiting abroad, in particular via US operators and online service providers. This legislation forces US digital enterprises to accept full digital security in the United States. If we think of the state not as a block with clearly identified contours (in the manner of jurists) but more as a set of practices and a rationality of governmentality, then it is clear that what these developments show is the incorporation of these private actors into the state. It is the co-option of their infrastructures and the dissemination of their know-how in the processing and analysis of masses of data now crucial in contemporary forms of government. It is therefore a merger that is taking place, much more than competition between the states and the Gafams who would seek to replace the governments.

China is opting for a global digital policy with results that are still incomplete. Both China and Russia have developed policies to guarantee their digital security and to emancipate themselves from American hegemony. These policies, which are far removed from Western democratic values, have met with mixed success but should not be neglected in any way. The American model is opposed to the authoritarian Chinese model, segmenting the digital space in order to have perfect control over it, prohibiting foreign enterprises from transferring their electronic data to their national headquarters and using the personal data of its citizens to establish the domination of the Chinese Communist Party. Is this model really sovereign?

China's shift to cyberspace is noteworthy. China's digital power has grown very strongly. In terms of cloud computing capabilities, China is in second place behind the United States and is experiencing extremely strong growth in activity, so it tends to challenge the American omnipotence in this field. The number of Internet users between 2000 and 2016 has shifted significantly in favour of China. Thus, in 2000, out of 412.8 million Internet users, 122 million were located in the United States, 77 million in the European Union, 38 million in Japan, 22 million in China, 21 million in South Korea, 16 million in Canada and 9 million in Australia.

Brazil, Mexico and Malaysia each had 5 million users and India 6 million. In 2016, the Internet had 3.4 billion users, including 733 million located in China, 414 million in the European Union, 391 million in India and 246 million in the United States. Brazil had 126 million users and Japan 118 million. Russia, which had less than 5 million Internet users in 2000, will have 106 million in 2016. Next come Mexico with 76 million, Indonesia with 66 million and South Korea and Nigeria with 48 million each, followed by Turkey with 46 million and Iran with 43 million. This development is no coincidence: the Chinese have been able to measure the importance of pursuing a policy of power in cyberspace. China came into cyberspace in the second half of the 1990s on its own terms. From the outset, it adopted the segmentation of cyberspace into three layers and decided to become sovereign over these three layers, at least in its own national space. The Great Golden Wall operates data control on the first layer, in the form of a gigantic firewall allowing the Chinese state to control, with great efficiency, everything that enters and leaves the Chinese information space.

At the second layer, the Chinese population can benefit from the services of national operators who offer in local and easily controllable versions, with legislation requiring data to be stored on the national territory, the equivalent of what international operators offer. The big Gafam (Google, Apple, Facebook, Amazon, Microsoft) are replicated, with, for example, Baidu for Google, Alibaba for Amazon, or Sina Weibo as the local Twitter.

At the semantic layer, an army of operators are paid to carry out checks to prevent the emergence of criticism of China's political and social system. The Chinese state is thus showing its desire to keep control over the entire architecture of its cyberspace, allowing China to enter cyberspace on its own terms. Nevertheless, we are witnessing a still relative Chinese digital security. BATX2s compete with Gafam, and this policy has enabled China to keep two-thirds of its national digital traffic on its soil.

Moreover, the control of the population by digital technologies is being established with a social rating system whose acceptability by democratic western societies seems unthinkable at the present time. However, it is relative to China's ability to maintain its "digital Chinese wall" in the long term. Two things corroborate this:

- While China is doing a good job of keeping its digital traffic on its soil, only 24% of visits to websites ending in the United States, 87% of the advertising components contained in web pages, called "trackers," end up in the United States.
- The Chinese digital value chain is not immune to American decisions. The decision to ban Chinese giant Huawei from US soil and, as far as possible, from the soil of US allies has shown the importance of the interdependent ties between China and the United States. This interdependence is complex and handicaps both China and the United States, as the recent turmoil in the semiconductor industry has shown.

What about China's dirigiste economic policy and legal arsenal in the service of digital security? China has modelled itself on the old Western model of technical administration that was once the success story of Europe and the United States. It has thus defined the main lines of its power policy in the 2015–2025 "Made in China" five-year plan and the 13th five-year plan 2016–2020. Beijing is aiming for autonomy and digital security in many areas, including new information technologies, robotics, aerospace, biotechnology and electric and low-energy vehicles. Artificial intelligence is also a priority area under the 13th Plan.

Beijing has not yet achieved the degree of autonomy and digital security defined by its programming documents but is continuing its efforts: for example, by funding research and innovation in strategic digital areas such as artificial intelligence or space policy. Similarly, China aims to emancipate itself from American hegemony in the field of submarine cables. In 2021, within the framework of the "PEACE" project (for Pakistan and East Africa Connecting Europe) participating in the New Chinese Silk Roads strategy, several countries are expected to host the first Chinese cable. It will be 12,000 km long and will link Pakistan, Djibouti, Kenya, Egypt and France. The Chinese authorities are streamlining their players in the field of submarine cables with the acquisition by the Hengtong Group (the world's largest manufacturer of land) and submarine optical cables (of 51% of the capital of Huawei Marine Networks), Huawei's submarine cable subsidiary, jointly owned with Global Marine, and the fourth largest cable producer in the world behind the American TE Subcom, the Japanese NEC and the French Alcatel Submarine Networks. This takeover will enable the emergence of a powerful economic player.

Another string to the Chinese bow is the establishment of a legal arsenal to guarantee the relocation of Chinese data to China. In 2016, China passed a Cyber Security Law which, in the name of protecting national security and privacy, gives security officials and regulators a wide range of options for monitoring the Internet. So-called crypto security policies have also provided for the prohibition of the use of US-made terminal equipment on certain occasions and in certain locations. China's New Silk Roads policy extends to the digital and space domains: the accelerated deployment of global Chinese satellite coverage, similar to the American GPS, by 2020 would extend Chinese navigation, communication and e-commerce services along the New Silk Roads.

China is thus encouraging countries adhering to its policy to use its services to launch their satellites, providing financial support for these projects and offering "all-in-one" services including the supply of the satellite and the launch by the Chinese Long March-5 rocket. In 2017, an Algerian satellite was put into orbit by a Chinese rocket. Contracts have been concluded with Cambodia and Indonesia. China's first moon landing on the far side of the Moon in January 2019 gives credibility to Chinese space policy.

On 1 January 2017, the Chinese government announced a plan to regain China's digital security on the Internet requiring telecommunications enterprises to close all access to VPN1, a means of circumventing China's isolationist digital measures. On 1 June 2017, the Cyber Security Law came into force, requiring enterprises engaged in the collection of personal data and network infrastructure to physically store such data on servers located in China. A 19-month grace period was provided to enable enterprises to comply with this legislation. The Gafams have signed partnership agreements with Chinese enterprises, with the exception of Apple, which has opened a data centre in China. The Cyberspace Administration of China (CAC) drafted new regulations in May, which state that if the acquisition of products and services disrupts key information infrastructure, or results in significant loss of personal information and important data, or poses other security risks, it must be reported to the CAC's Cyber Security Review Office. If China does not exercise complete digital security, it is implementing dirigiste or even authoritarian means to remedy it.

What about Russia? It adopts an authoritarian digital strategy adapted to its means and ambitions. Russia is investing the layers of cyberspace within its reach. The importance of the semantic layer of the Internet made a resounding comeback, with Russia's invasion of the Crimea and then the Cambridge Analytica scandal. Russia has invested in the semantic layer of the web to the point of speaking of information space to refer to cyberspace [the Russian model] focuses on the ability to have information operators broadcasting in Russian language, beyond the Russian borders, in a relatively large post-Soviet space. This model makes its weakness clear by concentrating on the international layer to the detriment of the two technical layers.

The action of the Russian authorities is focused on this informational layer of the Internet. This strategy could be explained by a certain pragmatism, as Russia does not have world champions in the digital field in the same way as Gafam or BATX. However, recent Russian advances in computing should enable them to no longer depend on either Microsoft or Intel for their sensitive systems. Although its industrial players are not world-class, they apparently manage to develop autonomous tools. On the semantic layer, Russia also has national players: Mail.ru (owner of the "Russian Facebook" VKontakte) and Yandex, the search engine dominating the Russian market, which launched its Yandex phone in 2018, a mid-range product of moderate cost. Mail.ru recently announced an alliance with Chinese e-commerce giant Alibaba, while Yandex has teamed up with the country's leading bank, Sberbank, to create a billion-dollar e-commerce joint venture.

It is therefore deploying a legal arsenal aimed at guaranteeing its digital security. Russia has, in fact, implemented a very authoritarian policy to protect its digital security in cyberspace. From 20,122 onwards, and in response to citizen protest movements, Internet censorship was centralized and organized. Rules for locating data of Russian nationals have been defined: storage must be exclusively on servers physically located in Russia. Likewise, web monitoring activities are facilitated by the increased powers of the Federal Service for Monitoring Telecommunications, Information Technologies and Means of Communication, the Roskomnadzor. Blocking (of internet addresses and inspection of data packets) is becoming commonplace.

Thus, the electronics holding company "Rosselektronika," part of Rostec, the Russian champion of military technologies, is a major player in high technology in Russia in both the military and civilian fields (notably creating integrated circuits and quantum electronics). A microprocessor called Baikal should be produced in Russia for government structures, avoiding possible NSA "backdoors" in American microprocessors. It would be implemented by the Rusnano Alliance (an investment fund aimed at developing, in partnership with private enterprises, the production of high-tech equipment in Russia, particularly in the fields of energy, nano-materials, biotechnology, mechanical engineering, optoelectronics, etc.), Rostec and T-Platforms (its latest supercomputer is the 22nd most powerful in the world; it also produces cash registers).

In 2015, the Roskomnadzor was able to demand that Reddit, and later Google, Facebook and Twitter, censor hundreds of pages of their users, based on the "Bloggers Law," passed in 2014, which prohibits the anonymity of bloggers and other Internet users who influence the population through their writings. The penalty incurred by the undertakings concerned is the suspension of access to their services by Russian users. In 2016, the "Yarovaya" laws to strengthen the fight against terrorism also included a digital component with very heavy obligations for enterprises distributing content on the Internet. They must now retain for 1 year, on Russian territory, data relating to the reception and transmission of calls, text messages, photos and audio and video content. At the request of security bodies, social network messaging using complementary message encryption systems such as WhatsApp and Telegram must provide the keys to decrypt content.

This system was further supplemented by two laws passed in the summer of 2017 prohibiting the use of VPNs, controlling instant messaging applications (operators must now cooperate in identifying their users and block messages at the request of the authorities) and censoring search engines, which are obliged to remove all references to sites blocked in Russia. Finally, in order to protect itself from the most destructive cyber attacks, Russia has begun examining a law designed to create a "sovereign Internet" in the country. The text was presented as a response to the "bellicose nature of the new US cyber security strategy" adopted in September 2018. The authorities are looking for a way to shut down the Internet in their territory in order, they say, to protect their strategic infrastructures that could continue to function in the event of a disruption of the world's major servers.

In this perspective, Russian Internet service providers will also have to ensure that "technical means" provided by "Roskomnadzor" are put in place on the network, allowing centralized control of traffic to counter possible threats. This centralized control, seen as a means of intervening directly, instead of operators, in the management of the network to block content banned in Russia, has been the subject of much criticism. Having a sovereign Internet makes it more credible to take action that could harm the global network, as national provisions can protect against the disastrous consequences of a large-scale cyber attack. Finally, Russia has the capacity to profoundly destabilize the web because it does not hesitate to exploit the physical dimension of the Internet from a strategic point of view. This is a major digital security issue for governments and businesses.

On 16 April 2018, American and British experts reported "malicious cyber activity by Russian state-supported actors" whose targets are primarily governments and private sector organizations, critical infrastructure providers and Internet service providers. For many years, Russian authorities have been accused of spying on the critical infrastructures of Western countries in order to expand the arsenal of tools used in the event of a hybrid attack. In January 2019, the then British defence minister accused Moscow of spying on British infrastructure in order to find out how to degrade its economy, destroy its infrastructure and identify an element that could cause total chaos within the country. In March 2019, a report by the US Computer Emergency Readiness Team (US CERT) claimed that hackers acting on behalf of the Russian government had carried out a networked reconnaissance of the system controlling key elements of the US economy and attempted to cover their tracks by removing evidence of their infiltration.

The Kremlin has thus reshaped the Russian Internet according to its own authoritarian, centralized and even aggressive vision. Its digital security is expressed by the desire to display, on the one hand, a capacity for resilience for its own territory and, on the other hand, a capacity for serious harm to the global network. In this context, the responses of institutions and enterprises to this competition in the expression of aggressive digital security, which is not only Russia's doing, as evidenced, for example, by the cyber attacks carried out by North Korea, which, some experts believe, enable it to finance the development of its nuclear arsenal, may seem limited. However, the digital security of states is already the object of many threats that have more to do with the organization of the web and its actors than with the international competition mentioned above.

Chapter 5
Establishing Competition in Digital Markets

The major players in Internet services (search engines, social networks, operating systems, service platforms, cloud computing solution providers, etc.), whose activity is by nature globalized, may have to question the digital security of states. Some do not hesitate to describe these players as "sovereign enterprises." Admittedly, the balance of power is not yet so overwhelming, but there is nothing to prevent it from becoming so, because this is exactly the project of certain digital entrepreneurs, who benefit from the double advantage of coherence (the success of their project) and continuity (as long as the shareholders continue to hope for "final victory"). Governments have neither the same coherence nor the same continuity: the citizen votes, but the consumer often acts in contradiction to what his vote expresses!

In the economic field, we can see that the digital environment favours concentrations, which themselves open the way to anti-competitive practices, which partly undermine the economic potential of certain states by restricting competition and innovation. This is why it is no longer possible to wait: an economic regulatory framework adapted to the twenty-first century must be adopted. All the courses of action demonstrate that concrete, pragmatic and credible political action is possible. It is all the more so because the gigantic size of what we now call the Gafams paradoxically constitutes an opportunity for politics, inasmuch as any damage to their brand image can have a substantial effect on their share price. "Stock price regulation" is therefore a weapon that states must not deprive themselves of. Likewise, these giants can reveal their weaknesses when the ethical convictions of employees force them to change their commercial orientations.

So, is there a monopoly economy that undermines the economic potential of some countries? Two factors are driving the concentration of users on one or two digital platforms and thus the concentration on platform markets: network effects and returns to scale. Recent work adds to these two variables the role of mass data holding as a multiplier of these two elements (which is a significant barrier to entry). The network effects can be summarized by the following formula: the more users,

W. Amedzro St-Hilaire, *Digital Risk Governance*,
https://doi.org/10.1007/978-3-030-61386-0_5

the more value the service has. Perhaps the most telling example is the social network: it is only useful if our loved ones are there.

Network effects can be direct (when the utility of the network to the user increases as the number of users increases) or indirect (when the utility of the network to users on one side of the platform increases with the number of users on the other side of the platform). These network effects exist only if the possibility of switching from one service to another or the use of several services at the same time ("multi-homing") is not restricted. Returns to scale are characterized by the fact that the fixed cost of product development decreases as the number of users increases. Thus, in the digital world, the marginal cost of production tends to be almost zero.

This is why we often find that "the winner takes all." There is thus a trend toward the creation of monopolies and then conglomerates. The unprecedented size of Gafam can be seen in the number of users, market capitalization, turnover and global market share, but the strong rise of Chinese digital players should not be forgotten either. One of the founders of PayPal and the enterprise Palantir, Peter Thiel, who also sits on the board of directors of Facebook, even theorized the need to build a monopoly. According to him, monopoly is the condition of every successful business. The author proposes a successful monopoly: start in a niche market in order to be dominant before expanding to nearby markets. This is, for example, the case of Amazon, which started with a bookstore service before expanding its online store to other markets.

In fact, many digital markets worldwide are dominated by one or two Gafams: Google has more than 90% of the search engine market; Facebook has nearly three-quarters of the social networking market; Google (Android) and Apple (iOS) have 76.03% and 22.04% of the smartphone operating system market, respectively; Microsoft (Windows) and Apple (OS X) have 78.43% and 13.53%, respectively, of the market for operating systems for personal computers, with Linux accounting for only 1.6% of the market; Google (Chrome) has nearly 65% and Apple (Safari) 15.15% of the web browser market; Google and Facebook have more than half of the online advertising market; Amazon accounts for nearly or more than half of the e-commerce market in many countries; Amazon (33%), Microsoft (16%) and Google (8%) account for more than half (57%) of the cloud computing services infrastructure market.

This dynamic also leads to the formation of conglomerates, where a company is able to increase its activities in one segment of its business by playing on the market power it holds in another product or market – this is the case, for example, with Amazon Web Services (AWS) for its Amazon market platform. Economists call this "economies of scope," which could be translated as "economies of diversification": large platforms that already offer multiple services are more efficient when they enter a new market. This is increasingly leading to competition between ecosystems, which may be made up of several online services but also of online services attached to terminals (smartphones, voice assistants, etc.).

These positions would not be acquired, "competition being within clicks' reach." While it is undeniable that some of the major digital players may have been overtaken in the past – such as the social network MySpace – these enterprises, whose scale is unprecedented, now have the means to avoid the emergence of free and undistorted competition, abuse of dominant position and aggressive external growth strategies. While the dominant position is not in itself condemnable under positive law, there have already been numerous abuses of dominant position by the digital giants. As early as 1969, IBM in the United States was forced to separate its software and services activities from its hardware business. In 2000 and 2008, Microsoft in Europe had to decouple its Windows operating system from services such as Internet Explorer browser and Media Player.

More recently, Google was fined more than $8 billion over 3 years by the European Commission for breaching competition rules with AdSense, Android and Shopping applications. Urgent measures in the dispute between Google and Amadeus in the online advertising market were discussed. Similarly, Facebook's authorization to acquire WhatsApp and Instagram has been criticized. Monopolistic market dynamics can provide an incentive for platforms to resort to anti-competitive practices. For example, the platforms, which are in a situation of virtual natural monopoly, have a right of life and death over a whole range of actors.

All they have to do is change the APIs (Application Programming Interface). This phenomenon is sometimes referred to as the "regulatory platform." The positioning of Amazon, which, on the one hand, as a marketplace, resells on behalf of merchants and, on the other hand, as an online trading platform, resells directly the products it purchases, also raises questions about the potential competitive harm it generates – indeed, Amazon is being investigated to determine whether the use of sensitive data from independent retailers using its marketplace violates competition rules.

There was also evidence of behaviour that was detrimental to consumers, such as Apple's deliberate curtailment of the performance of components in some of its smartphones to preserve their aging batteries. This dominant position in certain markets allows the enterprise to amass sufficient cash to carry out numerous company buyouts and equity investments. This external growth policy of the digital giants can be described as aggressive, as it leads, in some cases, to the acquisition of young enterprises that challenge their dominant position, so-called "predatory acquisitions," which aim to appropriate customers, technologies and human resources.

At the same time, large digital enterprises are buying up start-ups and highly innovative enterprises in the emerging new technology segments. The previous graph also shows the growing importance of equity investments via their internal investment vehicles, which enables digital giants to secure privileged access to innovations developed by target enterprises. Such a buyout policy guides entrepreneurs' choices: instead of growing their business to become a digital giant, they hope to be bought out by a giant. This can result in locally developed enterprises supported by public capital being taken over by foreign enterprises that appropriate the fruits.

Finally, two other factors are also indicative of the decline in competitive intensity in the new technology markets: the profits of the American technology giants have been disproportionately high compared with those of other industries over the last 20 years; their substantial cash flow also enables them to undertake colossal research and development (R&D) efforts compared with more traditional industries, with investment ratios five to six times higher. From this, it is clear that digital security can only be exercised through a dynamic economic and entrepreneurial fabric that must be protected from abuses of dominant positions or monopolistic situations created by large foreign groups. Massive anti-competitive practices are carried out by foreign enterprises and have the effect of undermining the economic development potential of local enterprises that might compete with them.

It should also be noted that domestic enterprises are dependent on foreign digital giants in several states, giving rise to sometimes illegitimate business practices. They may also be detrimental to consumers in terms of price, quality of service, or protection of personal data. Beyond the malfunctioning of the market, it is therefore economic security which is threatened by such behaviour, namely the possibility for every domestic entrepreneur to develop his activity under satisfactory conditions of competition. This is not to deny that the digital giants are providing ever more efficient services but to realize that economic power must not become domination. Ways and means of restoring competition and the possibility of entering the markets of the digital economy should therefore be examined.

Under such conditions, is it not necessary to renew competition law? A consensus seems to be emerging on the need to implement more effective economic regulation of the digital environment. Inaction should no longer be an option, even if the dismantling track does not seem to provide sufficient guarantees. The possibility of dismantling the digital giants is being discussed more and more seriously on the other side of the Atlantic, particularly by the Democrats. It is also defended by Chris Hughes, the co-founder of Facebook, and law professor Tim Wu. The dismantling of Google had been requested by several states. However, its concrete modalities are rarely specified.

While the precedents of Standard Oil in 1911 and AT&T in 1982 are regularly invoked, it should be recalled that Microsoft was nearly dismantled when a court ordered it to do so in June 2000. However, the decision was reviewed on appeal, and the enterprise was finally able to enter into an agreement (with the US Government in 2001) which is sometimes considered to be the initiating act of the waiver of US competition policy. This track should not be seen as a panacea for competition policy 2. 0. Indeed, many consider that, like the Hydra of Lerne, the enterprise, even if split, would continue to develop its power. The investigation will take 5 to 10 years and will not solve all the problems. Even if Facebook were divided into ten entities, there would still be 240 million users in each entity.

Finally, it is often argued that severely regulating Gafam or dismantling it would favour the emergence of Chinese digital giants beyond the Asian market. While this should not be a determining factor, since the severity of the competition authorities should be the same for American, Chinese and European enterprises, it should be recognized that in the absence of "local Gafam," BATX could benefit from the weakening of Gafam in their domestic markets. This is all the more true since the dismantling of the BATXs by the Chinese government, in the name of respect for competition law, is more than unlikely to date.

However, the American authorities have launched several actions against the digital giants. A committee of the House of Representatives has opened an inquiry into competition in digital markets. The Department of Justice has launched an extensive investigation into possible abuses of dominance by the largest digital enterprises. The Federal Trade Commission (FTC) has fined Facebook a record $5 billion. On 6 September 2019, nine state prosecutors announced the opening of investigations against Facebook under competition law. On 9 September 2019, 50 state prosecutors took the same route regarding Google. There is therefore a movement toward greater regulation, which creates favourable political conditions for action on this side of the Atlantic.

A strengthening of competition law appears necessary here. As the recent sanctions against Google have shown, competition law can deal with many cases of abuse. But a consensus seems to be emerging in favour of introducing certain adjustments to the legal arsenal. A concept that has been somewhat forgotten in recent years, that of abuse of exploitation in the examination of anti-competitive practices, should be used more extensively. It would allow to respond to the case of Booking taking commissions on the earnings of hoteliers, or Apple charging a commission to the creators of applications. Faced with the problems arising from the use of the data, the interpretation of this local law must be more innovative than in the past. In this respect, in some countries, this has led to Facebook being condemned for disproportionate use of user data, which went far beyond what is necessary for the proper functioning of the social network. Illegitimate data capture can therefore be sanctioned, as this decision shows.

The main plea should be to update the methods used by competition authorities under constant law: giving more weight in the competitive analysis to the competitive harm test and taking into account access to data to the extent of market power. Thus, amendments to the existing law also appear necessary. These are: to relax the criteria for defining the risk of harm to competition resulting from the practice in question (serious and irreparable damage) in order to provide for a finding of "serious and immediate damage"; to lighten the commission's obligation to establish a "prima facie case of infringement" by replacing it with the obligation to establish that the practice in question does cause such damage; and to broaden the scope of the protected interests justifying interim measures by no longer focusing solely on the infringement of the competition rules but also on the general economy, the economy of the sector concerned, the interest of consumers, or the complainant undertaking.

Some local directives on the powers of competition authorities represent a step forward, as they allow these authorities to issue structural injunctions – for example, the obligation to divest a branch of activity – as part of the sanctions they impose for anti-competitive practices. An adjustment of merger law at the international level also appears necessary. This law enables competition authorities to prevent a merger of enterprises whose effects could be anticompetitive. In order to effectively combat "predatory" acquisitions, local laws for digital enterprises need to be supplemented by lowering the revenue thresholds requiring authorization. It might also be interesting to introduce a new threshold based on redemption value, which may be a better indicator than turnover. Indeed, while WhatsApp had sales of around $20 million, Facebook acquired it for $19 billion. Such a criterion is already in force in Germany and Austria.

Will it be necessary to establish a general framework for ex ante regulation of systemic players? Drawing lessons from past initiatives and noting that while adaptations of competition law are necessary in states and must be completed, these measures alone will not be able to respond to all digital security issues, it now seems desirable to adopt a general framework for ex ante regulation of systemic digital players. The idea of imposing proactive, specific and multisectoral obligations on systemic digital players is beginning to be explicitly considered within administrations – it is expressly advocated in the reflections conducted by certain inspection bodies, and it is called for by civil society as well as by regulators: as soon as a player is a basic building block of the economy, then systemic regulation, which can resemble banking regulation, based on supervision, a dedicated technical regulator and the technological capacity of the regulator at the right level, must be developed.

For example, recent regulations in several states tend toward greater transparency in the platforms' relations with consumers and professionals. Normative provisions have in fact been adopted in recent years to strengthen the information provided to consumers and then to professionals using the platforms. Their proper implementation should be ensured. The objective is to better balance the relationship between platforms and consumers:

- Platforms that promote content, goods, or services offered by third parties, such as search engines, social networks and comparators, must specify the referencing and ranking criteria they use.
- Sites publishing consumer reviews must specify whether they have been verified and according to what methodology.
- Marketplaces and collaborative economy sites must provide essential information that can guide consumers' choices: the quality of the seller, the amount of the connection fees charged by the platform, the existence of a right of withdrawal, the existence of a legal guarantee of conformity, or the methods for settling disputes.

In addition, platforms with more than five million monthly unique visitors are required to adopt best practices to increase the clarity, transparency and fairness of their online offerings. The so-called "Platform-to-Business" regulation in some countries aims to increase the transparency of the platforms for their professional users. It provides for two main sets of measures to balance relations between platforms and enterprises: upstream, information and transparency obligations (on contractual clauses, on the parameters used by the ranking algorithms), and downstream, mechanisms for resolving disputes and mediating between platforms and professionals – internal system for handling complaints, appointment of a mediator and possibility for representative associations and public bodies to bring actions before the courts to stop or prohibit any failure to comply with the requirements laid down by the regulation.

The regulation is the first building block for transparency in the digital economy at the local level. However, it is limited to transparency, without considering any action on practices. Nor does it address the regulatory distortions between physical and online commerce: the absence of constraints imposed on the digital giant Amazon contrasts with the cumbersome rules weighing on physical retailing. There is now an urgent need to harmonize the fiscal and regulatory framework in which these two forms of trade operate. Finally, algorithms should be audited rather than made public. Algorithms are subject to many biases. They are also receiving increasing attention in view of their potential anti-competitive effects.

Several voices were raised calling for the publication of the algorithms. However, an algorithm may be protected as information by business secrecy, in the manner provided for in the Law on the Protection of Business Secrecy. In addition, once published, an algorithm can be bypassed. Firms that are aware of the benchmarking criteria, especially those with sufficient computing power, could delude the algorithm to improve their ranking. Finally, it is above all the knowledge of the data and the results, on the one hand, and the principles and methods of the algorithm's constitution, on the other hand, that allow a better understanding of how it works. Even if the algorithms were to be made public, deep learning algorithms are subject to the "black box" phenomenon: we know the input and output data, but we do not understand how they work internally.

The explicability of these algorithms is, however, one of the conditions of their social acceptability. While it is neither realistic nor advisable to provide for the publication of algorithms, their auditability must be organized in order to ensure compliance with competition rules, data protection, etc. This presupposes that the public authorities have the human and technical resources to do so. Moreover, the American model of the Office of Technology Research and Investigation (created in March 2015 within the Federal Trade Commission) should be generalized, and a specialized Office of Control Technologies for the Digital Economy (responsible for developing and implementing control techniques adapted to a range of new themes in the digital economy) should be created. This office could be approached by the entire interested community, including independent administrative authorities.

On this point, consideration should be given to setting up a body of sworn public experts capable of carrying out audits, which could be called upon in the course of investigations or administrative or judicial disputes. Let's face it, in many states today, no one is able to talk to Facebook programmers. States must be at the right technological level to understand, test, decode and even reverse the functioning of the algorithms. It is interesting to note that some governments have made algorithm transparency one of their innovation policy thrusts: it is one of the "big challenges" to be financed by state innovation and industry funds.

Chapter 6
Preserve the Legal Order by Strengthening Data Control and the Ability to Regulate Platforms

Data, especially personal data, is the raw material of the information society. As such, they represent a strategic economic issue and now form not "oil" but "soil." Indeed, it is the particular nature of data that makes the digital revolution so unique: unlike previous major industrial transformations based on the discovery and exploitation of new but limited physical resources, data deposits do not dry up over time or with the use made of them.

On the one hand, the increasing digitization and irreversible dematerialization of entire sectors of goods and services contribute to constantly feeding an exponential production of data: the latter is the result of the activity of individuals themselves (citizens through their activity on social networks, consumers through their online purchases) but also of enterprises and institutions (through their production, management or administration activities), and it even stems passively from sensors routinely and automatically analysing our daily environment (connected objects, "intelligent vehicles," etc.). On the other hand, this data constitutes a "non-rival" good, in the economic sense of the term: the fact that it is used – analysed, cross-referenced – once by one actor does not normally prevent its simultaneous, or even subsequent, use by another actor.

The value of these data is essentially the result of their processing and linking: aggregation, reconciliation of datasets from various sources, analyses and extrapolations. Taken in isolation, a single piece of data generally generates very little value. The now unprecedented capacity to collect and accumulate data is matched by the development of new processing technologies by the major players in the digital sector: very large-scale aggregation and massive processing (big data), algorithms including automatic learning mechanisms (machine learning), use of artificial intelligence, etc. However, the massive exploitation of data is made possible by the reduction in processing costs. Costs (of data storage and computing power) continue to fall drastically, thanks to technological advances.

The value generated by the "data revolution" lies in the new opportunities offered to economic actors: creation of new digital services, but also, even for traditional

W. Amedzro St-Hilaire, *Digital Risk Governance*,
https://doi.org/10.1007/978-3-030-61386-0_6

sectors of the economy, efficiency gains in the production of goods or the provision of services (through improved resource allocation and reduced transaction costs); the possibility of extreme customization of services to increase their quality or profitability (adaptation and targeting of the offer, advertising profiling) and predictive analysis to support decision-making or investment; etc. What is the nature and legal status of personal data? A piece of data is a piece of information. Digital is the particular format that this information takes – it then corresponds to a certain number of bits (composed of 0 and 1) for its processing by computer tools. Economically, it is a non-competing good (whose use by one person does not degrade that of another) and has a low production cost. Numerical data may fall under various legal regimes, as public information (code of relations between the public and the administration) or as "personal data" understood globally as any information relating to an identified or identifiable natural person.

Although the processing of data may be de facto controlled by the entities that collect them, the data are not, in law, the subject of ownership. The IT laws of several states are in fact part of a human rights approach. The possibility of having a private life is seen as a right that is at the very essence of the person, fundamental to his or her dignity and the free development of his or her personality. This conception of personal data thus constitutes the affirmation of ethical and humanist convictions: A commercialization of personal data would hinder the effective exercise of the right to informational self-determination, in particular by depriving individuals of the ability to revoke their consent once their data has been sold.

Thus, the question of the challenges of the "data revolution" for the legal order of states arises. The economic models of the major dominant players (free access, massive collection, use and enhancement of personal data, sale of targeted advertising) now require the implementation of avoidance strategies that allow them to escape the traditional constraints of our legal system. Their development, based on the search for the greatest number of users (for its network effects), has indeed every interest in being carried out independently of national borders: the interconnection of communication networks and technologies now naturally allows this, and the apparent free nature of these numerous services reinforces their attractiveness: [free] access has been conceived as the best way to create as quickly as possible an audience that is as wide and as captive as possible. It should be noted that non-payment leads to extraordinarily strong addictions to certain services, against which neither legal frameworks nor political will carries much weight.

In addition, these largely foreign-based actors may resist attempts to legislate in the states in which they operate through administrative complexities. These "sovereign enterprises" thus create their own standards (their general conditions of use – CGU; some of them incorporating an autonomous definition of "community standards," a true charter framing freedom of expression on social networks), to the point that invoking a violation of the CGU on certain platforms is often more effective than waiting for a formal complaint to be processed by the competent national authorities. Some digital players are even likely to be local vectors – with or without consent – of foreign legal orders: the American giants are obliged to apply extraterritorial sanctions regimes or rules of access to electronic evidence (such as the

Cloud Act), and major Chinese digital industrial players remain marked by a certain porosity with their country's military interests. What government, even a Liberal one, could live with a system that might in the long run render ineffective the prescriptions of its legal system?

From there, should we develop the digital identity guaranteed by the states? A striking example of this challenge to the legal system is the authentication of persons, a privilege of the state, which is increasingly being challenged by private enterprises, first and foremost Facebook and Google. Their identification solutions, which can then be reused on other private websites, generally for non-sensitive uses, have become the first means of proving one's identity on the Internet. Stakeholders deny any desire to supplant states and simply claim to provide their users with the services they need. In the long term, these solutions run the risk of becoming digital identities in use, especially since no tool proposed by states will be able to impose itself if it is not at least as easy to use, as effective and as practical as those proposed by digital enterprises. In the future, one of the major roles of states could be to guarantee the "commons," of which digital identity is a part. However, the identification instruments currently proposed by the state do not, strictly speaking, constitute a "digital identity." These are more like identity aggregators: the user uses a provider's digital identity to authenticate himself to service providers.

In view of the sensitivity and the mass of data processed, it is crucial that states finally take up this subject. Enterprises can use the data transmitted by users to resell them to targeted advertising services, reveal consumption habits and track individuals. An identification solution carried by states could not only enable them to reaffirm their digital sovereignty over this historic regalian monopoly, but it would also give citizens back control over their own data. The use of such data for public policy purposes should only be possible with the free consent of the users. Above all, we must avoid disrupting administrative architectures that work. The idea of creating a single digital regulator is regularly raised in the public debate. It would thus be a question of adapting a supervision exercised by the public authorities in a hitherto sectoral manner (telecom networks, audiovisual content, personal data, online counterfeiting) to the consequences of the convergence between services and networks caused by the digital revolution: to take account of the changing media environment and what looks like an "extension of the field of the fight," the law should also outline the future landscape of state regulation. On the other hand, support should be given to the idea of strengthening digital expertise, in particular auditing and algorithm control capabilities. This strengthening could be accompanied by their pooling at the state level.

It is also necessary to strengthen the human resources of the regulators and to deepen the pooling of these resources. It should be noted that more than ever before, regulatory authorities appear to be confronted with a lack of resources and an asymmetry of information in relation to the major digital players, at the risk of paralyzing them. Thus, the lack of resources is putting a serious strain on the activity of regulators, which is crucial for the preservation of the digital security of states. Would it be better to make certain platforms more accountable by fine-tuning the system of adjusted liability for technical intermediaries? A number of discussions are underway on whether and how to update the "electronic commerce" or "e-commerce" directives in the light of the imperfections of the reduced liability regimes that they grant to certain technical intermediaries.

It should be noted that technological evolution has enabled the creation of new types of digital players, making the hoster/publisher duality obsolete (interactive platforms, social networks, sorting and algorithmic promotion of content), which now occupy a much more important social and economic place than 20 years ago. These new digital players are today at the centre of the process of circulating information for citizens, with their own economic model based on free access, data exploitation and the ever more rapid dissemination of content without prior control obligations. A new status for the platforms must therefore be considered, imposing binding specifications on them: today, apart from the traditional rules of law, they assume too few responsibilities. However, it must be stressed that while promoting, and in some cases even imposing, an obligation to locate data on a specific territory is an idea that may seem interesting at first glance; the real usefulness in terms of digital security of such an approach must today be largely qualified. These initiatives may be of limited value in some cases:

- Above all to protect certain particularly sensitive data (sovereign public processing, private financial or strategic commercial data); as such, it would not be productive to use an "internal" geographically localized cloud for the most sensitive data, in a logic of concentric circles with decreasing security requirements. Indeed, we cannot impose a particular method of storage on enterprises without offering them high-performance and accessible industrial solutions that meet their needs. Such solutions could thus be imposed in the more general framework of the regimes for vital or essential service operators.
- Also to ensure greater accessibility, either from the point of view of businesses in a risk management perspective (when data are no longer located locally, it is more difficult in practice to monitor them and to have an assurance of the use made of them by providers or partners located abroad) or from the point of view of public authorities (to facilitate access to these data by the judiciary or national regulators in the exercise of their sectoral monitoring powers).
- And finally, generally speaking, by stimulating demand, to support the industrial ecosystem of Cloud players and the development of data processing capacities.

Such initiatives must nevertheless take into account recent developments in national law and foreign legal systems, and it appears that a data location obligation would not meet the challenge posed by some extraterritorial legislation. On the one hand, with regard to non-personal data, national laws drastically limit the possibility to impose location requirements. They are now prohibited unless they are justified on grounds of public security in accordance with the principle of proportionality. On the other hand, and in any event, data location clauses do not offer guarantees in the face of new foreign legislation or practices with extraterritorial scope (international sanctions, Cloud Act adopted in the United States in March 2018, etc.) nor against the porosity between certain industrial players and their government (some Chinese equipment manufacturers, for example). Thus, even if data are physically located in other territories, the entities that control the data centres (data centres) will, because of their nationality, also continue to be subject to legal regimes that require them to cooperate with foreign powers.

One example is the porosity of the major Chinese digital players with their government. China's 2017 intelligence law is generating the same concerns as the Cloud Act in the United States. Its article 14 states, inter alia, that China's intelligence services may request the cooperation of any Chinese citizen or organization. The legal analyses – which also cover the Counter Espionage Law of 2017, the Anti-terrorism Law of 2018 and the Computer Network Security Law of 2016 – confirm that this law is not applicable outside Chinese territory. These provisions do not have extraterritorial effect, so they do not apply to enterprises and individuals located outside the territory of the People's Republic of China. It is, moreover, important to note that these provisions are not linked to a nationality criterion. Consequently, any company located in China will be subject to these laws. However, particularly succinctly, it is expressly stated that Chinese citizens and subsidiaries of Chinese enterprises are not subject to these laws. Moreover, some studies on the Intelligence Law contradict the claim that the law does not apply to enterprises and individuals outside China.

In fact, several legal or technical solutions exist to preserve the digital security of states despite provisions with extraterritorial scope. The following should be considered:

- The legal separation of the business into different watertight subsidiary entities according to the geographical location of the services (this is the solution chosen by OVH to enable it to extend its activities to the United States).
- The strategy of mobilizing enterprises on a case-by-case basis to challenge in court administrative claims that would not go through the channel of international judicial cooperation.
- And, above all, the extensive use of robust data encryption technologies for which only the client would have the key and not the technical intermediary. This makes it impossible for the local authorities to decipher the information, even if the enterprise is forced to cooperate.

However, these solutions are limited in scope: they have a cost and depend on the legal and technical means that enterprises are willing to deploy or that their customers can afford. It is therefore more interesting to look for lasting solutions for which the public authorities would be responsible. As such:

- As the law has become a weapon at the service of the United States' economic war against the rest of the world, enterprises must not be left powerless in the face of the application of a panoply of extraterritorial laws (anti-corruption legislation, economic sanctions against states, intelligence laws, laws allowing the collection of data within the framework of administrative or judicial procedures, such as the Cloud Act of March 2018).
- The states must respond with a proactive strategy, which notably implies a modernization and a tightening of their law, known as the "blocking law" (creation of a mandatory early warning mechanism; implementation of support for enterprises targeted by such measures, thanks to a dedicated administration; increase in the penalties provided for in the event of violation of the law).

- An extension of the principles protecting liberties to non-personal data of legal persons would make it possible to protect local businesses by sanctioning the undue transmission by hosts of their strategic data to foreign judicial authorities outside the channels of administrative or judicial mutual assistance.

It should be noted that the general regulation on data protection in some states has established an ambitious (and powerful) legal framework and regulation commensurate with the challenges of digital security. The regulation aims to adapt the legislation on the processing of personal data to developments in digital technologies by making it uniform. It is directly applicable but also allows states to make certain national adjustments. It has three main objectives:

- Strengthen the rights of individuals whose data are used; it reaffirms the basic principles (transparency and consent), creates new ones, better adapted to the evolution of digital uses ("right to forget" and right to portability), and facilitates their exercise so that individuals can take them up and have them respected (right to recourse by proxy or even collective recourse, compensation for damages).
- Make all actors processing data responsible by grading their obligations according to the risks to privacy; it favours the use of impact studies and flexible legal tools, generalizes the appointment of "data protection officers" and abolishes or lightens prior administrative formalities.
- Give credibility to regulation commensurate with digital security issues; the regulation can be applied extraterritorially, the authorities are called upon to cooperate in the event of cross-border data processing, and the penalties are finally a real deterrent.

Its territorial and material scope of application is wide: the regulation must be applied as soon as the controller is established in the territory ("residence criterion"). However, it is also intended to apply outside the EU, when a resident is targeted by data processing (by an offer of goods and services, or behavioural monitoring), including via the Internet ("targeting criterion"). Sanctions are graduated and considerably strengthened: in addition to the traditional remedies, national authorities also have the power to impose record fines or, in the case of a company, fines of between 2% and 4% of the annual worldwide turnover (whichever is higher). The general data protection regulation thus provides for administrative sanctions that are now dissuasive in the event of failure to comply with its provisions, commensurate with the resources mobilized by the digital giants and the seriousness of the risks posed by massive data processing.

Finally, among the legal innovations introduced for the benefit of individuals whose personal data are processed, the regulation enshrines a right to data portability. In its individual dimension, digital security can also be presented as a capacity for informational self-determination, i.e. the possibility for each individual to "remain in control of his or her destiny on the networks." In this respect, the general data protection regulation aims to contribute to raising awareness among Internet users of the use made of their data: it reinforces the right to information and obliges those responsible for processing personal data to make the explanations given on the purposes and use of their data more intelligible.

But in a digital world marked by a strong asymmetry between, on the one hand, those who control data and algorithms and, on the other hand, those who use the platforms, imposing respect for these rights and making them effective for individuals still remains to be concretely accomplished. The tools developed to make the information presented to users effective and systematic are recent and can be improved. It is necessary to highlight the "dashboard" now allowing access to the history of use of the personal data provided and also recognize that Internet users had not yet grasped the right to portability and that there is still room for improvement, particularly to improve the transparency of the recommendations made to Internet users on the YouTube platform.

The collection of data by digital players is based mainly on the use of tracers when Internet users browse the web, particularly cookies, which make it possible to collect extremely detailed data. These are frequently used to create detailed profiles for targeted advertising purposes, with insufficient transparency and control by the user. However, these operations are mainly carried out by players located outside the countries of connection, which raises digital security issues due to the nature of the data collected and the uses made of it. Thus, Google's advertising agency collected data on nearly 45% of the websites in the panel tested, while the statistical analysis service of the same player was present on nearly 70% of the panel sites. More generally, on more than 91% of the panel's sites, Internet users' browsing is tracked by a third party. Thus, digital security can only be ensured if these devices, which are particularly intrusive and framed, in particular by the ePrivacy Directive, are used only in a way that allows data subjects to retain control over their data.

We must go further by introducing an obligation of interoperability: the need to go beyond the right to portability of personal data across platforms. As we have seen, portability allows a user to leave a platform with a copy of their personal data in their state at the time of the request. In principle, interoperability guarantees that the activity initially carried out on a platform can be continued elsewhere without losing the contacts and social links established. It would allow communication from one platform to another, along the lines of e-mail: being subscribed to one provider does not prevent you from receiving e-mails from people who have subscribed to other providers. In concrete terms, interoperability allows anyone to read from service A, the content disseminated by his contacts on service B, and to respond to it as if he were there himself.

However, a distinction must be made between protocol interoperability and data interoperability. Interoperability must be made a possible vehicle for promoting competition adapted, under certain conditions, to the specific features of a platform economy dominated by giant players that are difficult to challenge because of high entry costs. In addition, where equivalent services exist, the regulatory framework should take into account the emerging application of existing rules on data portability and explore other options to facilitate data transfers and improve interoperability of services where such interoperability is logical and technically feasible and can increase consumer choice without hindering the ability to grow (especially of small businesses). Such initiatives could be accompanied by appropriate standardization initiatives and co-regulatory approaches.

Chapter 7
Responding to the Fiscal Challenge Launched by the Major Digital Enterprises: A Digital Security and Equity Issue

After the economic and legal order, the power acquired by certain digital enterprises, particularly American and increasingly Asian ones, is calling into question two other regalian missions of the state, at the heart of its digital security: to levy taxes and to mint coins. However, these two areas could also prove to be powerful instruments for regaining our digital security, whether individual or collective. While multinationals use "traditional" methods to optimize their taxation, they also take advantage of the specific characteristics of the digital sector: the difficulty of locating the value added created in the digital economy, due to the decoupling that these enterprises can easily operate between their place of establishment and place of consumption (e.g. the fact that they can easily operate between their place of residence and place of consumption), and the fact that they have a high proportion of intangible assets, which makes it more difficult to value them on the books. The so-called "Irish double" or "Dutch sandwich" strategies; the prevalence in this economy of the intermediary model, which captures the margin to the detriment of traditional players.

Since international tax rules are largely unsuited to value creation in the digital economy, states cannot fully fulfil one of their regalian missions, that of tax collection. Their digital security on the digital players and in the digital world is therefore weakened, especially since these enterprises sometimes benefit from the support of partner countries. For example, the European Commission has finally qualified as state aid the specific tax scheme granted by Ireland to Apple. States were therefore powerless in the face of the practices of these multinationals. The only lever they could rely on, and still use, is the litigation process. For example, Google has entered into a public interest litigation agreement with the National Financial Prosecutor's Office in certain countries and an agreement with certain tax authorities. The total amount of these two agreements is close to one billion dollars and puts an end to proceedings launched by these states in 2015, through the filing of a complaint for aggravated tax fraud and money laundering in an organized gang of aggravated tax

W. Amedzro St-Hilaire, *Digital Risk Governance*,
https://doi.org/10.1007/978-3-030-61386-0_7

fraud. Despite some successes, recourse to the courts does not remedy the causes but the consequences of the underlying problem of lack of tax fairness.

On this subject, as on others, it is recommended that states move forward at the national level before the international level. Governments are heeding these exhortations, first by proposing a tax on digital services and then by putting forward the idea of a "name and shame" scheme, which would blacklist non-collaborative digital platforms. In this area, it almost always happens that when the immediate consequence is favourable, the subsequent consequences are disastrous, and vice versa. By deciding to go it alone on the taxation of the digital giants, in order to meet an objective that cannot be blamed on them (that of restoring tax fairness between enterprises), these states are exposing themselves to American reprisals.

This threat is, moreover, one of the most striking illustrations of the limits of states' digital security towards digital actors. The US President has asked the Office of the US Trade Representative to investigate possible discrimination against US enterprises in these proceedings. US Senators Chuck Grassley (Republican) and Ron Wyden (Democrat) sent a letter to Treasury Secretary Steven Mnuchin urging him to encourage these countries to back down. While the states concerned reacted quickly to these threats, arguing that these taxes were sovereign prerogatives and that they had not been designed to target exclusively US enterprises, the risks are nonetheless great.

American digital enterprises have therefore strongly criticized the system, condemning an initiative that undermines the ongoing OECD negotiations, discriminates against them and imposes high compliance costs on them. It should also be noted that such pressures are very unusual among Allied countries. The use by the United States of the procedure known as Section 301 of the 1974 Trade Act, used by Washington in its dispute with Beijing over the violation of intellectual property rights, is indeed unprecedented in the history of its trade relations with other countries. In addition to raising tariffs on certain goods, such as wine and luxury goods, the United States has also doubled the taxes applied to businesses and nationals residing on US soil, as authorized by Article 891 of the US Code.

Above all, we need to change the states' taxation rules, because let us stress the inequity of the current taxation rules: the large digital enterprises, specialists in tax optimization, take advantage of local infrastructures and training financed by the taxes of their users and customers. The tax differential between digital multinationals and traditional multinationals is 14 points (9.5% versus 23.2%). This observation elicits two types of reaction, with a common purpose. The first is the project of some states of a tax on digital services, which was aborted but is being pursued at scale. The second is the relaunch of international negotiations, within the framework of the OECD, on the revision of tax rules.

As a reminder, if it is a first answer, the tax on digital services is incomplete. It covers two types of services: (i) intermediation services, which enable users to contact and interact with each other, in particular with a view to directly providing goods and services; (ii) targeted advertising and the sale of data for advertising purposes. The aim is to capture the value generated by the "free work" of local users. In fact, this scope excludes digital content delivery services (e.g. the provision of digital content to the public, Netflix, iTunes) or selling online for own account (which is, for example, a significant part of Amazon's business). This action, which is limited in scope, does not address issues such as the localization of profits, the harmonization of transfer pricing regulations and the fight against fraud through e-commerce.

A tax is always, at least in part, borne by the final consumer, especially when enterprises are in an ultra-dominant position, as is the case with Gafams. Despite the administration's denials, the costs of this attempt by states to reassert their sovereign monopolies may well be borne by their businesses and citizens. On 1 August 2019, Amazon announced its intention to pass on these taxes on the services offered to businesses using its online commerce platform. Moreover, the collection of these taxes will be complex: it is based on a declaratory procedure and the transmission of data that are difficult to analyse. In the absence of a declaration, it will be very complicated for the administration to tax the enterprise ex officio: in the event of a dispute, the departments will have to set out the data on which they have based the amount of tax due, which could make the tax base withheld fragile and questionable.

It is necessary to take note of the fact that the Internet has transformed the value creation chain. This does not imply revolutionizing tax standards or making the rules more complex; it simply means taking the measure of the changes brought about and modifying the principles, which cannot be done without constant work and an increased presence in international negotiating forums. It should be remembered that the initial draft on digital taxation had a twofold objective: the short-term introduction of a tax on digital services and, in the longer term, the introduction of a new criterion for qualifying a permanent establishment (that of "significant digital presence"). The digitization of the economy makes the concept of permanent establishment, according to which an enterprise must have a physical presence in the territory of a state in order for the latter to be able to tax it, obsolete. The review was also intended to provide a better understanding of the role played by data and the "free work" provided by users for the benefit of digital businesses.

In the framework of the project (Erosion of the tax base and transfer of profits), launched in 2013 in St. Petersburg, the OECD has launched a work cycle to adapt the international tax system to the strategies of multinationals and in particular to those of digital multinationals. According to the OECD work program, the envisaged reform would be based on two pillars: (i) defining the place and basis for paying corporate income tax and (ii) introducing a minimum tax rate for all multinationals. On the first pillar, the options diverge. The United States and the United Kingdom are more in favour of separating profits between so-called "routine" profits from traditional activities such as production, distribution and research and development and so-called "non-routine" profits, which are then allocated between countries to determine the amount of tax due. The second option would be to split the enterprise's overall profit according to the countries in which it operates. Nor does the OECD give up defending a third, more specific option for Gafams, with taxation based not on the country of production but on the country of distribution of services.

Also, taxation should be an issue of attractiveness. States would be wrong to consider their sovereign prerogatives only in terms of sanctions, which would punish the behaviour of digital multinationals. Taxation must also be conceived and thought out as a tool for the future to maintain the competitiveness and attractiveness of states, whether by facilitating the installation of strategic digital infrastructures or by attracting the financial and human capital necessary for the development of innovations (the subject of further development).

Also, states will have to become proactive and innovative in the monetary field. In this regard. The question is: Are cryptoactives competing currencies? Cryptoactives are defined by their private, totally virtual character and by their lack of physical or financial backing. Today, there are close to 1600 of them, with an estimated capitalization of close to \$270 billion. It is important to note that there was a strong ambivalence about cryptoactives: a strong attraction for the proposed innovations but a constant concern to protect investors, consumers and the stability of the financial system. In view of their development and to meet their potential, the PACTE Act provides a more explicit framework for intermediaries in digital assets, with two regulatory aspects.

The first part is optional: intermediaries, such as cryptoactives exchange platforms, will be able to apply for approval from the Financial Markets Authority, which is a guarantee of reliability and seriousness. The second part is binding. It provides for the mandatory registration of all exchange platforms between cryptoactives and conventional currencies as part of the fight against money laundering. In its activity report for the year 2018, TRACFIN (Intelligence processing and action against clandestine financial channels) noted that there is room for improvement in terms of the volume of declarations among all cryptoactives professionals even though the number of declarations has already more than doubled between 2017 and 2018 (250 against 528). It remains to be seen, of course, whether the public authorities will have the necessary capacity to draw up a comprehensive list of these platforms and to monitor them.

The public authorities must not relax their efforts and not reduce the resources allocated to the regulation of these cryptoactives, particularly at a time when digital players, such as Facebook, are showing increasing interest in their potential. Like any innovation, cryptoactives can be both positive and threatening in their use, especially if states do not take them up at the right time and in the right way. They then risk seeing themselves competing and eventually being overtaken by private actors, on whom the strength of their regulations could be weakened.

It should be stressed that central banks and financial authorities now consider that cryptoactives do not pose a threat to global financial stability due to their limited volume and low acceptability. However, the G20 countries constantly recall that states must, through their regulations, ensure that these digital assets are not used for money laundering or terrorist financing, it being understood that they can guarantee quasi-anonymity to their holders. The European Central Bank, for example, set up an informal working group in May 2018 to increase its knowledge of the issues raised by cryptoactives and to monitor their potential negative effects.

Until now, national or international supervisory authorities have tended to consider cryptoactives as risky assets, reserved for the most sophisticated investors. Most states have thus adopted the so-called "sandbox" approach, easing the obligations on these players so that they can test their technologies and enter the market more easily. The regulator is then led to assess the changes brought about by these products and, if necessary, to strengthen the obligations towards the players concerned. Moreover, not all cryptoactives have the ambition to become true "private currencies"; some are above all financial assets or means of payment and are not intended to compete with banks, but rather to offer a new financial service.

In this context, the announcement by Facebook in June 2019 of the launch of its own cryptoactive in early 2020, libra, sent shock waves. It is indeed Facebook's market power and its striking power, with 2.4 billion users, that have led all national and international regulators to worry about the enterprise's wishes. What are the ambitions of the libra? Referring to the libra file and the statutes of Libra Networks, the libra's field of intervention is potentially very broad. The libra aims to "provide services in the fields of finance and technology." The libra could be used as a means of payment on the Internet and on Facebook group applications. It could also be bought on exchange platforms, stored and resold. It would be convertible into official units of account, unlike Bitcoin. Who are the Facebook partners? Facebook already has nearly 30 partners, most of which are large commercial or payment enterprises (Uber, Visa-Mastercard, PayPal, Kiva, Spotify and Iliad). What are the interests of the project stakeholders?

Facebook is aware of the limits of its model, based on the sale of personalized advertising on its social networks. By launching its own encryption system, Facebook would gain speed with its direct competitors and could eventually develop associated financial services, as other enterprises, such as Apple, are considering. Finally, Facebook is seeking to be at the forefront of the global competition between social networks: in China, WeChat has successfully integrated a payment system into its application. In Asia, also in South America, the rise of "super-applications" precedes by a few years the one we are now seeing in the West: they aim to complement a sometimes failing public service offer and offer payment solutions with a very wide scope (e.g. the Chinese can pay their electricity supplier via WeChat).

For Facebook's partners, the interest is twofold: to broaden their customer base, especially in developing countries, and, for established payment players such as Visa-Mastercard or PayPal, not to be overwhelmed by the new solutions offered by Facebook by joining them. For merchants who would come to accept this payment system, commissions could be reduced, as systems operating on blockchain technology are considered to be less expensive. What is the governance of this project? According to the first information communicated and confirmed by the hearing of Facebook's representative in France by your rapporteur on 18 July, the decision-making structure, i.e. a non-profit association based in Switzerland, will be collegial. Facebook would then be just one of many partners within the association. What technology is the libra based on? The operation of the libra will be based on "blockchain" technology, a transparent and encrypted information transmission technology. The nodes of the chain will be operated by the partners. In order to measure the resilience of systems, standards and supervisory authorities in the face of the emergence of this new type of cryptoactive, a distinction must be made between the three possible applications:

(1) The libra would first of all be a means of payment, enabling individuals to pay or transfer funds in libra. There is room for progress in this area, as cross-border payments are still subject to cumbersome and costly procedures. In order to be used as a means of payment and to ensure that its launch does not result in a regression in the progress made in this area, the libra would have to comply with all anti-money laundering regulations. The issue of data protection should also be closely observed, as the data associated with payments are both very numerous and very sensitive. This seems to be the option chosen by the association since, on 11 September 2019, the Swiss Federal Financial Market Supervisory Authority (FINMA) confirmed that Facebook had applied to it for approval of libra as a payment system.
(2) If the association intends to offer banking services, whether deposit, credit, or savings instruments, it may not operate in any major country without first obtaining a banking license.
(3) In the long run, the libra could be purchased anywhere in the world as a local currency in substitution for the national currency. This is a particularly strong threat to the digital security of countries where the financial system is not stable or has lost the confidence of the population (e.g. in the case of the United States). Venezuela and periods of hyperinflation, Argentina).

Regulatory intervention is required to decide on the classification of the libra. He also called on European citizens to refuse to be swept away by "the seductive but perfidious promises of Facebook's siren song." The ability for libra to reach a large part of the world's population only reinforces the risks associated with the very nature of cryptoactives:

- Data protection. For the moment, there is no reason to share data between libra and Facebook. Does this mean that this separation may one day be called into question, depending on the needs of Facebook and its partners? A second risk is that of the patrimonialization of data: Facebook could propose to grant libras in exchange for personal data.
- Facebook's ability to lead such a project, after several scandals related to the diversion of its products for malicious acts, including against the digital security of states (e.g. the use of the Internet for the protection of the Internet, attempts to manipulate elections).
- The emergence of a superstructure, with the increasing integration of Facebook services with WhatsApp and Instagram and the development of new financial services; the loss of monetary digital security, particularly in developing countries with unstable currencies; financial stability and investor protection.
- The circumvention of international sanctions and the normative framework for combating money laundering and the financing of terrorism, the use of libra to remunerate the perpetrators of criminal acts (cyber attacks or others).

Three of these risks must be highlighted: the circumvention of regulations aimed at combating money laundering, the systemic risk due to the number of Facebook users and the risk to the monetary digital security of states. In response to these concerns, Facebook has consistently explained that it is not about competing with the states or going it alone. The enterprise stated that it had already begun consulting with national and international regulators and that it intended to take the time to answer all doubts and receive the approval of the relevant authorities before launching the libra. It should be considered that this change of method only reflects the sensitivity of this new project, the fragility of Facebook's position and the risk it runs of losing the trust of its users.

It is to be noted that the libra project is carried by Facebook, an American company. If Facebook did not launch its project, other countries would do so, with different values, and over which the US regulator would have less control. There is a need for the United States to be a pioneer in this field and to seize this opportunity to be the first to set the standards in this still relatively unexplored field of digital innovation. The close relationship between the US government and digital enterprises, which is at the origin of the development of the largest multinationals, should not be underestimated here and is reinforced by a real convergence of interests. There is thus a profound link between the development of an innovative project and the affirmation of state digital security.

This project must be monitored with the utmost vigilance, because of the risks it represents, and know how to take the right measure of it. First of all, it is not certain that the libra will emerge and certainly not as a currency in its own right. Secondly, history has shown that private currencies always stumble over their lack of backing: in the event of financial panic, savers and investors always end up turning to the public authorities, the guarantor of the currency and their deposits. Finally, the states have no intention of abandoning their prerogatives: taxes, accounting documents, benefits in public money, etc. All this is expressed only in legal tender.

Cautionary, Facebook has suggested in its quarterly filings with the Securities and Exchange Commission (SEC) that it may delay, or even never launch, the libra project, in the face of mistrust from regulators and national representatives. Nevertheless, even if the libra project were never to happen, the strength of the reactions it has aroused and the ambitions it carries must lead our financial authorities to act more quickly and more forcefully in the area of cryptoactives. The libra project presents less of a threat to states and their monetary digital security than to the traditional banking system. Libra intends to take advantage of the benefits of blockchain technology: faster and cheaper money transfer, smoother transactions, transparent transaction logging, security of exchanges and opportunity for people who have lost their money. The launch of this project is therefore based on an observation: how is it that it has become so easy today to transfer data, documents and photographs but not money in this age of globalized services?

It is interesting to note that Bitcoin, the most famous of the cryptoactives, appeared in 2009, at a time when the financial system was going through one of the most serious crises in its history. The promises of cryptoactives, particularly in terms of transparency and decentralization, would be assets that could be seized by national central banks. The birth of a central bank digital currency (CBDC) could thus support the raising of funds in tokens and the financing of digital innovations, with investors being able to call on this guaranteed asset, without the risk of suffering the uncertainties linked to the volatility of private cryptoactives. Also pleads in favour of a CBDC, reducing the use of cash.

The question is therefore whether businesses and individuals need access to dematerialized payment services in central bank money and whether the central bank can offer economic agents reliable and secure services while maintaining its traditional tasks (supervising and ensuring the smooth functioning of the interbank market, guaranteeing the fluidity of payments, providing liquidity to commercial banks). The development of central bank cryptography would have development costs and could have unexpected implications for financial stability, for the transmission of monetary policy decisions to the real economy, for the efficiency of the payment system, or for the ability to respond to banking "panics."

Indeed, it is not a question here of playing "sorcerer's apprentice"; nothing says that this central bank cryptography should be immediately accessible to all economic actors. It is true that the use of cash remains important and that some central banks have just launched very efficient cross-border payment systems. However, if central banks do not act, they once again run the risk of being overtaken by private actors in a field where everything changes very quickly. At the very least, national central banks need to deepen their knowledge of the possible impacts of issuing a CBDC. Maintaining a wait-and-see attitude will not enable them to respond quickly to competition from private players. It must be said that, on this point, the libra project has acted as an accelerator.

In this respect, it would be necessary to support the development of payment system players: a little-known but crucial digital security issue. This means that in the questioning of the fiscal and monetary order, the subject of payment systems is rarely raised. It is, however, crucial and much less hypothetical than the libra. It is one of the "commons" whose neutrality should be guaranteed by the state. The example of India, a country that is very active on the payment systems front, is worth noting. Since the end of 2010, India has indeed adopted two major reforms aimed both at giving every citizen access to means of payment and at promoting the development of national actors:

- In 2016: the government launches the Aadhaar Payment application, which allows everyone to pay for purchases using their fingerprints. Aadhaar is a project of India's Unique Identification Authority, which aims to provide every citizen with a virtual identity card. It should be noted that Morpho, a Safran subsidiary until 2017, and IDEMIA, resulting from the merger between Morpho and Oberthur Technologies, are collaborating on this project by supplying biometric sensors. However, this system is still fragile and has already been the victim of several cyberattacks. It presents significant risks for the protection of these very sensitive personal data.
- In 2018: the Central Bank of India (RBI) decides that all information relating to payments made in India will have to be recorded locally. While this restriction

was justified by the need for better supervision of transactions, it was considered by some to be primarily intended to impede the collection and resale of data from more than 1.3 billion citizens for the benefit of US enterprises, in order to encourage the emergence of national start-ups instead.

The American digital giants were quick to adapt to the new regulations. After attempting to postpone the entry into force of the reform and being briefly banned from operating in India, Visa and Mastercard quickly made the necessary investments to locate the data in India (without, however, specifying whether they did not keep a copy elsewhere). While it is entirely possible to make digital and instantaneous payments in all countries, payment systems are still largely national, with no harmonization between countries, and the dominant players in the cross-border payments market are all foreign.

What is the interest of the digital giants in developing in the field of payment systems, long considered as a simple stewardship activity? This sector is actually an interface between the banking world and the rest of the world. Digital enterprises, whose model is based on the exploitation of data, can collect, through payments, valuable and marketable data, without having to submit to the strong regulatory constraints on players offering "real" banking services (deposit, savings, credit, etc.). This combination of low barriers to entry and high economic interests explains the penetration of American and Asian digital players in this sector.

It is to address all of these risks that we need to support efforts towards a National Payments Strategy that prevents our citizens from becoming consumers of services produced by others and having their most personal and sensitive data exploited and processed by American or Asian actors. In the past, banks in several countries had failed to respond to Visa and Mastercard; it would be damaging to continue to fall further behind in this area today. It should be stressed that time is now short: states have 2 years to promote an initiative before finding themselves effectively excluded from this strategic market.

Chapter 8
Strengths and Weaknesses of the Enterprise's Information System

The enterprise is at the heart of the economic activities of modern societies, where it has a special status as a consumer of goods and services within the commercial sphere but also as a producer. In addition, this special status allows it to interact with other state and private spheres. The societal exchanges of the firm can be represented in several ways that mark the difference with an individual exchange: a decision-making centre acting with others, in a responsible and enlightened way; a mesh network where each, in turn, produces and consumes the goods produced by others and a production centre to manufacture a good or offer a service.

The enterprise buys a material, in a more or less raw form, to transform it into a product, more or less finished, with the aim of selling it at a profit. Systems theory distinguishes three main systems that will condition the success of the production process: the decision system, the information and communication system and the production system. All these systems have been transformed by digital technology. They have become more efficient, but the analysis of possible numerical flaws in these systems is imperative. The aim of the decision-making system is to produce informed action by relying on knowledge from information that comes from the context and know-how, reasoning and methods capitalized on as experience is gained. In particular, the decision-making system incorporates, in the definition of its strategies, modes of organization according to norms, rules or laws. Today's enterprises are orienting their management towards a so-called agile mode in order to anticipate the threats that weigh on their activity and to develop several business models. The tools of the decision-making system are based on three pivots: knowledge of the ecosystem, the definition of a clearly stated and disseminated strategy and indicators.

The knowledge concerns the enterprise's business lines, inseparable today from a mastery of digital, the market, rules, standards and laws. The absence of such knowledge is a direct threat to the life of the enterprise. A distinction is generally made between the strategic management of the enterprise, which is based on governance linking it to its ecosystem, and operational management focused on

W. Amedzro St-Hilaire, *Digital Risk Governance*,
https://doi.org/10.1007/978-3-030-61386-0_8

production. Several joint processes are necessary to guarantee the functioning of the enterprise within its ecosystem: identity, regulation towards the outside world and market knowledge, management of the enterprise's knowledge and internal regulation using rules of use and charters.

The first step in a strategy is to define the identity of the enterprise, the one that will federate the collaborations. For a long time, organizations have developed their logical divisions or services based on their physical locations: the "management" division building and the "study" division pavilion. In such a model, the boundary of the enterprise is modelled on that of its real estate assets. In organizational theory, this way of structuring itself is called "group identity" where an organization builds its identity and recognition within the physical boundary of the territory it occupies: it is therefore not surprising that the concepts of identity and boundary do not fit well with the digital world. This strategy has the advantage of closing the organization as a system to external disturbances and changes of state, thereby facilitating its defence system. But today, the enterprise's boundaries have become blurred and shifting. Then, the decision-maker must write down in the collective the goals, objectives or purposes that he or she wishes to achieve. It federates administrative mechanisms, all based on regulation. The market-oriented stage is the utility of the good or service produced. This point has become one of the founding concepts of micro-economics, where the satisfaction of the basic need expressed by a consumer is evaluated by the utility function. A good or service is evaluated by this same function; a service also provides satisfaction to its user.

Among the strategic processes, expert knowledge management is fundamental, as well as the collection and storage of various information related to the enterprise's activity: business intelligence. The lack of this knowledge could lead the enterprise into a memoryless mode which, in the extreme, would produce a system that always reproduces the same error. The decision-maker must also set out the enterprise's preferences and rules for dealing with certain situations with the help of usage charters or security policies, particularly in digital matters; these preferences are generally based on the enterprise's utility or survival functions. Finally, the decision-maker sets up a value system that also includes the evaluation of management processes. Dashboards are essential management tools to enable decision-makers to keep a global vision of the enterprise's activities in a synthetic and analytical way, in time and space. The methods for deploying such indicators within enterprises are very complex and require several skills: business and managerial expertise to define the need. Methodological systems (ITIL or ISO/IEC 20000) are developed by specialists. However, this remains a sensitive issue since key performance indicators (KPIs) that measure different service providers in the same process sometimes come up against incompatible objectives.

For example, the amount of an investment related to digital security may be considered excessive compared to other investments with a clear short-term return. The efficiency of the decision-making system is based on the quality of the information that comes from the environment, which gives full dimension to the role of the information and communication system. The challenge of the information system is to provide relevant value for decisions. This property, which is generally difficult to evaluate, is the basis for a quality decision. The information system ensures the quality of the information in both directions:

- Top-down: the information transmitted to the production system enables activities to be carried out in the best possible way.
- Bottom-up: the information transmitted to the decision-making system notes deviations and enables the enterprise's operations to be corrected and optimized. This is control information with which the decision-maker acts.

The information system incorporates information storage capabilities that are essential for the enterprise to keep records of its experiences and capitalize on its know-how. The information system also incorporates a communication system. The challenge of the communication system will be the cohesion of all the internal and external parts of the enterprise. In order to preserve its balance, the enterprise can opt for two forms of relationships:

- Asymmetrical based on power, expertise and psychological status of one in relation to the other
- Symmetrical or egalitarian based on trust

The role of the communication system will be to ensure the appropriate circulation to make these interactions effective. Indeed, both forms of relationships can expose the enterprise if the flows between them are poorly managed. Too much authority or too much trust in a quasi-isolated system can lead to blockages. For this reason, the role of the communication system will play a regulatory role with the help of both internal and external circulations. All levels of the enterprise are irrigated by ascending, descending or transverse flows, to communicate the instructions in the form of information and the effects they have produced.

Company organization charts generally reflect these forms of relationships. The exclusion of a member of the enterprise due to a lack of circulation of information can produce disorganizing relationships that could become dangerous. This is why enterprises are currently moving towards leaner, more agile structures with regard to multi-level hierarchical structures. A company forms an ecosystem from which it interacts with other enterprises, either in adversity or in cohesion, for example, during a digital attack or resilience to it. External circulations are the only means of exchange with other ecosystems. Communications, especially in their digital components, can nevertheless weaken the enterprise, which is why one of the enterprise's duties is also to protect itself.

The challenge of the production system is to carry out the instructions without error. The enterprise carries out basic operational activities by executing and controlling actions based on instructions issued by the strategic level. In the early 1990s, the reference model for the information system of an industrial company was based on the CIM (Computer Integrated Manufacturing) model. The objective was to automate industrial processes and the management of their data, from the data produced by the sensors to the management data of the information system. The interest of a tiered structure is likely to facilitate the progressive evolution of the processes to be automated. In the different levels of the enterprise structure according to the

CIM model, levels 1 and 2 concern the "control-command" mode linked to the sensors. Levels 3 and 4 concern the supervision and planning of manufacturing. For example, computer-aided production management (CAPM) software is at level 4. Today, this management is directly linked to the enterprise's ERP (Enterprise Resource Planning).

The Manufacturing Execution System (MES) is the control and monitoring system for work in progress on the shop floor. Its role is to collect all traces of manufacturing activities in real time from sensors and actuators controlled by PLCs; it is as close as possible to the manufacturing process that has to meet time requirements of the order of a minute. Thus, the MES is located between levels 1 and 2 of the CIM, occupied by the supervision of the actuator sensors and their controllers, and level 4 of the planning, occupied by the CAMM.

Control systems, called SCADA in computer scientists terminology, are increasingly being built with traditional computer components. For example, the Transmission Control Protocol/Internet Protocol (TCP/IP) of Microsoft or Linux software is used in SCADA. These systems are therefore increasingly vulnerable. It was therefore decided to secure industrial information systems on all Shell sites, whether platforms, refineries or depots, to effectively complement the current system. Today, at Shell, there are monitoring devices installed in turbines on oil platforms; these sensors continuously measure many parameters – temperature and rotation speed – and this information is analysed using big data technologies to determine the beginnings of breakdowns; this prevents being the victim of a turbine rupture forcing a platform to stop production.

The decisions taken at the MES level are of an operational nature, more of a reflex to adapt to the hazards of the environment of a temporal and/or spatial nature. The production system receives instructions through the information system and reports hazards through the information system. The entire process is based on the proper functioning of the enterprise's digital system in all its components. The protection of the enterprise's production capacity is fundamental because it is a prerequisite for its survival. Generally, enterprises ensure that actions are managed in advance and implement industrial risk management to this end. Risk management is a method that aims to control production processes. Its complexity required the development of a method at an early stage; the best known is the Failure Mode, Effects and Criticality Analysis (FMECA) method based on cause and effect trees.

The information system is therefore at the heart of the enterprise's processes. It is designed to perform several functions generally grouped around the collection of information related to the organization's activity, its processing, storage and dissemination. This is why the electronic form of the information system is a considerable asset, never before known, to facilitate the gaining and obtaining of information. The activities of a company's information system business lines are modelled to determine the functions to be automated based on the expression of needs. Modelling is carried out using reference models that express all the enterprise's knowledge and business data, as well as their relationships.

Increasingly, an information system is seen as a building constructed for and by the cooperation of people or other information systems to the point of constituting a real knowledge network. It seems that the functions of the information system are nowadays evolving in order to promote the circulation of knowledge in addition to the circulation of information. To do this, an information system covers several functions of:

- Communication system: it couples operational and management modules in order to guarantee the achievement of a service objective with regard to the information: its speed of transmission, its reliability, its suitability for the recipient and its completeness.
- Network and application services: a service relationship is established between the information system and the user where the system formats the information to facilitate access.
- File management: it allows to build up the enterprise's memory through storage: servers, computers, data and knowledge.
- Security: it must guarantee the availability, integrity and confidentiality (AIC) of the elements contributing to their transport and storage Gillet.

Cybersecurity in its three dimensions: its physical component, i.e. telecoms, pipes, computers; its virtual component, software, protocols, servers, etc.; and, in its informational component, information, ownership of information, information processing. It is essential to screen the various functions of the information system to detect possible digital vulnerabilities. Modelling is a complex activity that requires a method. For a long time, modelling methods were based on a so-called entity-relationship approach; then the proposal of a so-called object modelling came, and finally, today, process modelling is carried out using "agile" methods. The Deming wheel (plan, do, check, act) defines the four major functions that serve as a basis for the organization of information systems.

Since the 1990s, enterprises have connected in a variety of ways to facilitate their communications with external partners. In order to optimize the costs of the basic elements of the information system, these are mutualized with the help of a network to manage the sharing between users. This organization, which is increasingly effective in inventing new business models conducive to the development of corporate profits, nevertheless opens, by this same digital path, opportunities to connect to intruders and unwanted uses. The majority of enterprises have set up Local Area Networks (LANs) to share different types of resources such as printers, servers, storage, scanners, network and office applications. These networks can be wired or wireless. The technology used in both cases is to provide a connection medium shared by several users, usually employees.

The first step in setting up a local business network is to set up its physical support. Within each company, there is a technical room (TR) that hosts the network equipment, i.e. one or more switches depending on the size of the enterprise and the switch. On each switch, between 24 and 48 workstations are connected; beyond that, other switches are stacked. The role of a switch is to concentrate all network flows; this means that all users share the same equipment. Generally, the technical room is designed to filter access and reserve it for the enterprise's network administrators. From there, the switch distributes the flow to workstations, servers or shared resources such as backups, printers and scanners. The cabling runs along the baseboards from the switches to one or more network jacks deployed in each office. Each equipment connected as a workstation has its cable to the switch when the deployed standard is IEEE 10baseT.

Certain areas of the enterprise must benefit from special conditions: more confidentiality or performance. There is a technology called Virtual Local Area Network (VLAN) that performs this function. A special setting at the switch assigns a logical channel to a work centre that is reserved for it (red dotted line in the simplified representation of the Business Information System above). When the wiring and configuration of the distribution equipment are complete, the network interface of each computer is connected to the network socket of each office.

Telephony cabling is often coupled with workstation cabling to optimize deployment costs. Today, telephony is carried out from the IP network using the technology known as "voice over IP," which is then connected directly to the network infrastructure. In order to avoid disturbances between voice and data flows, the principle of Virtual Local Area Networks or VLANs will be implemented. At this stage, equipment communicates but cannot exchange Internet services until it is identified by its IP (Internet Protocol) address. Each company sets up an IP addressing plan to associate each piece of equipment with a unique IP address. Administrators configure the IP address on each device and server: workstation, file server, printer, etc.

The technical room also hosts the router whose role is to manage the Internet routes. The simplified representation of the enterprise's management information system shown above shows the IP network flow in black dotted lines. The example shows two IP networks; one would be that of users with IP address ranges in 192.168.1.x; the other would be that of the server farm 120.10.10.x where x represents the address of each piece of equipment, workstation or server. In order to use IP-based services, knowledge of the address of each of them is essential. For example, if the user with the IP address 192.168.1.21 wishes to access the web service of the server 120.10.10.16, he will use the IP address of the server as the URL of his web browser.

Changes in the physical perimeters of enterprises have sometimes led some of them to integrate cheaper, faster and/or more aesthetic solutions to distribute the network as close as possible to its users. For these different reasons, wireless networks (Wi-Fi: Wireless Fidelity) have been a great success with the majority of enterprises. When compared to wiring solutions that can cost up to several hundred thousand dollars, wireless solutions were a less expensive alternative, especially since a simple Wi-Fi antenna represents a deployment time of the order of the day, whereas a wiring solution is of the order of the year.

The principle consists of setting up a radio access point (AP) that broadcasts a network identifier called SSID (Service Set Identifier) on a given channel. Each station equipped with a wireless network card and present in the radio coverage area of the terminal can connect to the SSID network on the same channel. Communication is established; the operation is simple. In order to benefit from Internet services, most kiosks incorporate a Dynamic Host Configuration Protocol (DHCP) server that automatically distributes an IP address to the user. In the illustration below, this mechanism is implemented. Here, the user is hosted in a small room outside the enterprise, which has preferred to provide this room with a network service via a wireless gateway, the cost being very low and offering users direct access to the enterprise's information system. The wireless terminal is connected to the distribution switch.

Wi-Fi configuration is currently widely deployed, especially in businesses. The Wi-Fi connection is quite easy since the user can consult the list of available networks. This list also provides other information on the network concerned such as the security mechanisms implemented, the channel and the available bandwidth. The Wi-Fi configuration could nevertheless, due to the lack of control over radio coverage, offer access opportunities and lead to undesired uses. The efficiency of firms depends on their ability to react to market developments. When manufacturing products from heavy production lines, agility is not obvious due to design delays, consideration of standards and regulations in this market, and communication operations on finished products. The MES (Manufacturing Execution System) already described above is a valuable decision-making aid for these enterprises. Originally, the MES was designed, as advocated by the Computer Integrated Manufacturing (CIM) model, as a stand-alone system. Nevertheless, it is becoming increasingly integrated with enterprise resource planning to improve productivity and reduce costs. Tomorrow, Enterprise 4.0 will be a major challenge for industries: to enable proactivity by ensuring delivery of products on demand while preserving quality and optimizing costs.

Large enterprises are also at the heart of the problem with subcontractors around them. Their security systems are connected with that of the main company with which they have permanent exchanges, therefore interconnections. If these subcontractors do not have serious security systems in place, they will be a conduit for hackers seeking to enter the main system. This problem also exists for all small SMEs and SMIs working in the orbit of large enterprises. The era of sensors and electronic chips is now beginning. More and more, sensors placed on the body will report testimonials, active or passive, of each person's behaviour. Sensors in the individuals' environment will be continuously monitoring. There will increasingly be a quantification of people (standard of living, purchasing power, professional competence, connections between individuals, permanent knowledge of the online student, etc.), which leads to ongoing behavioural awareness.

Many mobile digital objects now access company networks. This can be the motives of employees or people visiting the enterprise. It could also be a passer-by on an adjacent street, as the coverage of the wireless gateway is not easily verified, so anyone could use company resources in this way. The implementation of wireless gateways creates opportunities for unwanted uses. In everyday life, the problem is that physical security and information security are very much intertwined: for example, when a computer controls an air-conditioning system, or an electric generator that itself controls a door opening or something else.

A network service is an application generally hosted on a computer called a "server" for this reason. The role of a server is to process requests or queries from workstations, known as "clients." In order to perform these processes for several clients, the processing and storage capacities of the servers are very important. In the IP environment, a service can be accessed directly from the network by means of an identifier called a "port number" that completes the IP address of a server. Thus, a server can host several services: mail and web on the same physical server. Note that a server that responds positively to a request (120.10.10.80) gives information about the origin of the request.

Information about the presence of the service, for example, of mail on this server, could lead to misuse. The network allows to share services within the enterprise. All these services are generally hosted in the server farm. It consists of one or more isolated IP networks located in a special room called a "clean room" (CR) with access controlled and restricted to IT staff. These services aim to optimize the infrastructure in terms of safety or performance, or to improve the work tool of the employees. These network infrastructure services generally facilitate administrative tasks as well as those of users.

The first service, Dynamic Host Configuration Protocol (DHCP), is commonly implemented in corporate LANs to automate the configuration of IP addresses on users' workstations. The customer's workstation is usually configured by the administrators when it is put into operation. This service has several advantages: hosting a number of IP addresses, reduced configuration time, fewer errors and easier hardware changes. The DHCP service usually hosted within the server farm automatically assigns an IP address to a workstation when it connects. Servers are configured with fixed IP addresses so that they can be contacted by users and administrators. The image would be that of a city hall department whose address would be constantly changing. The DHCP service nevertheless requires tracking to verify the use of IP addresses.

The second service, Domain Name System (DNS), offers users a name resolution service that avoids the tedious entry of IP addresses in the URL of their browser. Each resource is associated with a host name and a DNS domain, for example, www.intranet.entreprise for the web server which becomes the Uniform Resource Locator (URL) of the server. The user then only needs to enter the address to access this server; his workstation will address the DNS server of the infrastructure for each request. Simple Network Management Protocol (SNMP) is another infrastructure service often used to facilitate network management. The SNMP is a protocol to automate the collection of management alerts to alert the administrator of defects requiring his intervention.

There are other infrastructure services such as virtual network services or network redundancy services. Infrastructure services are very useful to assist the administrator in his daily tasks, but they often open up opportunities for undesired uses. Some of these services will also be essential for user and administrator authentication. These aspects will be developed further. The so-called application services provide facilities to the users of the information system. In a very general way, these are office automation applications or applications related to the user's job. The use of these services takes the form of so-called client applications. Currently, the trend is to use a "universal" client, the web browser, to use these applications.

In this way, users use Uniform Resource Identifiers (URIs) that encompass URLs to locate and access their resources. The file service is a service intended for the storage of files created, modified or deleted by the users of the enterprise during the realization of their mission in the enterprise. In a way, such a service is the repository of all the enterprise's knowledge. Employees benefit from shared or personal spaces, hosted on the common file server. The advantage is that the enterprise centralizes all the knowledge and can regularly ensure the backups of these valuable elements of the information system. It also makes it possible to guarantee access to the information it holds in complete confidence since this service is accompanied by a prior authentication service.

The centralization of shared directories allows the administrator to manage each directory for these users. It ensures that the available space on the servers is maintained and then administers usage profile rules to guarantee the proper use of this storage space. At present, 64% of the file management system deployed in enterprises is provided by Microsoft servers, the rest being Linux, IBM AIX servers, etc. The personal storage spaces on company servers facilitate in this way the inlaying of the private life of employees in the enterprise through these directories, and it is legitimate to question the consequences which result from this with regard to legal and normative aspects.

Conversely, employees not connected to this service would have professional knowledge that would not be deposited on the enterprise's information system. This is often the case with mobile terminals such as laptops or smartphones. Finally, resources are pooled to be hosted in data centres mixing system configuration data with user data. However, not all departments within a company can share all data. There is a need for a finer empowerment system. The navigation service is at the heart of Internet services; it allows access to the majority of services; it could very well be the only navigation tool to access messaging services, directories, etc.

The first principle of a web client or browser is based on the Hypertext Transfer Protocol (HTTP). It is a thin client in the sense that the tool is universal, with few settings on the user's side. The request is built by the client from a URL. A URL is a user-entered data composed of several parts:

- The protocol that defines the HTTP language and allows the exchange of pages in HTML (Hypertext Markup Language) format. It is the most widely used, but it is possible to exchange via many other protocols such as https, ldap and ftp.
- An identifier and a password transmitted to connect to a secure server and to specify an access profile; but this method is no longer used because the traces would make it possible to decipher it.
- The name of the server hosting the requested resource or its IP address.
- The port number associated with the service, as already mentioned above.
- The resource path to specify the location of the resource and, in particular, the directory and file name.

At the enterprise level, access to web services is provided through access to the enterprise's Intranet or through Internet browsing. The ability of the webmaster is of great importance; he will guide users as accurately as possible in their navigation to avoid typing addresses or errors that lead to misuse. The messaging service, unlike instant messaging services, allows for "stop and wait" communication, adapted to each person's rhythm. The messaging service mostly deployed in enterprises is Microsoft's. The open source software solution, Zimbra, is also increasingly deployed in public enterprises. A single mail client can configure multiple mailboxes, including external mailboxes.

This capability introduces elements of employees' private lives into the enterprise and conversely leaks elements of the enterprise into employees' private messaging. The principle of messaging has made great strides in the last decade: transmission of a message accompanied by attachments in multiple formats (photos, URLs), in order to quickly share opinions, advice or emotions. These characteristics have revolutionized practices. Nevertheless, they lead to numerous possibilities of undesired uses.

The directory service lists all the enterprise's employees in order to associate certain characteristics such as their telephone number and job title. This service, similar to a "white pages" service in the La Poste directory, can be coupled with the enterprise's authentication service to control access to shared resources. In most enterprises, the directory is MS Active Directory. On the user's side, the overall structure of the directory service is not directly visible to the user; it is difficult for the user to visualize the service; only the names are accessible. Often, the user does not know where the names of the contacts in his mailbox and directory are stored, all the more so if the directory is managed by network administrators. Knowledge of the directory's bases represents a sum of information which, if exploited in an inventive way, could lead to undesired use.

Some applications not yet available in collaborative environments are based on so-called proprietary applications. Many applications have often been developed for the specific needs of a particular company. These developments are carried out by service enterprises specialized in their field. The languages as well as the architectures have responded to a need expressed at a given time by the enterprise, but for some, the rapid evolutions of information systems technologies have made these applications less well adapted than they were originally. For other enterprises, the developments were carried out at low cost and resulted in loopholes that could later be exploited. Moreover, the constraints and cumbersome nature of developments have not always allowed their adaptation.

In order to avoid such pitfalls, the IT departments have used so-called integrated software. This is particularly the case for Enterprise Resource Planning (ERP) software integrating the management of sales, invoicing, accounting, payroll, finance and also production linked to industrial systems. The current market is shared between SAP, ORACLE Application and PeopleSoft/JDE. This type of software is equipped, from its conception, with a multitude of functions. During an expensive implementation phase that best meets the enterprise's needs, functions that are not useful for the enterprise may not be deactivated due to ignorance or negligence on the part of the expert. However, they can leave room for unwanted uses.

The world of industrial computing and the world of general computing are increasingly connected. As for industrial and on-board computing, an example illustrates this: a Boeing already has seven points of entry, one link for logistical incidents, one link with the plant or with Air Canada, another with passengers, one with the police, and so on. Next year your car and your refrigerator will have their entrances; this is irreversible. So, the number of entries into the system will probably increase tenfold in less than 10 years. Not to panic the crowds, but it is still a cause for concern.

The Internet has represented fantastic advances in productivity and growth, but it also brings vulnerabilities. It is also a chance for the industry to develop new products. It is a world that is fairly fragmented between large, highly specialized groups and a myriad of fragile and subcritical SMEs that have virtually no access to exports. This is an area where we have a lot of assets but also a lot of things to do.

Chapter 9
Securing the Information System of Enterprises and Institutions

As described above, for both human and digital exchange, the exchange comes with an object, the stake of the exchange: a good or a service is, first and foremost, a precious resource. The environment presents many dangers that lead everyone to put protective measures in place. The fundamental approach to security in general develops protective measures. What about the protection of the enterprise's information systems?

The fundamental approach to security is to design the components of an information system to ensure and maintain the properties of availability, integrity and confidentiality (AIC). A defence model consists of a triple vision: strategic, organizational and operational. The strategic vision elaborates the principles of information system defence. It is based on a number of general principles to ensure that the safety objectives set are maintained. The first principle covers all the others; it defines a global policy whose mission is to monitor security operations in a uniform manner in space and time.

The second principle is that of unity, which makes visible only one authority, one common policy with shared values, and does not allow any semantic division. The third principle defines a security perimeter for the defence force and its permanent presence. Finally, the temporal and spatial division necessary for the deployment of these principles must be ensured by decentralizing the defence forces in accordance with the principle of globality.

The organizational vision sets up the human organization; it defines the responsibilities of people, the governors of safety, for the maintenance of safety. These individuals must be chosen according to established professional criteria to ensure unconditional compliance with the law. Their role is the anticipation of threats and dangerous events, the planning of predominantly protective and preventive plans, the implementation of plans and compliance with laws and standards, the circulation of information aimed at the defence of the system, their control and the conduct of crisis operations. Their mission will be to ensure that dangers are averted and, in

W. Amedzro St-Hilaire, *Digital Risk Governance*,
https://doi.org/10.1007/978-3-030-61386-0_9

particular, to act to protect the resources vital to the defended system and to take the measures that best meet the needs of users and their objectives.

The operational vision defines and applies tactics. Operational security, enriched by monitoring mechanisms hosted in an operational security centre or Security Operations Centre (SOC), enables both curative and short-term preventive security activities to be carried out on a daily basis. It incorporates threat management, vulnerability monitoring and analysis, and investigation. A safety property characterizes the value of one or more states for which the safe operation of a system is satisfied and outside of which it fails. Three properties are sought: availability, integrity and confidentiality, better known under the acronym AIC. Nevertheless, other security properties can be considered from these three basic properties, for example, accountability, which stores user or machine activities in "event logs."

Availability is the ability of a system to be used only by authorized persons, entities or processes, authorized under the conditions of access and use normally provided by authorized system administrators. It guarantees the operation and does not release it to unauthorized persons, entities or processes; it uses security services such as authentication and backups; and it does not use any other means of authentication. Unavailability may result from major attacks on the integrity of the system or from failures in the technical or human environment contributing to its operation. Availability is controlled using metrics defined by authorized persons according to user authorizations.

For example, the availability of a service is measured by the number of requests per second that it processes; a breach in availability will result in a significant decrease or a total halt in their processing. It may also be an unauthorized change in usage rights that makes the use of this service unavailable. Denial of service vulnerabilities in devices can lead to denial of service attacks. In both cases, the requests are no longer able to be processed. But a denial of service attack can also occur through other means. Stopping a server after a power outage results in a denial of service.

Integrity ensures that knowledge, data, information or configurations have not been modified by unauthorized persons, entities or processes; that they will only be modified by authorized persons, entities or processes; and that the data have not been accidentally or intentionally modified without authorization. The modification of data by an unauthorized individual may, in turn, lead to behaviour that is unwanted by legitimate users but desired by an attacker for manipulation purposes. This is the case of a "suspicious" email forged by an individual; the insertion of a malicious URL is an illustration of this. When securing an information system, these security requirements lead to several questions concerning:

- The authorizations and their links with system assets
- The authorizations and their links with persons, processes and entities
- The authorizations and their links with authorized activities: logging in, reading a file, etc.
- The management of histories to monitor past activities

- The identification and evaluation of properties: knowledge, data and configuration
- The linking chains, also called dependencies, which present human processes or actors that may interact with others

Confidentiality ensures that knowledge, data, information or configuration is not revealed to unauthorized persons, entities or processes but will be revealed to persons, entities or processes according to their authorization. The revelations of IP packets constitute a breach of confidentiality insofar as the information contained in these packets does not, by default, have its own authorization: the use of an IP address, for example, is not linked to an identity. The security of the information system is based on several functions:

- Prevention includes security policies to specify the conditions of use of the system as well as a bastion architecture to provide the most robust line of defence possible. Security experts and architects are the key players.
- Systems monitoring carries out detection and analysis operations when security policies are violated, issuing an alarm in such cases to inform the security analyst.
- The analysis is based on reasoning to understand the source of the safety deviation from the standard and to define whether it is an incident; knowledge of the chains of links or dependencies between processes and humans is an essential question.
- The reaction, rather oriented towards the search for "symptoms," uses the results of detection and analysis; the decision is the key phase for defining and organising countermeasures, parries and reconfiguration actions.
- The investigation, which is more focused on the search for the causes of the incident and its remediation; this stage makes it possible to reconstruct the modus operandi for in-depth remediation of the incident – the investigation also makes it possible to reconstruct the scene and the criminal's motive in order to assist justice in gathering the necessary evidence of the existence of a misdemeanour or crime.
- Repression reinforces acts of prevention; it is carried out by judicial actors.

In this highly dynamic context, and in order to maintain control over systems, the technological fields of telecommunications security are varied and include both proven techniques and others that are the subject of research work to anticipate security breaches. These technologies aim to drastically ensure that each link in the security chain maintains its properties of availability, integrity and confidentiality. In order to be able to monitor such a system, all mechanisms must be designed to provide the monitoring systems with the ability to maintain control over these three fundamental properties. When designing IT assets and/or services, the absence of security mechanisms to alert administrators would hamper their supervision and encourage surprise attacks on the properties of availability, integrity and confidentiality.

The exchange opens up new opportunities for the enterprise's development but also exposes it to external or internal attacks. The enterprise operates in a balance of power between an attack system and a defence system. Nevertheless, this relationship is often uneven in the field of computer security because attackers are often "one step ahead" and have a greater knowledge of information systems, so that the changes of state produced by the attack system call for a process of continuous improvement on the part of the defence system. At each step, the improvement represented in the figure below by the letter guarantees by a permanent reconfiguration activity the availability, integrity and confidentiality properties of the system until the next attack.

Attack 1: Illegal copying of files to the user's system directory by connecting from the hacker's computer.

Response 1: Setting up firewall rules to block unwanted external connections.

Attack 2: Sending a malicious program to the user's system: this program initiates a connection to the hacker's workstation for an illicit copy of files.

Response 2: Setting up an antivirus program on the user's system to detect and eradicate malware.

Attack 3: Sending a trapped email to the user by the pirate asking him to connect to his site – which will allow an automatic and illicit copy of the user's files.

Response 3: The user is aware of the malicious e-mail and does not respond, but since an error message is not returned to the attacker, the user's "e-mail" address is ipso facto confirmed.

Attack 4: The attacker forges a malicious email by social engineering to incite the user to open the email through ignorance, reflex, fear, etc. The attacker is not aware of the user's identity. Although aware of the malicious e-mail, the user, manipulated, executes the hacker's request.

Response 4: The user looks for ways to cancel the action that he imprudently triggered on the order of a stranger.

In this confrontation that mixes human and cybernetic actors, inventiveness seems to characterize the human. This is why the introduction of machines into this spiral must be controlled; otherwise, the risks of drift could lead to a total loss of control of the information system. We may think that this is a utopia and that the aggressor will always be one step ahead. We are currently faced with simple problems. First of all, you only find what you are looking for. Second, when an attack is detected, it has already succeeded.

Third, computer attack detection equipment is not sovereign. There is a dominant state when it comes to detection equipment. It is therefore necessary to develop detection tools in our turn in order to deal with possible attacks coming from this country. The Future Investment Program has made the necessary funds available to national equipment manufacturers.

Some add security to the four pillars of the future cyberspace: cloud, mobility, social networks and big data. The winners are those who first ignore security in favour of the easy way out and then lock down their digital ecosystem rather than protect us from the bad guys. The prevention phase is not sufficient in terms of mastering a technological environment; however, it is indispensable insofar as the implementation of safety by design is always superior, if only to apprehend the risks and set up their monitoring by design.

Currently, the implementation of design-based monitoring is sorely lacking in enterprises due to the massive pragmatic deployment of digital equipment within them for several years. The prevention phase includes the implementation of security policies to specify the conditions of use of the system and bastion architectures to delimit the system's line of defence and develop access control mechanisms to keep it as robust as possible.

The national defence model was designed by governments to protect the nation from external and internal aggressors. The defence code often sets out the basis of the defence model: The defence policy aims to ensure the integrity of the territory and the protection of the population against armed aggression. It contributes to the fight against dangers that could jeopardize national security. It is within this framework that, recently, the Policy on the Security of State Information Systems sets the protection rules applicable to state information systems. These texts are based on the experience in preventing and responding to cyberattacks of state surveillance agencies as well as ministerial participants. Ten principles are essential.

When the control of its information systems requires it, the administration calls upon trusted operators and service providers. All government information systems must be subject to a risk analysis that allows preventive consideration of their security, adapted to the challenges of the system in question. This analysis is part of a process of continuous improvement of the system's safety throughout its life. This approach should also make it possible to maintain an accurate map of the information systems in use. The human and financial resources devoted to the security of the state's information systems must be planned, quantified and identified within the overall resources of the information systems.

Means of strong authentication of public officials on information systems must be put in place. The use of a smart card should be preferred. The state's information systems security policy requires the use of strong authentication means (including smart cards) for sensitive data, which is more secure than a simple password. Then you have to manage all the usual and daily cases of card loss, not to forget it, think about recovering it, etc. This real constraint must be integrated with its initial cost and its daily constraints of no loss and procedures to be implemented, in particular to find one's access card when it has been lost.

The management and administration of the state's information systems must be traced and controlled. The protection of information systems must be ensured by the rigorous application of precise rules. Every public official, as a user of an information system, must be informed of his or her rights and duties but also trained and made aware of cyber security. The technical measures put in place by the state in this area must be known to all. Information systems administrators must apply, after training, the basic rules of computer hygiene. Products and services acquired by administrations and intended to ensure the security of the state's information systems must be subject to a prior evaluation and certification of their security level, according to a recognized procedure (labelling). Administrative information considered sensitive, because of its need for availability, integrity or confidentiality, is hosted on national territory.

The architecture for securing a company's information system is based on a perimeter line of defence, of which the firewall is the key element, supplemented by access zones with varying degrees of restriction depending on the sensitivity of the resources to be protected. The implementation of a defence model is based on a tactical vision of raising a line of defence and protecting it from external aggression. The traditional perimeter image is that of fortified towns whose security was based on controlled accesses concentrating incoming and outgoing flows and continuous surveillance at all points: doors, windows and ramparts. The guards are placed on deployed bastions so that they are linked to each other to monitor each other and communicate with a common code.

A demilitarized zone (DMZ) forges its robustness on a perimeter defence linked to the physical location of its components. It is designed to analyse incoming and outgoing network flows on independent channels. The security model of digital exchange applies these same principles. Within an information system, the line of defence is developed through a demilitarized zone, the aim of which is to concentrate the incoming and outgoing flows of the information system at a single point. The filtering of these flows is concentrated at a point whose basic technical element is the firewall.

The centrepiece of a demilitarized zone (DMZ) is a firewall. Entering via WAN (Wide Area Network) access, each packet is subjected to a fine analysis before being allowed to transit the system. Moreover, the firewall keeps several packets in memory in order to validate their possibly suspicious links. A firewall is mainly used at the edge of the private corporate network and the public network. It contains a set of predefined rules to either allow only those communications that have been explicitly authorized or to prevent those exchanges that have been explicitly prohibited.

The choice of one or the other of these methods depends on the security policy adopted by the entity wishing to implement communications filtering. The first method is the safest, but it requires a precise and binding definition of communication needs. A firewall uses two types of filtering: application and packet based. Packets contain headers: source and destination IP address, packet type (TCP, UDP, etc.), port number, etc.

When an external machine connects to a machine in the local network, and vice versa, the firewall analyses the headers of the exchanged flows. When filtering is based on IP addresses, the term address filtering is used, while the term protocol filtering is used when packet type and port are analysed. This time, application-to-application feeds are filtered at the content level. The firewall is a powerful system for network protection, subject to daily administration. In order to help determine a balance between the need to exchange and the exposure to threats and vulnerabilities, the interconnection zone makes it possible to define two types of zones:

- One rather open to Internet users and potentially to enemies: the systems are said to be "sacrificial"; they are publicly accessible servers such as those of e-commerce or web or FTP. It also contains technical data for the need for services such as DNS and SMTP (Simple Mail Transfer Protocol).

- The other rather open to partners and potentially friends, also hosting common and specific data for public and private areas such as certificates or authentication servers.

The first step will be to make a partition between private and public at each level: cabling, network and applications. For monitoring purposes, probes will be deployed at strategic points in the DMZ. Today, information system managers are reaching their limits, since the enormous quantity of alerts emitted by the surveillance probes are transmitted in a disordered manner and make it impossible to monitor, i.e. to interpret the meaning of the multiple alerts emitted by the surveillance probes. An antivirus is a software in the form of a program, developed by a software publisher, which analyses system, network or application flows. It acts as a filter; it extracts from the stream the content that it compares to reference models it knows, better known as signatures.

If the values are identical, it means he has found a virus. In this case, the antivirus software stores the file in a specific space called the quarantine and sends an alert to the administrator so that he can analyse this anomaly by himself. The administrator will then take the necessary measures. Some antivirus software needs to be tested to prove its interception capability. There are antivirus self-test sites, but this feature should be built into the software. Similarly, it should be possible to test these signatures. An antivirus is there to protect, but it cannot be infallible. On the other hand, this global system will be above all layers of information.

The moral contract that IAD (International Antivirus Demonstrators) has with the state is to be able to provide a tool that goes much further than what antivirus programs do today. We are very well on our way to achieving this; the results are very encouraging. The first part of the modules, which is currently being tested, already allows to do much more than what current antivirus software allows, especially on the detection capabilities of unknown codes, which is the real technical challenge and the real operational need.

From the thumbprint signature, in commerce in Babylon less than 3000 years B.C., to the first access control equipment of the 1980s, the notion of identity and recognition is a fundamental human concept. Several models were proposed as early as the 1970s to address the implementation of access control principles. Bell-LaPadula's (1975) access control model is the reference model still in use today. The major problem is the authentication of the interlocutor. This also concerns the administration. For example, when the tax department notifies an adjustment to an individual, some people will check whether it is really the tax department, but others will not. The origin of the electronic mail seems to be the proof of the pudding.

The problem of authenticating who is talking to you, who is calling you, or who you want to talk to or exchange with is a major problem. Today, faced with that, we are totally under-equipped. However, there are small enterprises, both local and foreign, that have developed effective authentication systems. At the national level, it will be necessary to seek a system that satisfies everyone and to implement it by gradually imposing it, starting with the administration. For tax returns today, formalities start with an identification certificate, followed by the entry of several codes. The tax authorities are the only ones to take such precautions.

That being said, if the tax department gets caught, they will never say so. In enterprises, an internal authentication system must already be in place to verify that it is the enterprise's employees, customers and subcontractors with whom contact is made. Large enterprises are also at the heart of the problem with subcontractors around them. Their security systems are connected with that of the main company with which they have permanent exchanges, therefore interconnections. If these subcontractors do not have serious security systems in place, these subcontractors will be a conduit for hackers seeking to enter the main system. This problem also exists for all small SMEs and SMIs working in the orbit of large enterprises.

Access control is the cornerstone for maintaining confidentiality. During this operation (schematized below), the client (1) contacts the server which returns a response called a challenge (2) in the sense that the client must prove its identity by taking up this challenge (3); the server checks and accepts, or not, the access (4); the client then receives the information sought (5).

This authentication mechanism is not sufficient to guarantee that the information contained has not been read or manipulated by a third party. Integrity is the second component developed in flow control models. Many attacks are aimed at "capturing identifiers." These identifiers are valuable elements that are a key condition for system penetration. For this reason, exchanges 1, 2, 3 and 5 in the above diagram can be encrypted during authentication operations to raise the level of protection to a higher level of robustness.

From social engineering to man-in-the-middle attacks, from passive network eavesdropping to phishing, from dictionary attacks to brute force attacks, authentication and, in particular, identifiers are targeted by a large proportion of computer attacks. This is why the processes for generating identifiers and then verifying them are probably the most sensitive steps. In order to verify the credentials of a client wishing to access resources whose access it controls, an authentication server must have identity verification elements.

To do this, the client and the server carried out a common preliminary step of distribution of the login/password couple. This phase constitutes identification. Identification protocols are designed to optimize the exposure phase during the distribution and verification of identifiers and then to strengthen the evidence of identity. An identification mechanism will respect several properties and conditions in order to maximize exposure.

To optimize the distribution and verification phase of identifiers and to avoid attacks based on identity theft, an identification and authentication protocol will have to comply with several properties. Non-repudiation, close to imputability, ensures that the source that emits the data cannot contest its emission; it must be identified and identifiable without qualification. The non-replay, or non-reuse of the object, ensures that resources such as main memory or disk storage areas can be reused in a safe manner. Auditing is the ability to collect information on the use of resources in order to monitor or bill a user according to his consumption. An alarm ensures that specific relationships between different data are maintained and reported without being altered.

The identification phase is based on evidence of a purely human identity. To develop a digital identity, elements of the identity must be extracted such that they are unique, obvious, unambiguous and securely authenticatable. For this reason, this step will favour weak or strong evidentiary factors developed from human identities of a memorial, physical and/or physiological nature.

1. "What I know," which represents a memory element, is a weak element because it is based on an element of memory such as a password or a favourite musical instrument.
2. "What I own," which represents a material element, is a strong element because it uses a reference such as an identity card or a smart card with a certificate.
3. "What I show," which represents a bodily element, is a strong element because it uses a physical reference such as a fingerprint, voice, gestures and biometrics.
4. "What I do," which represents knowledge about behavioural habits as a habitual gesture or signature, is a strong element.

In addition, the combination of several of these factors significantly increases their complexity, thereby introducing a hard point in the face of identity theft attacks. Instead of using these evidentiary factors or a combination of them, the most widely deployed technique for authentication is often based on the login/password when it does not sufficiently protect users and/or processes.

Identity management is a key process in corporate security. It enables all the prerogatives of an employee to be grouped together on the information system. All computerized processes such as messaging, human resources management and IT equipment assignments for employees are grouped in one point in order to assign authorizations. Identity management also makes it possible to put the management of employees back under the direction of human resources while often still under the responsibility of the IT department. Nevertheless, the implementation of this function must be deployed with caution so as not to omit to block or authorize certain resources, which could lead to undesired uses of the information system.

In order to group together all the users of the same entity, a common database is set up in which each user will be seen as an object. In order to classify each of them, a directory is used. The directory follows a hierarchical organization in order to adapt to the multiple forms of company organization. The most widely deployed standard is the X.500 standard, which allows a hierarchical structure of the directory to be defined. Cryptography is used to reduce the exposure of identifiers during their transfer; it can be combined with biometrics to increase the complexity of evidence.

The principle of a cryptosystem is based on the transformation of a source message into a cryptogram using a key while retaining certain properties for decryption. The key is calculated using more or less complex algorithms and mathematical functions; in the case of an asymmetric cryptosystem, the two keys are linked by a mathematical function. The first asymmetric cryptography protocol allowing the distribution of a cryptographic key via the network was proposed by Diffie-Hellman in 1978 with the objective of authentication and not only protection for transport.

This protocol makes it possible to generate keys between the server and the client without transferring them over the network. In addition, it creates a mathematical link between the sender of the message and the owner of the key, thus ensuring its non-repudiation properties equivalent to the acknowledgement principle used to guarantee the source and recipient of a postal mail. In addition, the protocol uses a pair of keys, dependent on each other, each of which is specialized in encryption or decryption operations, hence the qualification of asymmetric.

Turning a message into a cryptogram is not an end but a step; the encryption process has a dual purpose: encryption is done with the aim of deciphering easily while being low exposure during transport. To make decryption efficient, operations will be performed on bitstreams for both the key and the message. The basic principle is based on two operations: XOR and concatenation. According to the following basic principle: in Boolean algebra, the eXclusive OR function, also called XOR, is a logical operator. An XOR function applied to its own result allows you to return to its initial result. For example, the function "XOR 1" applied to 0 gives 1; applying "XOR 1" to 1 gives 0.

Cryptographic functions transform a message into a bitstream, slice it into blocks to adapt it to the application of cryptographic algorithms and apply XOR operations with the preset key. Nevertheless, algorithms use increasingly complex functions for the transformation of keys and data streams. Encryption is achieved by combining a binary key with a bitstream such that the protocol is complex enough not to reveal all or part of the identifiers and structured enough for decryption.

The following is a challenge authentication protocol. This protocol is widely deployed because it is simple to implement. In the case of a login/password login, the user receives a "login" test pattern from the server so that he can enter his name and password. In order to enable this to work, the server is configured beforehand so that it can know the passwords corresponding to the user's identifier. A storage space is reserved on the server to store all the enterprise's identifiers (login and password). This space is particularly protected, and passwords are encrypted to prevent unauthorized access to this server, making the identifiers unreadable. Thus, the server only knows the encrypted value of the password. At the time of authentication, the client encrypts the password, on the one hand, to keep it confidential during transport and, on the other hand, so that the server can compare it with the value it holds in its database.

If the comparison between the encrypted value provided by the client and the encrypted value held by the server is successful, the authentication is pronounced. The WBS technique is intended to use a password only once, with another password being provided for each subsequent session. A first deployment is carried out; this is the preliminary phase of setting up; then a matrix card held by the customer is used to calculate the code at the time of login. The following example shows a dynamic raster map calculated by a terminal synchronized with the authentication server. This principle, widely deployed by enterprises, guarantees strong encryption as well as the certainty that the server is authentic. However, it does not guarantee that the user is legitimate in case of theft of the key.

A digital certificate solves the problem of the authenticity of the actors of an exchange. It relies on an asymmetric cryptosystem for this purpose. This principle, by design, states that, given two keys dependent on each other, a message decrypted with one of the two keys proves that it could only be encrypted with its complementary key. These two keys are called, respectively, public key because it can be published to everyone and private key because the complete security of the cryptosystem relies on its confidentiality. The advantage is that the link between the two keys is based on a complex mathematical function (discrete logarithms, factorization of prime numbers) to which the encryption key is associated as a parameter. To deduce the key, the attacker would have to find one of a very large number of solutions, especially since the key values will be generated from very large prime numbers.

The only weakness, however, is to ensure the authenticity of the certificate during its generation. To this end, complex certificate infrastructures called Public Key Infrastructures (PKI) are deployed. Technologies that are important for the digital security of enterprises and the nation, such as Public Key Infrastructures (PKI) – which are authentication or encryption systems – should be identified in order to invest in the most reliable offers and encourage their local production. The use of a public-private key method with signature to secure messages is done in several phases.

Phase 1: tools for securing messages

1. Anne-Yvonne and Bruno each develop a private key and a public key.
2. Anne-Yvonne and Bruno each obtain a certificate of their public key from a certification authority – it can be the same authority or two different authorities.
3. From each person's computer, several cryptographic functions can be used, in particular hash functions. It is assumed that Anne-Yvonne and Bruno have the same functions.

Phase 2: exchanging message security tools

1. Anne-Yvonne addresses her public key – which can be compared to an open padlock of which only Anne-Yvonne holds the private key – as well as the certificate associated with Bruno and vice versa.
2. Each one can check the certificate to verify that it is indeed the public key of the other.

Phase 3: sending a secure message and its fingerprint

1. Anne-Yvonne encrypts the message she wishes to send to Bruno with Bruno's public key – the open padlock addressed by Bruno.
2. Anne-Yvonne hacks her message and signs the result with her private key to obtain a signed imprint.
3. Anne-Yvonne sends her encrypted message and the signed print of this message to Bruno.

Phase 4: reception of the secure message and her fingerprint, reading and authentication

1. Upon receipt of the encrypted message by Anne-Yvonne using Bruno's public key, Bruno decrypts this message with his private key.
2. Bruno hacks Anne-Yvonne's message to obtain a print.
3. Bruno compares the fingerprint addressed by Anne-Yvonne with the one he obtained to verify their similarity.
4. To be sure that it is indeed a message from Anne-Yvonne, Bruno verifies, with Anne-Yvonne's public key, that it is indeed Anne-Yvonne's signature.

The application of the use of a certificate to web services is a principle that makes it possible to guarantee the authenticity of the message since a message received and decrypted with a key could only be issued by the holder of the complementary key. This principle is used in certificate-based protocols. The Secure Sockets Layer (SSL) protocol used in many authentication mechanisms on the Internet applies this principle. Biometrics involves an additional physical factor, making authentication strong.

Generally, biometrics uses several recognition methods based on a single characteristic or behaviour: fingerprints, retina, venous network, voice, behavioural signature and DNA. Credentials relate to the rights that users obtain over computer resources. These are of all types ranging from a simple file to a printer or scanner.

The most sensitive resources, i.e. the enterprise's data, are often pooled. The value of the clearances will be to allow discretionary access to this information using profiles. To grant authorizations, the administrator defines profile types corresponding to authorization levels that associate resources (assets) with possible actions such as reading, writing and modifying.

Once this profile has been defined, the administrator will be able to associate the user's name with this profile. (1) The administrator chooses the resource to be protected. (2) The administrator selects the user to be enabled from the enterprise directory. (3) The administrator defines the actions on this resource that this user will have the right and the possibility to perform.

When the user John Smith logs on, he accesses this resource. The principle of authorization mechanisms is based on authentication protocols. Once authenticated, the server assigns the requested resource to the user: the resource can be a printer, a file or a virtual directory. There are multiple protocols for managing authorizations within a network, either proprietary or open source. The following example details the Kerberos protocol and its authorization architecture. This protocol is implemented by Microsoft in its Active Directory and file management system. The different steps to obtain a resource go through classical authentication and then by obtaining rights in the form of a ticket.

- 1: access to the Kerberos service and client authentication
- 2: winning a ticket to access the ticket service
- 3: authentication by the ticket server
- 4: request for access to the resource server
- 5: winning a ticket to access the resource server
- 6: authorized access to the resource server

Browsing on shared resources is impossible due to rights management. Nevertheless, particular attention must be paid to this management on a daily basis, as an error on the part of the administrator could lead to unwanted visits to sensitive directories. In addition, the administration of this protocol is sometimes difficult due to users belonging to several profiles. A rights mapping should help the administrator to improve the consistency of entitlements. In some situations, company data must be transmitted over wide area networks. The attractiveness of the cost of the Internet has led software manufacturers and publishers to propose new principles for securing architectures.

A network is said to be virtual when it connects two physical enterprise networks (LANs) by a link that tends to be considered private: only the computers on the LANs on either side of the Virtual Private Network (VPN) can exchange, see each other and access shared data. In order to secure the data transmitted, it is necessary to use secure tunneling protocols, i.e. to create an opaque envelope for everyone except those who have the authorization to use it. Encryption is widely used to create a tunnel. A distinction is made between level 2 VPNs, where almost the entire frame header is encrypted (Layer Two Tunneling Protocol, L2TP); level 3 VPNs (IPSec), where source and destination addresses can circulate in clear text; and level 5 VPNs (SSL: Secure Sockets Layer).

The Virtual Private Network (VPN) is the most widely used and robust technology today, especially when it is accompanied by the certification of interlocutors, machines and users via signed certificates. While a VPN provides a secure link at a lower cost, it does not provide a quality of service comparable to a leased line.

The SSL VPN, used for remote access, is a flexible solution allowing simple, fast and secure access to corporate network data, but more suitable for mobile workers (teleworkers, nomadic users, etc.). To date, the IPSec VPN remains the most robust and agile solution for interconnecting remote sites or networks. This is the solution chosen for the private digital cloud in order to interconnect the customer's site with that of its cloud host. Among the other technologies used to link remote sites, dedicated links are non-shared links, reserved for a company, whose cost has become a deterrent even though their security principle is the most robust to date.

In order to transport data outside the enterprise in a secure manner, the most common means of transport is the establishment of secure links. The idea is to establish a unique relationship between the source and recipient using an end-to-end protocol. Two successive phases will therefore be completed: first the establishment of a logical channel between the source and the recipient, sealed by means of encryption protocols, and then the transfer of encrypted data in this channel.

Several countries have also taken the initiative to issue their safety standards. They recommended that it should be a widespread national standard. I put forward exactly the same idea to the Department of Productive Recovery. This could be universal, but it is possible to create, or at least use, existing "adapted" standards to ensure that they are very safe. We know, for example, that there are some very significant flaws in SSL, a standard that is used massively and that is still being used despite everything. As it is an aging standard, it tends to disappear, but it is a breakthrough standard that continues to be used.

Chapter 10
Digital Vulnerabilities and Attacks Compromising the Security of Enterprises and Institutions

After having described the hostile environment in which enterprises operate, not always able to design their digital security, including material or human vulnerabilities and attacks of various kinds against the enterprise's information system, let us take a closer look at complex attacks and experienced attackers and then at the means of anticipating and dealing with them. Beyond the security vulnerabilities inherent in the networks or digital products used and the exploitation of these vulnerabilities during use, these vulnerabilities can be contained in very mainstream digital products that have become familiar through habituation and therefore have a sometimes-deceptive aura of security.

These loopholes may also exist at the heart of enterprises or even states. When the Ministry of Economy and Finance of a rich country was attacked on the eve of a summit between Heads of State, it was considered that this was not a marginal issue even if no figures could be given in terms of impact. The Stuxnet virus attack on the centrifuges of the Iranian military-industrial complex broke the constitution of a nuclear force; similarly, Saudi Aramco had 30,000 computers destroyed. But what exactly is a digital security breach? Where can it come from? Are software developers, hardware and network designers, or the hardware and networks themselves solely responsible? Do digital users have their share of responsibility in exploiting these loopholes?

As the stake of the enterprise is to develop its capacity to invent and create, through exchange, the enterprise brings an answer to this challenge; it creates wealth, produces, sells, communicates and evolves. However, these issues are also those of its competitors, or even its enemies, hostile individuals or organizations with whom it trades and against whom it will have to fight.

Within such an ecosystem where technology should be the undisputed asset of enterprises, helping them in their decisions, accelerating their production, guiding them in their purchases, carrying their image and ensuring their cohesion, the role that technology sometimes plays is still uncertain. Who controls it? Can it become a serious threat to business productivity?

W. Amedzro St-Hilaire, *Digital Risk Governance*,
https://doi.org/10.1007/978-3-030-61386-0_10

Who are the victims? All actors in the societal spheres but also all actors in the technological sphere. From software publishers to manufacturers of connected objects, all are likely to become victims. Who are the winners? Cybercriminals or networked organizations, ever more ingenious in exploiting the immaturity of technologies, are expanding their activities in cyberspace, while these threats also bring enormous gains for other players.

Some exploit them, others suffer them. Winners or victims, they all have in common their links to vulnerabilities in digital systems. Current knowledge about these vulnerabilities is immense, and the way in which this knowledge is organized has been widely studied. Most of the time, we realize that the design of the systems is sufficient in terms of security because many attacks are not very "strong." They become efficient when the overall architecture has not been well thought out. There is a need to disseminate a culture of security among enterprises, especially SMEs, which are particularly vulnerable.

A vulnerability characterizes an accidental or intentional failed state caused, during the design, development or operation of the information system and susceptible to exploitation by a malicious individual. Vulnerability is carried by the target. The concept of vulnerability can often be confused with that of threat. Vulnerability can be seen as fixed in the face of the phenomenon that reveals it, whereas threat is a state that depends on the context in which the target is operating.

Thus, a development fault in a software is a vulnerability, whereas a development fault intentionally provoked by a competing developer will be a threat. The nature of a threat/vulnerability/attack model depends on many parameters. Just as the detection of an infinite number of threats may be impossible, so the detection of system-related vulnerabilities can be structured. From this perspective, the identification of vulnerabilities is based on a complex process of analysis. Security properties are based on maintaining availability, integrity and confidentiality. Vulnerability will be assessed on the basis of its capacity to be exploited by a malicious individual.

Moreover, the identification of a vulnerability is often carried out after an initial effect because the discovery of a vulnerability is long, complex, expensive and sometimes linked to chance. In addition, a vulnerability can have a local effect of global origin. For example, a subcontractor is asked to configure software that is deemed reliable on behalf of a company, but during this adaptation by the subcontractor, an unprecedented vulnerability appears.

Finally, some players may find it beneficial to develop a climate of mistrust towards certain technologies competing with their own or, on the contrary, to conceal the presence of certain vulnerabilities. It is not uncommon to find suspicious vulnerabilities that look much more like backdoors left on purpose. This is, for example, the case of a number of commands hidden by operators (notably Huawei), which allow certain functionalities to be reactivated or deactivated remotely. For all these reasons, the detection of vulnerabilities and their dissemination must be shared or even carried out by an institutional service.

The watch principle originated in the United States of America in the late 1980s as a result of computer security incidents. As part of the 2Centre project, training needs related to new security professions were identified, such as the need for people to intervene in incidents, analysts who are also in charge of monitoring, intrusion testers (to find vulnerabilities before attackers do) and also engineers in charge of incident response. There are some in large enterprises, such as banks. State security agencies are planning to recruit hundreds of security specialists, while the number of staff at the Defensive Computer Warfare Analysis Centres is expected to double in the near future. Indeed, why wait to be attacked?

The incident management organization has been set up to allow community enrichment of computer system vulnerabilities. Among the key players and organizations that have made efforts to achieve this, the National Institute of Standards and Technology (NIST) (along with the Mitre, a non-profit organization focused on the global identification of security vulnerabilities) should be mentioned first. Since then, the Mitre, close to the Massachusetts Institute of Technology (MIT), manages the vulnerability lists for NIST. The Mitre is historically a non-profit entity with a mission to provide technical engineering for the North American government with a focus on defence requirements.

Together with NIST, the Mitre helps organizations secure their critical infrastructure and data by fostering public/private collaboration to identify and resolve complex cyber security threats. For their part, the software publishers whose developments are at the origin of the flaws are working to correct them.

Finally, the CERT/CC (Computer Emergency Response Team Coordination Center), a specialized and accredited organization, provides emergency response to computer security incidents. CERTs are organized and certified to carry out the following activities: centralization of security incident tickets on networks and information systems; analysis and processing of incidents: solutions, information exchanges and technical studies; enrichment of the vulnerability base; dissemination of information on measures and good practices and coordination of actions with the other actors involved in the incident.

Security professionals are users of the information provided by CERTs. The "bugtraq" site of the "SecurityFocus" is intended for the general public publication of "bugs" and vulnerabilities. The software publisher or equipment manufacturer detects a flaw from network information (1) and then analyses this flaw. In order to allow a large-scale deployment, it also disseminates information to SecurityFocus in the form of a newsletter also called bugtraq, and it also informs the CERTs.

From this step on, the patch update will be followed by the bugtraq, as shown in the diagram below in the "update" field. The bugtraq is transmitted to the Mitre symbolized by the CVE reference base in order to associate a unique identifier to this flaw. The Mitre thus holds a comprehensive global list of vulnerabilities. The Mitre lists vulnerabilities in a universal format: (CVE, Common Vulnerabilities and Exposures), references them and disseminates them to CERTs and the SecurityFocus website (3). Once the vulnerability has been referenced, a relationship is established between these different actors with, at the centre, the software publisher to initiate the correction of the vulnerability.

In the second scenario, only the entry point changes since the bugtraq is motivated by an alert from intrusion detection logs. This means that, in scenario 2, the incident is a security incident. As part of its overall mission, the Mitre is responsible for assigning vulnerability identification numbers. The process is that of a global addressing process using centralized management. The identifier is based on three fields: the CVE prefix, the year and a serial number within the year. Referencing vulnerabilities on a global scale is the asset of cybersecurity actors in their defensive approach, or at least it will become one if they are allowed to exploit them. For several decades, these actors, Mitre, NIST and SecurityFocus, have been addressing the issue of vulnerabilities; many classifications have emerged.

Currently, as shown on the Mitre site page above, there are more than 23 basic classes to describe vulnerabilities. In particular, the Cross-Site Scripting class (XSS, on the eighth line of the list in the diagram above) is the cause of many attacks. This classification is evolving; most recently, NIST has proposed a new CVE identifier with new classes and is also preparing a classification for managing activities within a cloud computing centre.

A zero-day vulnerability is a new vulnerability, discovered during its exploitation by an attacker. It is often present in software and is usually related to a simple programming error, but it can also occur in a system or equipment. It is called zero-day because the software patch for the vulnerability is not available or could not yet be tested for its application at the time it is discovered. The developer in charge of the patch has the minimum amount of time, zero days, to offer users a reliable solution as quickly as possible and stop the spread of the attack. Until the patch is introduced, the vulnerability will be called zero-day. When scenario 1, entitled "Fault/attack/corrective ecosystem," is used, for a variety of reasons, it is possible not to reveal the flaw, the so-called zero-day vulnerability.

As always, a security breach also leads to new forms of exploitation; we are talking about new business models. The discovery of a vulnerability may be worthwhile to governments wishing to wage cyberwar or to organizations with malicious intent. Indeed, a non-public flaw that will not be corrected by the software publisher or programmer will only have a stronger effect.

This was the case of the famous Stuxnet virus, for example, a priori developed jointly by the United States of America and Israel, or Aurora which developed four zero-day vulnerabilities to penetrate systems. If a computer flaw is not published, or known to the general public, and therefore not corrected by the publisher of the targeted software or the hacker who intends to exploit the flaw benefits from a total surprise effect, he can then take control of a computer, software or network, or even carry out a denial of service attack, without the targeted structure having had time to prepare for it.

The combination of vulnerabilities and threats can have a considerable impact on enterprises' information systems. During their digital exchanges, interlocutors expose themselves, putting at stake the availability, integrity and confidentiality of objects and/or interlocutors during their transport. For this reason, weaknesses relate to the entry and exit points of transport systems and the people who use them. The principle of risk analysis is to bring together the elements of assessment in order to better control these weaknesses and make a company's activities as safe as possible, bearing in mind that complete safety cannot be guaranteed. The assessment of this safest possible state is therefore based on two key elements:

- The potential for an incident which is generally measured by the history of similar events that have occurred or the particular exposure of an element of the information system
- The impact of an incident, which is usually measured by a financial assessment

A level 4 impact and a level 4 potential result in a level 4 risk for the enterprise: the enterprise commits to address it, whereas a rare but high-impact incident will only represent a level 2 priority in addressing the risk. Nevertheless, while the use of risk analysis methods remains a considerable asset for obtaining an objective knowledge of a company's environment, this process is cumbersome in the face of enterprises' need for agility to ensure their day-to-day security.

To conduct this analysis, the different levels of the enterprise must be studied. Every business has goods and services that make up its value. Assets within the information system are data, information, knowledge or know-how. Indeed, Total has established a regime for classifying data into four categories: up to level 2, it is possible to use the cloud, but above level 2, for security reasons, it is forbidden to use the cloud.

Risk analysis examines the exposure of these goods and services to their vulnerabilities or the threats they pose. Services represent the algorithms for disseminating these goods or producing them in a transportable form (packaging). All the services implemented with the same production objective form a process. Processes are the enterprise's knowledge and know-how to produce or transform values by promoting the circulation of goods and services. The enterprise's information system consists mainly of processes and assets, the former aiming to enhance the latter.

From the point of view of exchanges, services represent the algorithms for disseminating the good or producing it in a transportable form (packaging). From the point of view of vulnerability analysis, the exposure of processes and assets takes place at specific points in the information system. It is therefore necessary to identify and locate the memories that house the assets, the places where the processes or services attached to them are executed, as well as their points of exchange, their transport and interconnection networks that support their circulation.

The risk analysis should cover all of these assets by addressing their level of sensitivity to breaches of confidentiality, integrity and availability (CIA). Risk analysis methods facilitate the identification of assets using the classifications they propose. For example, the method developed by CLUSIF is a method to help enterprises conduct a risk analysis of their information system. It offers an analysis of the processes of a company's information system: invoicing, production, etc. For each process, it allows assets to be classified into several categories: the services involved, applications, data, files, paper documents and electronic and paper messages. This analysis work is tedious and difficult to automate.

It is important to identify the different locations involved, directly or indirectly, in the valuation of the enterprise's assets and services. These key elements of the information system are carried by different entities: administrative sites composed of physical or digital memories (computers), industrial sites composed of physical or digital memories (computers, MES, etc.), mobile staff laptops, mobile phones or smartphones, USB keys, sensors, etc. Employees are also to be included as key elements of the enterprise's memory and services. It is also important to identify the components of the link chain because it is important to determine if this component is:

1. Private, and in this case, it should be possible to keep control of it by means of security rules and policies.
2. Public and/or shared, and then access becomes open to everyone without restriction or to groups; the robustness of the components depends on external factors, human and technological, which are difficult to control.

In addition, the security of the chain of links of the connected company's information system should be analysed to identify the elements involved in transport operations and, in particular, packaging/unpackaging. These are the points of exchange that are mostly sensitive to intrusions and information leaks.

(1) Private interconnections between different sites: interconnection "administrative site - industrial site" based on the "local loop - Internet-local loop - industrial site"; interconnection "administrative site - operator" based on the "local loop - Internet-local loop on the operator's side"; interconnection "industrial site - operator" based on the "local loop - Internet-local loop on the operator's side"; public interconnections between different sites: interconnection "mobile network - Internet"; interconnection "mobile network - PSTN"; interconnection "Internet-PSTN".
(2) In the case of Local or Remote Networks, the various media federating these interconnections are:

   - Private media: wireless local area network for business users; wireless industrial local area network made up of sensors
   - Public media: Internet network composed of access networks, or local loop, connected to the Internet core network; 3G, 4G or 5G mobile network composed of access networks via antennas and core network; PSTN network

(3) In the case of private/public interconnections, the valuation of assets and services involves exchanges with external actors, which makes them vulnerable. Because of information technology, the transport of these assets and services requires that they be transformed into a binary form, the only one compatible with the medium. These media are sometimes public, in which case these flows will be more exposed.

Within a corporate information system, risk analysis implies knowledge of each flow by identifying their interlocutors as well as the nature of the assets transported. Among these key elements, some of them constitute points of exchange with the outside world, which can be public and shared: public and private life of company staff with the outside world, public DMZ of the administrative site, Internet access for laptops of mobile staff and Internet access for mobile phones of mobile staff. Within an extensive information system, a multitude of services and flows are exchanged. The risk analysis proposes a method to identify them exhaustively and then classify them. It is a flow matrix specifying the function it performs, its direction (public to private or vice versa), its origin, its destination and the nature of the information it carries.

Once the flows have been identified, they can be analysed according to their source and destination in order to implement policies to authorize or block them. For example, the messaging flow involves DNS, SMTP and HTTPS type flows. Their description makes it possible to identify control rules that can be applied at the time of their transit through the public DMZ. This flow analysis will be used by security administrators to set up the filtering rules of a firewall. These rules are an important part of the enterprise's security policies.

Risk assessment is also based on numerous classifications. It includes several main categories that may change depending on the business and the specificities of the enterprise, namely temporary unavailability of resources, destruction of equipment, degraded performance, destruction of software, software alteration, data alteration, data manipulation, disclosure of data or information, misappropriation of data files, loss of data files or documents, total immaterial damage and non-compliance with legislation and regulations.

Concerning the risks combining the evaluation of the impacts and the probabilities of occurrence of a scenario, for each service, it is necessary to identify the different exchange points made up of the elements of the architecture. Each asset is evaluated according to its need for availability, integrity and confidentiality (AIC). For example, the line "commercial management" may indicate a level 4 sensitivity for the application, local and exchanged data and exchanged mail and a level 2 and 3 sensitivity for their availability. Concerning the assessment of potentiality, for each scenario, the probability of occurrence of each of them must be evaluated.

The global analysis of the enterprise's digital risks is important to identify the different entry points and angles of attack that can be exploited by a malicious person against a company's information system. In order to identify these very varied vulnerabilities, each component of the information system must be audited. An audit consists of probing a system by comparing it to different possible attack scenarios. An audit must be conducted methodically by an expert in the field. We have identified 14 areas of expertise covering fields as varied as system equipment, networks, software and compliance with standards and laws. There are several hundred scenarios in each area, which shows that a comprehensive audit would require more than 4000 checkpoints.

The states have the implementation of ISO 27001 and the following standards: the awareness of the general directorates, detection and control with the law of military programming, computer charters and awareness of personnel. But enterprises do not have all that. Eventually, they have the charter. We need to offer them standard and inexpensive charters because they cannot afford to pay for a real service. Moreover, a company with between 20 and 150 employees does not have the complexity of a large company. In any case, enterprises must be made aware of digital security and strongly encouraged to notify personal data breaches.

Although current auditing methods are at a high technological level capable of detecting numerous flaws, auditing faces three major difficulties:

- Accelerated audit obsolescence: auditing produces an instantaneous view of the state of a system, becoming inaccurate from the first change (addition of a disk, memory or change of configuration, etc.).
- The excessive variety of technologies: the audit must make it possible to simultaneously detect vulnerabilities on recent and old systems, which presupposes knowledge of the progressive constitution of the information system.

For their part, vital operators will be required to map their systems. You can challenge a major industrialist to show you what their information systems look like, especially their industrial information systems. In general, manufacturers do not even know how their system is configured, where the interconnections are and the gateways to the Internet. The blur is pretty abysmal. This is also the case for administrations. The obligation to map is therefore absolutely important.

- A partial view: in practice, the audit is concerned with an excessively local analysis that runs the risk of potential unaudited grey areas.

In the past, encryption meant intercepting the transmission. The advent of computers revolutionized that. Snowden revealed that it was not so much the algorithms that protected, like some kind of armoured doors in computer systems, but the strength of the walls around the doors, too often today the equivalents of cardboard walls. Therefore, rather than attacking the armoured door, it is easier to cut out the wall with a cutter. Most of the time, American standards allow you to extract what is on the computer by means of, for example, a hidden door (backdoor) located on the hard disk or in the operating system (firmware). We must therefore have a global vision of security, including doors and walls.

In the case of the analysis of new vulnerabilities for cloud computing, it should be noted that these threats concern all service models, except for the "abuse and malicious use of the cloud" threat, which only concerns IaaS and PaaS models. Indeed, there is no real threat specific to cloud computing because all of them already exist but, generally speaking, they are amplified in this environment where there is a relative loss of control over data and services, this control being delegated to the provider, all the more so if it is multi-tenant.

The latter offers a management of network links or the hosting of one of its websites. To do this, the enterprise must negotiate the business rules by signing a service contract. Hence the need, once again, to establish a service contract (or SLA) between all parties involved, which defines the level of responsibility of each. The various threats are listed below.

(a) Data breach: Poor database design of a multi-tenant cloud service. Access to confidential data of all customers, data theft.
(b) Data loss or leakage: Lack of vigilance, loss of key, data recovery (backup) measures not implemented by the cloud provider. Theft of data stored in the cloud by hackers, or involuntary losses for various reasons (forgetting to back up, but also in case of natural disaster, fire, etc.).

(c) Account/service hijacking: Due to insufficiently complex passwords, frequently repeated reuse of passwords, phishing, fraud and exploitation of software vulnerabilities. Hence the possible espionage of the activities and operations, the use in question, the manipulation of its data and the return of falsified information.
(d) Unreliable interfaces and APIs: Use weak APIs. The security and availability of cloud services depends on the security of these interfaces. Otherwise, there is a risk of exposure to data corruption, disclosure of information and circumvention of the security policy.
(e) Denial of service: There are vulnerabilities in web servers, databases or cloud resources. Flooding a cloud service with queries can prevent legitimate users from accessing their data or applications. The customer is then forced to cut off access to his service himself to avoid ruin, since billing is per use and therefore depends on the number of requests.
(f) Malicious “traitors”: Lack of transparency about cloud providers' processes and procedures and their recruitment standards can have adverse consequences. Access to confidential data and control of cloud services by an adversary – hacker, organized crime agent or industrial espionage.
(g) Abuse and misuse of the cloud: The flexible service registration model offered by some IaaS cloud providers lacks control. This can lead to password and key breaking, denial of service, malicious data hosting and control of “botnets” networks.
(h) Lack of foresight: Adopting the cloud model requires prior analysis of risks and consequences. But there is not enough training for employees on how to use the cloud. This makes it vulnerable to all kinds of attacks.
(i) Problems related to mutualization: These problems may stem from weak partitioning between different virtual machines – and therefore between different clients – and a weak hypervisor. Within the framework of the shared cloud, possibility of impact on the operations of other “co-tenants”, access to data belonging to them, to their network traffic.

In conclusion, exchanges can only be reliable and secure – reducing the risk to a minimum level of attack – if appropriate technologies are used at all times. To date, the most widespread and effective technology to secure these exchanges and allow remote access is the VPN (Virtual Private Network). Concerning vulnerabilities in authentication protocols, exposure analysis is usually based on the impact on security properties. There are a multitude of authentication protocols. In choosing between them, the trade-off between their ease of deployment and their speed versus their robustness is the main element. A comparison between some types of protocols is outlined below.

(a) Vulnerability of the one-time password (OTP): As already mentioned, the OTP technique consists of using a password only once, with another password being provided for each session. After the first deployment of the pre-setting phase, a matrix card held by the customer is used to calculate the code at the time of login. In summary, there is the use of a shared secret and the use of a matrix card (symmetrical cryptography); non-repudiation is not 100% guaranteed and the cost is limited.

(b) Digital certificate: It uses asymmetric cryptography; its non-repudiation is guaranteed and its cost is very high.
(c) Biometrics: Through the recognition of a unique characteristic or behaviour, non-repudiation is guaranteed and the cost is very high.

With regard to attacks against the information system, it has to be said that the news is increasingly frequent about successful digital attacks on increasingly official sites, increasingly large sums of money or involving an ever-increasing number of people. Anecdotal a few years ago, these attacks have become extremely professional and are becoming more widespread. The examples cited below cover only about 1 year and provide a glimpse of the magnitude of this new phenomenon, the expansion of which must be curbed. This will be all the more difficult since the attacks are not necessarily the work of extremely competent computer specialists. In addition, consumer piracy software is beginning to appear.

Some examples, far from being exhaustive, of recent digital attacks are:

1. International wave of wire fraud.
2. CAC 40 enterprises have been robbed of up to 20 million euros by a Franco-Israeli network.
3. Large-scale crackdown on users of consumer software piracy.
4. Easy to use, Blackshades allows you to remotely take control of a computer.
5. eBay, new victim of hackers. The auction site announced that it had been the subject of a large-scale intrusion: 145 million pieces of customer data were allegedly stolen.
6. The personal data of 70 million customers and the credit card information of 40 million customers of the North American hypermarket Target have been looted by hackers.

A problem of under-investment in computer security and payment systems has been diagnosed.

Chapter 11
The Nature of the Attacks and the Characteristics of a Cyber-Attitude

Not everything in the digital world can be described as an attack. The figures quoted in this regard are often very exaggerated. Moreover, the most successful attacks are those that are not perceived by their victims – sometimes for years. It is the specificity of the digital risk that a company may remain unaware of a computer attack in progress and fail to perceive the long-term consequences of this aggression. In reality, the lack of maturity of the systems and the fragility in their design or implementation have produced many vulnerabilities that remain. There is often confusion between the notions of attacks and vulnerabilities.

State security agencies identify vulnerabilities and attacks. The technical directorates draw up very complete daily statements of the vulnerabilities of the systems. These observatories take the form of Internet sites, at the country level, disseminating at an almost daily rate new vulnerabilities in systems and providing a basis for classifying and researching vulnerabilities.

All attacks concern physical resources (precious objects) or human resources. Many dependencies exist between these resources. The challenge in protecting these resources will be to understand this notion of property as a target of attack as well as the dependencies to which they are subject. Thus, a resource is not an isolated system, quite the contrary; it is therefore a question of expressing a resource through all its interconnections. All the traditional attacks of the societal domain can be found within electronic exchange; their general classification is based on the same modus operandi. The basic operating modes of a digital attack are reminiscent of well-proven techniques:

- Mystification: simulation of the behaviour of a machine to deceive a legitimate user and take his name and password (e.g. terminal simulation).
- Disguise: illegitimate access consisting of pretending to be someone else and obtaining the privileges or access rights of the person being imitated.
- Replay: consisting of entering a system by sending the reproduction of a prior connection sequence of a legitimate user.

W. Amedzro St-Hilaire, *Digital Risk Governance*,
https://doi.org/10.1007/978-3-030-61386-0_11

- Sneaking: an attack which consists of passing through the access control at the same time as a legitimate user.
- Substitution: eavesdropping on a line, intercepting a legitimate user's disconnection request and benefiting from the current session by substituting for him.
- Saturation: an attack on availability; it consists of filling a storage area or a communication channel until it can no longer be used.

Since attacks based on basic modus operandi are often blocked, attackers develop modus operandi combining several basic attacks. Scenario 1 allows the attacker to take the form of legitimate behaviour or to simulate it by disguise. The middle scenario allows passive listening to capture the elements of the identification; it analyses them by replaying and modifying them in order to build a new identity adapted to the access mechanism. Scenario 2 allows to intercept the elements of the exchange by making them non-functional for the source, for example, a denial of service, and then to take advantage of its malfunction to introduce its own elements. An attack using a browser history file or cookie is an illustration of this principle.

In the context of attacks on confidentiality and integrity, authentication is a central element in countering vulnerabilities. This process provides a guarantee when exchanging data or documents, and the analysis of the exposure of the authentication process is usually based on the impact of maintaining the properties of integrity and confidentiality. There are a multitude of authentication protocols; some have advantages in their deployment, others in their robustness. The protocols attempt to strike a compromise between ease of deployment, speed and robustness.

The modus operandi of complex and targeted attacks incorporates legitimate user actions, making these attacks difficult to detect and analyse. The majority of dangerous digital attacks ultimately take place in two phases: a social engineering phase and a phase of so-called technical attacks described above. Social engineering is the legitimate acquisition of information for unfair use or fraud.

This modus operandi is not technological in nature but exploits human and social flaws. The principle is to obtain from a person information whose use is not obvious to the person transmitting it but which will not be insignificant, quite the contrary, for the person trying to obtain a good, a service or information from that person. All kinds of examples show every day how the usurper exploits psychological levers to achieve his ends. This is the case of messages linked to pirate sites where the attacker's stake is to obtain a "click" from his target.

In the example of dissecting a complex attack, the attacker will use tricks to decide the user to click on the link sent with the email (spam). Attackers are currently taking more and more care in forging their email bombs: they put pressure on the user by offering to make money or pretending to be an IT department or banker. The use of browsing history or cookies is at the root of most security problems. It is specified that this history or cookie is a file held by a customer and containing information on past and current exchanges with a website. The identifier written in the cookie records the fact that the client has successfully authenticated to the server, but is mainly used to be recognized by the server.

The preparation carried out by the attacker involves the collection of information. In order to set up a strategy, the active attacker finds sites that manage sessions using JavaScript executables. The attacker starts by posting a review on e-commerce sites (1), for example, the one of the tested organizations (here, the bank). He finds that the web application does not validate the entry (2) correctly; he concludes that the application is vulnerable and that he can later forge an identifier in JavaScript format. In the course of normal operation between the Internet user client (victim) and the organization's Internet server (here the bank, also a victim), the user carries out purchase transactions on the site of his credit organization (3). The connection by means of which he has authenticated with a name and a password is secured by the Secure Sockets Layer (SSL) protocol. The user gets a cookie from the server.

During each of the authentication phases during which the user provides his or her name and password information, the server has generated a unique session identifier whose validity is limited to the duration of the session (by default, a session duration is 20 min). When the server sends the new identifier to the user, the user writes it into the cookie file following the previous expired identifiers. When the session expires, the user authenticates again, and a new session ID will be generated using the same process. The server always uses only the last identifier of the cookie. The attacker forges a message cunning enough to trick the user into opening an attachment (4-1). The user reads the malicious message according to the attacker's plan (4-2). JavaScript is running.

The attacker has already checked in. The JavaScript accesses the cookie corresponding to the session (4-3) and redirects the client to another server, malicious, sending the session as a parameter (4-4). The victim notices that the user interface of the e-commerce site has disappeared for 2 s but does not worry (4-5). The malicious server receives the victim's session and redirects the victim to the previous page (4-6). The malicious user now has a few minutes to access the bank user's account and act on his or her behalf (4-7).

This scenario shows one of the many attacks able to exploit vulnerabilities related to web application developments. These vulnerabilities can be deliberately hidden to exploit a zero-day vulnerability one day. The information contained in the files (cookies) is dangerous; they are the source of most attacks. More and more activities, especially the digital cloud, are using the principle of cookies. To eliminate the danger, it would suffice not to use cookies. However, as they contain valuable information for commercial exploitation, their removal is not being considered.

In cloud computing environments, three key aspects have introduced new vulnerabilities: data and services are delegated; the provider is multi-tenant; and one or more providers will be responsible for data and services. New threats concern almost all service models: IaaS, PaaS and SaaS; due to the loss of control, the vulnerabilities of traditional information systems are amplified.

Multi-tenancy: Data breach is a technological vulnerability related to the current failure to design multi-tenant databases to manage data access that poses a significant risk of data theft.

User-Friendliness: Data loss or leakage is a vulnerability related to users who, through ignorance or lack of vigilance, could lose their encryption keys or passwords without implementing backup procedures or, perhaps poorly implemented by the vendor, not having a recovery testing process in place. The lack of transparency on the part of the provider on the processes and tools for storing or sharing does not provide users with a dashboard for monitoring their data.

Uncontrolled Access to Data: The destruction of data is a vulnerability due to hackers or unintentional causes such as forgetting to back up or the occurrence of a natural disaster, fire, etc. An adversary accessing the provider's services can sneak in and gain access to confidential data.

Identity Management and Security Policies: Account hijacking is a vulnerability due to lack of requirements in password security policies or due to "phishing," fraud and exploitation of software vulnerabilities. Espionage, close to economic intelligence, is a vulnerability due to uncontrolled activities and operations by the user on his data, or in response to non-authenticated requests. The theft of data stored in the cloud is a vulnerability due to the undetected presence of hackers. Data alteration and disclosure is a vulnerability due to circumvention by users or hackers of existing security policies.

Services: Lack of reliability of the interfaces between applications or bad programming exposes them to attacks on their integrity and availability. Denial of service of web servers, databases or cloud resources are vulnerabilities related to "storm" flows of poorly configured services. Hackers flood a service with queries to prevent legitimate users from accessing their data and/or applications. For a company in this situation, the consequences will be a substantial loss of turnover, amplified if it is a payment server. Risk analysis should not be overshadowed by the fact that the responsibility lies with the service provider.

However, user training should not be neglected on the grounds that legal responsibility lies with the service provider. The lack of requirements of the service provider in its recruitment plan may result in the presence of hackers belonging to criminal organizations. The digital cloud model adopted must preserve misuse and provide basic controls such as password and key complexity, denial of service (DoS) resistance, control of potentially hosted malicious data and control of "botnets".

Mutualization: The weakness of the partitioning between virtual machines (systems, routers, etc.) within the framework of mutualization can lead to effects on users caused by the unreliability of its "roommates."

What about securing connected objects? Connected objects are mobile systems capable of carrying processing capabilities that make them autonomous to provide a service.

Today, the interest of connected objects is no longer to be demonstrated; they are already invading everyday life. The number of connected objects will increase in unimaginable proportions.

To stick to the orders of magnitude, which are quite diverse, mentioned by the people interviewed for this report, it could be fifty billion connected objects in the world before 2020, eighteen to eighty billion before 2018 and fifty billion in 2050, or even the hypothesis that with the future development of big data, there would be a thousand times more connected objects than humans. These quantities will represent a turnover that will grow very rapidly to extremely high amounts. Each person could be equipped with about a hundred connected objects and each dwelling with about five hundred. Some mobile phones already have around 50 sensors: gyroscope, etc.

The prospects offered by these new objects are impressive, both in the development of new business models, promising a flourishing economy, and in the services they will render to mankind. However, at present, these systems have been designed in disregard of serious security mechanisms. The difficulty of managing them also remains a major concern. These objects are already present on industrial sites of high criticality. How will businesses and, in particular, vitally important operators be able to protect themselves, especially since they will have invested considerable sums in security plans and these small items will thwart their efforts?

Several countries have called on state agencies to develop security standards for smart metering systems, a subject that no one has taken up until now. Today, we are finding that connected objects can be gateways for computer attackers when they are not necessarily secure, and when they are secure, they are not necessarily reconfigurable. It is important that security loopholes should not allow such objects to be taken over by malicious individuals.

Complex attacks highlighting digital vulnerability are designed by individuals with a certain psychology that your reporters have tried to understand – while being limited to a certain profile corresponding to a very high technical level. Digital security is generally considered to be most seriously threatened when hackers are involved – or, conversely, best protected if hackers are used – which is why your rapporteurs wanted to find out more about what lies behind this name, which is supposed to explain many misunderstood actions.

Hacker comes from axe. It refers to the person who uses an axe to break into a computer system rather than being burdened with passwords or protocols. This term also means that programs and software can be simplified to a simpler or even more elegant structure; the hacker is then more akin to the pruner. In the first sense, the hacker evokes the burglar. Like him, he is a specialist in breaking and entering things. Like him, he tries to leave as few traces as possible of his break-in. However, in the context of the construction of the Internet and the invention of microcomputers, those who are referred to as hackers have played an inventive, creative role that goes far beyond that of digital thieves or slashers.

The Internet was originally conceived as a place of total freedom of access to information, to free information – this information also included access to how components, computers, networks and those who use them are made and how they work. But it was not about free information about everyone or access to everyone. And this is where hackers intervened, notably to make microcomputers exist in front of the giant computers of the big computer firms. Little taken seriously at first, the hackers felt that the availability of microcomputers for everyone was bound to happen, and they did everything they could, as if driven by an obsession, to turn their intuition into reality.

Often studying at renowned American universities but also obsessed with computers from an early age – sometimes only around the age of 10 or 15 – those who were to be called hackers shared their knowledge for free and considered that money, the market and everything forbidden could only compromise their quest. Among these young enthusiasts were many brilliant inventors unknown to the public but renowned in the computer world and others whose careers and fortunes are known throughout the world today, in particular Steve Jobs and his partner Mr. Steve Wozniak, the founder of Apple, and Mr. Bill Gates, the founder of Microsoft, who was the first to believe that the technical ingenuity of hackers deserved a fair reward.

These hackers have frequently been right in the face of the established order of universities – often missing classes, using computers without authorization and at closed hours and neglecting to obtain degrees. The hacker spirit persists today, and penetrating computer systems remains a challenge. A challenge made all the more exciting by the fact that equipment manufacturers, enterprises, administrations and states claim that their computer systems are secure, even inviolable. This has led to multiple system penetrations by hackers followed by warnings, more or less public, drawing attention to flaws in computer systems. When these alerts are not taken seriously, when the victim of these attacks threatens repression, the situation can escalate.

Conversely, some firms and states immediately take advantage of these alerts and sometimes even go so far as to hire the hackers who have exposed the vulnerabilities. These elements show that, unlike the burglar, the hacker is not primarily motivated by the desire to steal but by the desire to break through the barriers designed to prevent entry. A bit like those obsessed with the discovery of the Parisian subsoil who explore all the possible entrances to the subsoil, which are often ignored by the owners of buildings located above galleries or underground rooms, or caves.

This is why enterprises, administrations and states consider that a good use of the hacker can consist of hiring him to, this time, help build a dynamic protection of a computer system. In the course of their visits and hearings, your rapporteurs were able to observe that enterprises, and even administrations, in charge of IT security had hired hackers, always cautiously presented as "former hackers," as if it was necessary to reassure the interlocutor and testify of a supposed repentance. It is to be hoped, on the contrary, that they are always hackers in a state of maximum inventiveness to be up to the attacks to be overcome.

This quick overview of the psychology of hackers could inspire several proposals for recommendations such as:

- Predispositions to computer science and its use do not wait for years or for official training, whether or not leading to a diploma, hence the need to develop computer awareness, education and training from a very early age, given the very sharply increasing need for specialists in this field.
- The need to identify hackers in order to benefit from the positive effects of this particular turn of mind.
- The interest of keeping people with hacker talents. Indeed, more and more often, those founding new small innovative digital enterprises are mostly recruited by American enterprises or engaged abroad.

- Hackers today constitute a national asset that could be used to strengthen digital security and resilience following successful attacks.

There is a significant fringe of young hackers, who are a first-rate resource. They are far from being autistic, and it would be interesting to listen to them. Rich countries have the major advantage of having many bright young people in the digital field even if they are not the most highly educated. Unfortunately, Google and other foreign enterprises are currently plundering this pool of young people. A national leap forward is needed to take advantage of this know-how and good will. The United States of America or Singapore welcome them with open arms.

It is important to stress the difference between the real, the virtual and the imaginary; it is important to underline that this distinction, not always easy to make in practice, has effects on the psyche of digital users. Digital technology is an incredible opportunity; it offers young people remarkable possibilities for knowledge, for taking action in the world and for developing their creativity. But it is also associated with a major risk. To understand it, one must have in mind a key concept in cyberpsychology: the concept of immersion.

When we immerse ourselves in a virtual world, in a digital world, in the mind of a subject, there are very original and specific mechanisms that are not reducible to what happens when we play a game with small figurines, when we read a book or when we watch a movie. With digital technology, we are actors of a virtual action. This placed the subject in a very special position of responsibility, since he or she performs both a real action and an action that takes place in a virtual world. So, there is a kind of irresponsibility of the act that makes it an in-between, a particular transitional space.

This transitional space can have interesting effects. Virtual worlds are, for example, used to care for a number of young people with difficulties. But this space also presents difficulties and risks. Five risks need to be identified: traumatic seduction, addictive behaviour, subversion of framework institutions, ideological manipulation and confusion of values.

Attacks of a technical nature are the privilege of malicious individuals using technology as a weapon of persuasion. These individuals, who are not systematically confused with the hackers described above, are specific criminals whose crimes fall within the scope of cybercrime, which studies its various forms.

The term "cybercrime" is a recent one, since it was first used at a G8 meeting in 1999, one of the purposes of which was to defend states against new electronic forms of crime. A few years later, a convention on cybercrime was proposed; it has now been ratified by 23 states, both members and non-members, including the United States of America.

It is criminology, also known as the "science of crime," which studies its various forms by looking at the circumstances that led an individual to commit the crime. Criminology relies on descriptive statistical methods to identify a certain form of normality and certain typologies of crime, even though, as the founding father of the concept, Emile Durkheim pointed out, these statistical models are probably inaccurate for many reasons, if only because the circumstances are not reproducible.

However, the difficulty in measuring "cybercrimes" has only served to reinforce criminal threats to societal spheres. For more than 2 years now, new institutional observatories have been appearing and organizing increasingly relevant instrumentation of cybercrimes. Consequently, the next few years will be decisive in providing a clear vision of cybercrime and restoring public confidence.

Marcus Rogers' taxonomy identifies several profiles characterized by two criteria: their competence and their motivation. It details eight profiles ranging from the novice to the most experienced in their actions and whose interest is gain or social recognition. In the late 1990s, the objectives of offenders (novice or cyberpunk cyber offenders, NV or CP) or criminals were varied but rarely commercial, since e-commerce was in its infancy. Rather, the goal was to defy law enforcement or to be recognized by the community by performing exploits; anonymity conferred natural impunity on the perpetrators of these offences.

The new commercial stakes, the almost universal acceptance of the Internet as a "daily companion" and the expertise easily shared between all the actors, for good and evil, have this time become the daily lot of mafias in search of financial profits. They have massively organized themselves and set up shop around the spheres of exchange: societal and technological. Thus, the success of electronic exchange has quickly given rise to the desires of dangerous individuals (PCs, PTs) acting alone or as mafias, taking advantage of clumsy users or administrators not yet experienced in their attack techniques. In the eyes of the law, these individuals are delinquents, swindlers and sometimes criminals, but do they make the Internet dangerous? Does the development of exchange crime threaten the security of electronic exchanges?

First of all, system vulnerabilities, whose fragility has been increased by the dexterity of VW and OG type hackers and the heterogeneity of communicating systems, have developed rapidly, taking worrying and still little-known forms: the marriage between "attacking robots" and "worms" or "viruses" activates their propagation and thus constitutes a mass attack under the weight of which the dike has difficulty in not giving way.

The risk study, leading to a risk mapping, is a prerequisite for the enterprise to build its in-depth digital security, which is also based on audit or investigation. This set of information determines the nature of the operational security to be implemented in response to digital attacks. It is never a question of total security because it would be false and dangerous to let people believe that the environment is perfectly secure, especially since a certain feeling of insecurity and constant vigilance must be maintained.

Moreover, rather than just using antivirus software, an in-depth approach is needed with barriers to network entry, walls (firewalls) that filter certain information with antivirus software and means of supervision to see if something abnormal happens, such as when a computer consults another computer or server too often; it is then possible to find out what is happening. Encryption tools, protections and filters are put in place in different places as needed to improve the level of security to an acceptable level. Faced with the significant escalation of security breaches, the role of operational security is becoming paramount. Oversight is one of the pillars of risk management.

Over the last 20 years or so, the study of risk has emerged in many fields as a framework for reducing uncertainty and complexity. Nevertheless, modern society is currently experiencing a curious paradox in which it is asserting its desire to project itself into the future through an accelerated race for innovation while preserving a prudential logic. As a result, risk control has become a pervasive societal phenomenon that some sociologists in the early 1990s called our modern societies a risk society. This observation leads us to believe that digital technology should not dominate society but should simply remain a new product of the risk that must be apprehended in order to return to a situation of technological mastery.

To meet this dual requirement effectively, it was decided to set up a monitoring function based on risk mapping determined from a risk analysis. This approach is consistent with the new governance models recently proposed within the ISO/IEC 31000 and ISO/IEC 27005 standards. The activities of operational security, a security operations centre (SOC), are very costly if not too expensive for enterprises, especially due to the high and continuous skills required by the experts.

In addition, the use of specific, powerful and expensive software such as Security Information and Event Management Systems (SIEM) and Intrusion Detection Systems (IDS) increases this difficulty. Security activities are usually carried out by experts in the field, either within an institution or in private enterprises. For investigation or audit, these activities are occasional and with a high level of expert competence, which fully justifies the use of these activities in the form of services.

An operational security centre (or OSC) is the part of the enterprise's information system designed to implement solutions for the detection, location and qualification of security events and the provision of response plans. An operational security centre acts on a given site but can intervene remotely using specific and particularly secure tools: this supervision is said to be centralized and distributed. SIEMs bring together a set of tools for analysis that takes into account a safety supervision need expressed by a customer.

The relationship between an operational security centre and its customer is established through a contract called SLA (Service Level Agreement) which seals beforehand the monitored perimeter, the modes and times of intervention, and the escalation mechanism in case of incident. An IT incident is a threat of imminent violation of IT security policies, usage policies or practices. The incident is then recorded on a ticket; the user who has been the victim of the incident reports it using a specialized tool that is usually accessed using a web browser. The user must describe the incident in order to benefit from the service.

NIST has defined incident reports to include a description of the incident or event, using the proposed taxonomy. A majority of operational security centres respond to incidents related to untested or modified applications and human errors due to ignorance or lack of documentation. Hardware, electrical and network problems account for only 20% of the incidents.

The expert is an incident responder, but in reality, it is a team of experts rather than an individual, due to the need for multiple and heterogeneous skills ranging from network expertise to "Java" expertise, but also due to the length of time it takes to resolve an incident, which can take up to several days on average, several months in the case of complex and targeted attacks. The security supervision part is based on the analysis of traces from the intrusion detection systems placed at the various locations of the information system for monitoring purposes.

The role of an SIEM will be to manage these traces and to interpret them. From a management point of view, the management of this data requires the organization of the EMIS functions on the governed system. It is a four-step cycle: collection, detection, analysis and treatment of security incidents. Each of them is also the subject of a decision-making process:

- Collect: decide on the relevance of a signal through observation.
- See: decide that this signal constitutes a security incident.
- Understand: analyse by locating, identifying and characterizing the incident.
- Decide on corrective actions.

The performance of such a monitoring system relies entirely on accuracy at each stage of the decision-making cycle. From the onset of the incident to its resolution, an escalation response methodology must be implemented. The security audit of an information system is a snapshot of this system, the aim of which is to detect vulnerabilities on different levels: organizational, technical, human resources, compliance with standards, rules of good practice and legal constraints.

The audit may also be combined with a risk analysis depending on the purpose of the audit: reaction to an attack, assessment of the level of security of the information system, evolution of the system incorporating new equipment or processes, etc. The audit should even be carried out each time the information system is modified.

The safety audit approach is close to that of the quality approach: it must be methodical and not omit to test one element of the system, namely the weak link. The audit is based on several methods: maintenance, intrusion tests and meticulous surveys of system configurations (programs, routers, workstations, servers, etc.). The technical audit can be conducted alone or as part of an organizational audit. It allows the expert to focus his attention on the workings of a new web application in order to ensure that it will not present any flaws when it goes online.

A methodical and periodic inspection of the information system is a considerable asset for its good health. However, the human resources involved in these operations are time-consuming and entail significant costs for a company of between $1500 and $2000 a day, easily involving several experts for several weeks. The "penetration test" is an interesting alternative since it involves a team for about a week at a cost of about 10,000 dollars and makes it possible to detect vulnerabilities before they are exploited by real hackers.

Investigation is a step in the search for the cause of an incident; for this reason, it is called "post-mortem," also known as forensic analysis to detect the modus operandi of an attacker or robot if it is a virus attack, or the intrusion of malicious software. Specialized teams intervene to determine and delimit the perimeter as well as the extent of the computer attack. On this occasion, digital evidence is collected and analysed to establish the origin of the malicious act or incident. The evidence collected can be used to support the legal or insurance process.

The difficulty of distinguishing an illegitimate individual or even an illegitimate system from a legitimate system has suggested an anomaly detection function that tends to consider as hostile any activity or flow taking place on the other side of a boundary called a line of defence. The same strategy has also been extended to internal activities. The general principle is to remove any exposed asset from the knowledge of the attackers. The communication zone is the seat of a multitude of filters, also called bastions.

Their role is to assign a pass to each legitimate flow whose source, destination and modus operandi can be identified: these are the controlled flows. Several flow filtering mechanisms are applied which can be linked together and complement each other: firewall filtering, intrusion detection system (IDS) filtering and antivirus software.

Firewall filtering embodies the rules defined by security policies in the form of "what you can do and what you should not do.". A violation of these rules causes alerts and results in a blockage of the flow. Security is said to be active. Intrusion detection, thanks to the intrusion detection system, is a passive security, the objective of which is to inform the analyst.

The principle is based on two different methods of analysis: signature-based analysis and behaviour-based analysis. The signature-based analysis will try to detect intrusions by looking for codes, texts and patterns previously learned. Behaviour-based analysis allows to elaborate behavioural reference profiles – users or system. These reference profiles are calibrated using indicators that allow to measure deviations. This method of analysis, complementary to the first one, offers the possibility to detect as yet unknown attacks.

The states will give a label to trusted providers responsible for detecting vulnerabilities, the failures of critical operators at the heart of their systems. They will be in touch with the state. There will be state-qualified detection providers who will be in contact with agencies to exchange on new threats, new technical signatures of attacker behaviour. These are the technical criteria that can be introduced into the automatic probes to detect that something abnormal is happening and that we are a priori victims of an attack. These signatures are now the most expensive asset of security agencies.

The question of deploying an uncontrolled tool then becomes a key issue. How can we ask everyone to be responsible for their safety if no control is possible? The analogy with the automobile seems appropriate: how can we control and meet legal and safety obligations without a speedometer, dashboard, etc.? It is through the three properties of availability, integrity and confidentiality that the operational reliability of systems is assessed. However, other security properties are indispensable, such as the "accountability" already mentioned. But digital systems are hardly instrumented at the design stage within their ecosystem. Why not set up a standardization requiring any system designed to control the three safety properties?

Chapter 12
IT Safety Education for Digital Literacy

This chapter intends to insist on the existing gap between the permanent recourse to the digital tool in perpetual evolution and the lack of mastery of this tool, coupled with a lack of hindsight as to the more or less opportune use of it. As businesses may be at a loss in the face of this situation, which is evolving according to multiple and sometimes contradictory timetables, agencies and business groups have developed methods and guides to help businesses build their digital security in a fast, consistent and effective manner. This is particularly necessary in the face of the extension of outsourcing and its declination in cloud computing.

Digital technology began by revealing that it made it possible to act, most often to work, "in real time," which meant immediately reducing the actions carried out without it to a kind of singular unreality. Then the techniques allowed not only an acceleration of the possibilities accompanying this "real time" but also a permanent ubiquity accompanied by unlimited access to information and knowledge. To illustrate the veracity and superiority of these new concepts and techniques, the rapid creation of new economic empires made the promises of this supposedly immaterial and limitless world very tangible.

Immersed very quickly in this new universe at the end of the twentieth century, the best proof of the adaptation of the connected man seemed to be hyperconnection. However, following this sustained tempo, there was not enough time for observation, or even reflection, let alone education and the construction of a digital culture. The need for such a construction is particularly felt in enterprises, all of which need not just digital but secure digital. Otherwise, it is their nervous system that could be affected to the point of compromising their existence.

This construction requires reliable materials: hardware, software and routers with various protocols. This is made difficult by the fact that the use of digital technology is still recent and that the staff are not very well adapted to the building of digital security.

Indeed, using the full range of digital tools on a daily basis, even with brilliance, is not enough to make users responsible, i.e. aware of the rigorous requirements of

W. Amedzro St-Hilaire, *Digital Risk Governance*,
https://doi.org/10.1007/978-3-030-61386-0_12

digital security. All the more so as this security can often only be ensured at the price of abandoning two principles accepted as superior to all the others without having been discussed: immediate and permanent connection and acceleration of speed. However, it emerged from a number of hearings that security first involves, for example, an analysis of the confidentiality of the data to be protected, of those that may be stored or transmitted in such and such a way, without forgetting to consider the security conditions offered by the recipient(s) of the message.

Not all data need to be protected in the same way. They should therefore be prioritized according to the degree of confidentiality without spending excessive time on this classification. Once classified, the categories of data will undergo different numerical treatments. Not everything can be stored in clouds; the question of using sovereign clouds will also arise on this occasion. The transmission channel should also be selected after considering the security guarantees it offers. This will also raise the question of consistency of security throughout the message transmission channel. For example, the use of an encrypted telephone only offers security if the caller is equipped with a device of the same technical standard.

To illustrate the basic precautions mentioned above in a very concrete manner, it is sufficient to review very common situations in the daily life of enterprises, to deduce practical rules of prudence before drawing from them general principles constituting computer hygiene. The Large Enterprise Networks had the excellent idea of staging, in a playful way, through a serious game called Keep eye, situations faced by company personnel, transforming each player, the supposed weak link in digital security, into a "guardian angel of a company employee."

For example, what to do when you find a USB stick? Can you take a computer abroad, recharge it at airports, or leave it in the safe in your hotel room? For example, some of the people interviewed indicated that when travelling to certain countries, it was prudent to take a computer and a telephone that had never been used and not to use it on the return journey. The most careful people perfect their password, encrypt their messages and avoid connecting to all the Wi-Fi networks on offer. However, the passwords chosen are often too simple, the encryption is unreliable, and trust in networks, other equipment or more or less usual interlocutors leads to a generally imprudent attitude even though it has certain appearances of prudence.

They can also be simple rules of behaviour to be observed and whose non-observance can be observed every day in all means of transport (trains, planes, etc.), in restaurants, hotels, on the phone, etc. Some enterprises find it useful to recommend to their staff that they ensure that no one else reads the messages displayed on their computer screen at the same time. Again, however, the priority given to the permanence of the connection is often detrimental to its security. Awareness of these various digital risks is growing, but without going so far as to translate into thoughtful acts of prevention and precaution, which have been established as permanent rules of conduct and need to be constantly adapted. These constraints are badly experienced and felt as antagonistic to the freedom that seems to characterize the digital world.

An anecdote illustrates the difficulty of reconciling efficiency and safety and the fact that immediate efficiency can compromise the goals it is supposed to achieve.

A well-known example, in terms of aircraft sales, is the competition between Airbus and Boeing: a head of government flew to Singapore, and there were only two people who knew the price that was going to be offered for the sale that was going to be signed. The political leader made a telephone call from the plane to one of the two people in charge of the negotiations mentioning this price, and on landing, it was noted that a financial offer just a little better had just been made by Boeing.

At the time, encrypted communications did not exist or were very inefficient. And the NSA had already set up Echelon. Now they exist, but this does not necessarily mean that politicians use them. Secure phones can encrypt data, encrypt voice and encrypt everything. But they stay in the glove compartment of the authorities' cars. Based on these daily observations and his technical knowledge, collected computer hygiene rules have been developed in searchable guides.

An example of a setback in the digital evolution is provided by the coexistence, for the time being not convergent, of global, international and national priorities partly already mentioned in more detail. Recently, a draft regulation and a draft directive are in the pipeline in international institutions. The desire to negotiate at a forced march and then to conclude as quickly as possible a Transatlantic Partnership Economic Treaty, including digital, is interfering with plans to change national rules. In addition, the need for an international text governing the global management of the Internet is increasingly mentioned.

These priorities are likely to be difficult to reconcile. If the treaties (transatlantic and Sino-American) are concluded first, the freedom of states will be curtailed accordingly. The same applies to Asian countries, where subsidiarity is likely to be affected by rules whose consistency is likely to be affected by the hierarchy of legal norms. In the face of global, international, Asian and national rhythms, ultimately influencing the meaning of digital arrangements, it is not clear that a sharp perception of the issue is permanently dictating government policy in the Southeast Asian states.

In this respect, we can put forward the new idea of taking digital technology into consideration, of a vital nature, in order to assert the need for a digital exception to be asserted in international negotiations. This would not be juxtaposed to the cultural exception but would encompass it. While government agencies are at the forefront of advances in digital security for businesses, other initiatives usefully complement its work, such as the recent creation of the Cyber Defence Industry Club. The contribution and the limits of the advice given by these agencies to industrialists are apparent from their various guides to good practice, including one on computer hygiene rules. Another example is provided by the guide entitled "Controlling the risks of outsourcing" relating to the outsourcing of information systems.

Without analysing this interesting document as a whole, some of the advice given in it does indeed situate the balance to be sought between increased use of digital technology and security, not only of the enterprise's information systems but also of the security of the enterprise as a whole (insofar as a weakening of its digital nervous system could lead to its disappearance). The use of a third party to manage its information system could be the definition of outsourcing. This may involve managing infrastructures, applications or even service hosting.

The question is whether or not the risks inherent in outsourcing (due to the simple or cascading outsourcing that the service provider may resort to, due to the uncertainty about the location of data, particularly in the cloud, and due to the risk of disclosure of sensitive data) outweigh the benefits to be expected from such outsourcing.

This risk is particularly sensitive with regard to personal data for which the data controller is accountable (criminal sanctions are even applied to any breaches). All of these elements must encourage the business manager who uses outsourcing to carefully weigh the terms of the contract between him and the secure outsourcing provider. This contract should specify that the customer has a right of control over the choice of subcontractors; the terms of payment of the subcontractors; the security of the data hosting facilities offered; the existence of a contract between the service provider and its subcontractors (including clauses relating to the security and confidentiality offered by the subcontractors); and the value for the customer of the service provider's choice of new hardware or software solutions (particularly if it is a question of using proprietary applications that are not widely used) because the customer must be able to obtain at any time the return of its data in a standard and open format.

The list of essential protective clauses to be included in the contract raises the question as to the practical possibility of implementing real control by the customer over these multiple and highly technical elements if the balance of power towards the outsourcing provider does not work to his advantage. A particular risk should also be highlighted, that of remote interventions. The enterprise will be tempted to ask for the possibility of this type of intervention in the hope of reducing the cost and speed of intervention times.

However, these two hoped-for gains must be weighed against the many risks inherent in remote interventions. Among these, we can cite passwords that are not sufficiently secure, flaws in access interfaces, operating systems that are not updated and the lack of traceability of actions, not to mention the insufficient consideration of IT security in general by remote maintenance personnel.

All these risks are likely to facilitate intrusions. It is therefore incumbent on the customer to protect himself against these risks by carrying out a real risk analysis which will enable him to request any document likely to reassure him about the technical and organizational security measures proposed by the service provider. For regulatory institutions, remote maintenance devices cannot be considered secure without the implementation of a secure gateway, which is the only way to guarantee a level of authentication, prevention, data confidentiality and integrity, traceability of actions carried out by the support centre, etc.

And this use of a secure gateway must be audited. In addition to the risk related to the loss of control of one's information system, increased by the risk resulting from remote interventions, there is also the risk of shared hosting, i.e. hosting several services on the same server. In this case, the service with the greatest vulnerability may increase the vulnerability of other services. For example, a denial of service attack that results in a loss of availability of one server may compromise other services hosted on the same server by making them unavailable as well.

In reality, security agencies believe that seeing services sharing the same physical environment can lead to cross-referencing of information (content of customer files from several sites in the same database, or the same subdirectory, etc.). The risks to which a cohesive service is exposed are therefore significantly increased in an uncontrolled environment. Moreover, it is estimated that shared hosting compromises a quick and relevant analysis of incidents (the host will refuse to communicate the event logs of the server and its peripheral equipment so as not to affect the confidentiality of other hosted services). Once again, it is essential that the contract concluded between the customer and the host be extremely precise regarding the hosting terms and conditions, including its reversibility, but also the communication of event logs, the careful monitoring of the hosted service (updates, maintenance, etc.), the attack prevention methods and the reactions to incidents.

In this form of cloud computing outsourcing, neither the location nor the operating methods of the cloud are made known to the customer. Cloud computing can offer:

- Virtual machines allowing the remote installation of the operating system and applications of its choice (Infrastructure as a Service)
- Platforms for remote application development (Platform as a Service)
- Applications that can be directly used remotely (Software as a Service)

The outsourcing risks described above are also present in cloud computing. The reservations previously expressed are even more relevant in the context of cloud computing because it is no longer just a question of the difficulty of negotiating a contract but of the impossibility of doing so, since it is generally a question of subscribing to offers by validating standard contracts! The localization of data at any time is impossible in the digital cloud, hence uncertainty about the applicable law; in the absence of certainty about this localization, the principle of territoriality is undermined.

So which courts have jurisdiction and which law applies? Added to these uncertainties is the loss of customer control over the management of security incidents. In addition, it will become difficult to change service providers because data portability is not always guaranteed in standard contracts. As already pointed out in relation to outsourcing in general, data integrity and confidentiality may be compromised due to significant storage and memory degradation. Finally, assuming that the customer has decided to leave an unsatisfactory cloud provider, there is no guarantee that the data entrusted to the cloud will be erased or not duplicated.

Particular attention should be paid to the nationality of cloud providers and the location of their servers in Southeast Asia or locally if one does not wish to give up any control over one's personal data. It should be noted, however, that location in itself does not constitute a guarantee of security but only a presumption. In contrast to this leap into the unknown, a risk analysis should make it possible to better identify the security objectives to be pursued in the face of risks accepted, refused or possibly transferred to an insurance company.

Such an analysis should make it possible to conclude the contract with the service provider in full knowledge of the facts and bearing in mind that, in this area, far from totally freezing a situation, the contract must provide for taking account of developments inherent in the digital field. This development can be observed through the establishment of a digital security monitoring committee to encourage the taking into account of new security loopholes, for example. Security audits would usefully complement the work of this committee.

Can all the risks outlined above be managed, even in a calculated way, by operators of critical infrastructure? No, they cannot. All the more so since countries' military planning laws, in the face of attacks, whether terrorist or not, governments have the power to decide on the implementation of specific measures to protect, in particular, the information systems and telecommunications networks of critical infrastructure operators. This may include, for example, increased trace backup.

Industrialists are the first to be aware of the vulnerabilities of the digital environment and the complementary nature of the solutions to be implemented to remedy them. This is why, in addition to initiatives taken within their own enterprises, they have set up a number of bodies for reflection and action. These include the network of large enterprises, the Committee for the Security Industry. These initiatives are in line with those taken in the field of cyber defence. Wherever there are computers and data exchanges, we are dealing with an attackable space that we must learn to defend. If we do not master cyberspace, we do not master any operational capability. That is why cyber defence is one of the two national priorities set by the national defence and national security directives of states.

Following the launch of national cyber defence plans in some countries, in the form of Cyber Defence Pacts with measures and the SME (small- and medium-sized enterprises) Defence Pact (which concern training and research as well as enterprises), governments wanted to speed up the implementation of the industrial component of these plans (as they see digital space as a new battleground for what could be a cyber war). Recently, an initiative to create the Cyber Defence Industry Club has been launched in some countries. To achieve this, the cyber defence industrial club should bring together, inter alia, multinational firms, with the addition of small- and medium-sized enterprises and major customers (including vital infrastructure operators in strategic sectors such as energy, transport and banking).

This gathering would make it possible to better define computer network protection needs so that suppliers' offers can be adapted to them. Through this initiative, the opportunity would be seized to improve the training of all the employees of these enterprises, to provide better protected know-how, to experiment with solutions and to qualify products and services. It should be noted that the armies of several states are already engaged in electronic warfare exercises. For example, some exercises are based on the scenario of an attack on the networks of an air base by hackers exploiting a vulnerability of one of the subcontractors of the military installations on that base. The detection of the attack, the identification and then the neutralization of the attackers were the phases of this exercise.

For the future, platforms will be set up to provide training, cyberattack management training and experimentation of new IT security products. Several of these defence-cyber pacts plan to foster the emergence of a national cyber defence community by relying on a circle of partners and the reserve networks. It should be noted that the military programming laws in place in these countries provide for a tripling of the resources allocated to cyber defence and an increase in manpower through the creation of posts. Beyond defensive capabilities, it is now asserted that there is a need for offensive cyber security capabilities. It is also from these angles that great importance is attached to the industrial base of technology and defence.

Despite the rules governing the protection of individual data at national and European levels, the protection of individual and company data within the enterprise does not appear to be ensured. To remedy this, educational efforts need to be undertaken, awareness needs to be raised and reliable materials and tools need to be made available. As for hardware, no state alone is in a position to guarantee profitable sovereign use of all the components, computers, software and networks used, whether or not they are designed or manufactured in other parts of the world. As for tools, since these materials are linked to each other, to other objects, to software and, finally, to their users, it is necessary to ensure that the chain of interaction between them can be the subject of legal recourse, either as a chain or as an individual element essential to the security of the whole.

It must be said that the technical elements of digital security often depend on legal rules that are independent of each other. There should be an overall coherence linking each element of the digital chain and guaranteeing their use. Some countries have a number of assets in the field of digital law, which it would be advisable to mobilize in order to turn them into instruments of economic power at the international level.

One example is cryptography, which is a key element in the secure transmission of digital messages. It so happens that, thanks to the research carried out in this field, in particular by the armed forces within the General Delegations for Armaments, this asset can be one of those to be developed as a priority in order to deal with digital insecurity (which is increasingly evident in the face of enterprises and society in general). Finally, states still have considerable capacity in the field of languages and linguistics, a capital that could also be used to the benefit of digital tools.

It would therefore seem to be a priority to train in cryptography, to promote research in this field, to help young people setting up a business to move into this activity and to support them until their business is consolidated – which means helping them to get past the stage where they are likely to accept that North American enterprises take over their business. At the same time, gaps in the digital security of businesses can lead to the adoption of new and sustainable legal rules to encourage the emergence of new markets.

What are the unmet needs? They are numerous and range from sovereign probes to risk mapping, from intrusion detectors to digital security audits, and from training in coding from kindergarten onwards to the creation of work games (or serious games) to accelerate and anchor the reflexes that condition digital security. Existing cooperation between security agencies can help to design and implement the necessary new legal rules and their practical translation. The recommendations are along these lines: simplifying access to digital technology by better protecting citizens and businesses.

Beyond that, in the framework of the industrial plans of the states, a large number of them are very directly related to digital (embedded software and systems, technical and intelligent textiles, intelligent electrical networks, digital health, big data, cloud computing, e-education, telecom sovereignty, connected objects, augmented reality, contactless services, supercomputers, robotics, the factory of the future), and one of them is cybersecurity. They need to be closely monitored by governments and by all players in the sector.

The cyber security plans of each state will aim to build "a homeland of security and digital confidence" through a high-performance cybersecurity industry to meet a sovereignty challenge and seize an opportunity. They should have ambitious objectives such as securing the most vital infrastructures (to ensure the defence as well as the security of countries and to protect the daily life of citizens: sovereignty objectives based on the protection of digital secrets). These plans represent an opportunity because they are conducive to job creation (since several states have world-class industrial players in this field and a fabric of SMEs capable of meeting this challenge).

The plans aim to significantly increase the demand for trusted cyber security solutions; develop, for national needs, trusted offers; organize the conquest of foreign markets; and strengthen national cybersecurity enterprises (so that a national trusted offer exists and is better taken into consideration by national public and private sponsors and better valued for export). This offer of confidence is based on an effort of governance and valorization of research and development to take full advantage of the national industrial fabric (large, but sometimes too dispersed – too many actors). It remains to consolidate them while avoiding the risks of sterile competition or inappropriate takeovers brought about by the current dispersal. Above all, we must not forget to take advantage of the extraordinary opportunities for market share conquest that consolidation or mergers can offer.

Moreover, manufacturers have not waited for these cyber security plans to mobilize and demonstrate their creativity. This is the case, for example, of the IT Security Managers' Clubs. And their efforts are being combined with those of training programs. We must insist on the need to clarify the legal rules to be imagined in future digital bills. The rules to be put in place must be carefully thought out so that digital technology is a factor of economic development that places these states at the forefront of regional and international development.

Powerful pressure groups are at work to delay the adoption of the draft regulation as long as possible so that it does not interfere with the negotiation of international trade treaties. Meanwhile, the manufacture of digital equipment and tools, some of which are indispensable and others parasitic, is gaining momentum.

Doing business with law? This is possible and necessary to be part of the ongoing digital revolution. It lends itself well to it, being present everywhere and in everything. This may involve somewhat disrupting the relationships that the various players, more or less aware of this revolution, are used to having with each other. This concerns researchers as well as young entrepreneurs, SME managers, vital operators, local authorities, administrations and governments. Finally, how can we not bear in mind that while this digital revolution with its essential and global stakes is being conceived and carried out, espionage and economic intelligence actions continue?

Chapter 13
How to Win the Digital Security Challenge in Terms of Governance?

Having considered the scenarios for responding to threats to the so-called traditional digital security of institutions and enterprises, it is necessary to consider how digital security, i.e. the capacity of states to act in cyberspace, can be exercised in two dimensions:

- The capacity to exercise digital security in digital space: which is based on an autonomous capacity for assessment, decision-making and action in cyberspace. This corresponds de facto to cyber defence.
- The ability to preserve or restore the digital security of states on digital tools in order to be able to control their networks, electronic communications and data, public or personal.

These actions to safeguard digital security must be piloted. To date, however, this evidence is still struggling to be translated into practice. In recent times, digital security has become a recurring theme in public debates. After a phase of utopia, which some might describe as naive, the development of digital technology has become a global battleground, with harmful consequences for societies and their digital security. In spite of high-profile cases (the revelations of Edward Snowden, Cambridge Analytica) and the revelations of unannounced eavesdropping (Alexa, Siri), the trust capital of digital enterprises has remained considerable, delaying government action towards them. The majority of states have long been procrastinating, with digital only very recently becoming one of the main strategic priorities.

The speed of digital developments and innovations alone cannot disqualify public action. The reign of complacency must come to an end, and leaders must accept responsibility for the challenges of the digital age. States must realize that our era is a "turning point," a crossroads. The energies, initiatives and forces exist to respond to this decisive moment. It remains to take the right direction, at the right pace. In other words, to give the necessary unifying impetus.

At a time when major decisions need to be taken, it is interesting to ask whether governments have a comprehensive digital strategy. There are many sectoral

W. Amedzro St-Hilaire, *Digital Risk Governance*,
https://doi.org/10.1007/978-3-030-61386-0_13

strategies, tens of millions of dollars released (on average by states) on a multitude of projects, but all this is far from offering an image of coherence and control. This is all the more alarming since digital technology is by definition a cross-cutting issue, a fact that is no longer reflected in government organizations. It is doubtful that some states have a good grasp of these cross-cutting issues. This is particularly striking when it comes to the crux of the matter: the funding of ambitious digital projects.

The architecture projects for the processing and massive exploitation of multi-source information, carried out by certain armaments directorates-general, are emblematic of this state of affairs. It is therefore regrettable that in the majority of states, the financial burden of these projects, which could benefit all ministries, is currently borne exclusively by the armed forces. It must be said that government action by states is based neither on a clear guideline nor on a shared vision.

This could be a source of inconsistencies that could be detrimental to the defence of their digital security. Depending on the country (and depending on the ministries and themes addressed), priorities and opinions change. A governance problem is emerging. It is partly the result of the contradictions of the digital age. How, under these conditions, can we arbitrate between digital security and civil liberties, security and defence, and effective economic presence in a necessarily global market?

To answer this question, this chapter promotes a new steering and the federation of all the players involved in the digital world. It must be said that in some countries, digital law has tried to move in this direction, without success. The National Digital Councils should be transformed into temporary institutional consultation forums. These would bring together public and private players, from administrations to industries, including academics and start-ups (not forgetting local authorities, which play a crucial role in digital regional planning).

These forums would make it possible to bring together individuals and entities with sometimes radically opposed positions, so that they can dialogue together and be a source of strong proposals to defend their digital security. These forums would then create a true digital culture and would bring together the most qualified people in this field (in order to take advantage of the treasure trove of skills and know-how available in these countries, where there is a real scientific and technological culture). It is on this culture that we must rely and on high-tech industrial know-how.

These forums, finally, would have a limited lifespan of up to 1 year. Indeed, it is not by working in "isolation" that states will succeed in defining a real strategy to assert their digital security: governments, parliaments, local elected officials, businesses and researchers will not succeed alone. While the institutional forums should make it possible to define strategies and put some order into initiatives that sometimes seem too disconnected from each other, these strategies should then be embodied at the legislative level. Parliaments are responsible for ensuring regular follow-up and monitoring the implementation of the priorities thus defined.

It is necessary to be aware of the scale of the task and the diversity of the fields of innovation that states must seize upon in order to defend their digital security and stem the hegemonic trends described. In order for this to work, there must be both flexible and long-term management: there must be long-term investment, based on a shared and permanent vision, but also a rapid reaction capacity to respond to new innovations.

As such, it recommends the development of standards for guiding and monitoring digital security. These standards, which would be triennial, would be based on military programming laws, which have already been tested in several countries. They would allow several countries to project themselves into sectors in which they can still defend a regional and/or world leadership position (such as edge computing, a blockchain that consumes less energy, or embedded artificial intelligence). Objectives related to training in these sectors under stress would also be included. It should be said that recruitment difficulties are the first limit to the expansion of the ecosystem of start-ups and unicorns in several countries. This is a political meeting that mobilizes public authorities around the strategic issues of their digital security.

Therefore, the implementation of a cyber defence for a real autonomy in cyberspace is desirable for the states. Cyber defence differs from the fight against cybercrime, but also from the digitization of armies and theatres of operation. It covers the policies put in place by states to actively protect networks and information systems that are essential to the life and digital security of their country. While cyberattacks and threats are significant and numerous and have been observed for more than a decade, the development of cyber defence in some countries has been gradual.

Since the first cyberattack on a state structure in Estonia in April 2007, the threat has become more concrete and more intense. Indeed, Estonia, wanting to mark its independence from Russia, had decided to move a Red Army monument from the centre of the capital in Tallinn to the suburbs. This decision showing the Estonian rapprochement with the Western powers would have triggered a Russian reaction, which has not been officially proven. Russia is said to have hired hackers to increase the number of computers involved in the denial-of-service attack against Estonia that lasted a few days. Hardly a day goes by without reports of targeted attacks against the networks of large public or private organizations somewhere in the world. There are three types of attacks:

- The disruption of institutional sites, such as parliamentary websites, made inaccessible during the discussion of the law on the Armenian genocide; this is what specialists call a "denial-of-service" attack: the website is made inaccessible because it is saturated with thousands of requests.
- The large-scale computer attack on certain economic and finance ministries in preparation for the G8 and G20 summits. This is a vast computer intrusion for espionage purposes: spyware is introduced by means of a "Trojan horse", which takes the form of a booby-trapped attachment opening a "back door". The attacker can then monitor and take control of his computer remotely and without the user's knowledge, for example, to extract data, read his e-mails, and even listen to his conversations or film his victim by triggering the computer's microphone or camera himself; he can then, by successive bounces, take control of other computers, or even the entire network.
- Spying on sensitive operators. Several years ago, the press reported on an operation suffered by industrial groups in the nuclear sector.

Armies are also the target of these cyberattacks. Armies are the target of particularly numerous computer attacks. Thus, in 2019, an average of 1200 significant events in Asian countries were recorded by the cyber defence commands (an increase of around 20% compared to 2018). About a hundred consist of proven cyberattacks, six of which are characteristic of modes of action of structured groups affiliated to states. All of these attacks were carried out for the purpose of spying on senior officials of ministries or operational functions.

It should be noted that, despite an awareness of what is at stake, many countries are still relatively late in implementing a cyber defence strategy. It was at the instigation of President Barack Obama that cyber security was designated as a strategic priority in the United States, mobilizing several agencies, within the Department of Homeland Security or the Pentagon, such as the National Security Agency (NSA) or Cyber Command. From 2010 to 2015, the United States spent $50 billion on cyber defence, and several tens of thousands of agents were working on the subject.

The British government has already adopted a new strategy, implemented by Government Communications Headquarters (GCHQ), the agency responsible for technical intelligence. At the time, some 700 officers were working on cyber defence issues, and despite a tight budget, an additional £650 million ($950 million) has since been provided for cyber defence. Finally, in Germany, a strategy was drawn up in February 2011, coordinated by the Federal Ministry of the Interior to which the Federal Office for Information Systems Security (BSI) is attached, with a budget of 80 million euros and more than 500 agents.

In several South Asian countries, recent policies have given real impetus to cyber defence which has led to the creation of digital security agencies, identified as national authorities for the defence of information systems. However, with an average staff of 230 and a budget of around 75 million dollars, the resources available at the time were far from those of the services of the world's major powers. The rise in power has been slow. Cyber defence has been established as a national priority in most states for digital defence and security.

It should be noted that, according to ExpertActions Group, digital security can be understood as the ability of states, on the one hand, to act sovereignly in the digital space, maintaining an autonomous capacity (for assessment, decision and action), and, on the other hand, to preserve the most traditional components of their digital security against new threats (taking advantage of the increasing digitization of society). Several countries have therefore opted to retain autonomy of decision-making in matters of defence and security in cyberspace. The achievement of this objective is based on the following elements:

- A sovereign capacity to detect computer attacks affecting the state and critical infrastructures. Thus, their intelligence agencies are developing their own detection systems for the supervision of administrations and work that has led to the emergence of trusted industrial solutions for the benefit of enterprises.
- A sovereign capacity to attribute cyber3attacks. The choice to develop and maintain such a capability is a major orientation. The mastery of such capabilities will

in the long term be accessible only to a very limited number of countries that have made the strategic choice to possess them.

- A national doctrine of deterrence and reaction, based in particular on a national method of assessing the seriousness of a cyberattack, incorporating legal standards (penal code, defence code, general regulations on data protection, etc.). This is a classification scheme for cyberattacks prepared by all those involved in cyber defence.
- A national response doctrine, based on the principle that the response is the result of a political decision formulated on a case-by-case basis in the light of the criteria established by international law. The response may take the form of a public attribution, the adoption of countermeasures or even, insofar as it is not excluded that a cyber-attack may reach the threshold of armed aggression, recourse to self-defence within the meaning of Article 51 of the United Nations Charter.
- Offensive capabilities that make it possible, in the face of the risk of armed aggression, to have response options of a military nature in the cyber environment as in other environments. Cyber weapons are now fully integrated into the operational capabilities of armies and are the subject of a doctrine that provides a framework for their use in military operations in external theatres of operation, in compliance with international law.

Successful actions in the area of cybersecurity have been taken by several states. The cyber governance of states must be organized around four pillars with specific governance: prevention (under the responsibility of the national information systems security agencies and supervised by the heads of government); intelligence (with the general directorates of security and the supervisory ministries); judicial action, which is the responsibility of the chancellery and, finally, military action (led by the chiefs of staff of the armed forces and the heads of state).

Each pillar has autonomous governance, and all are coordinated around a Cyber Crisis Coordination Committee, which articulates the cyber defence cycle (detection, attribution, response): the aim is to define response strategies that are submitted to and validated by the political authorities. From there, we should ask ourselves, in the context of strategic data protection issues, which encryption for which data?

In terms of data protection and communications protection of states, enterprises and citizens, the diversity of the stakes leads to the level of ambition of countries being broken down into different spheres: for classified data and communications, the obligation of result, guaranteeing their protection against targeted attacks by the most competent adversaries is indisputable. This ambition implies national mastery of certain technologies, first and foremost the encryption of communications. Several countries have a trusted industry in this field, capable of providing equipment with a very high level of security, approved to protect data exchanged at the Secret Defence classification level. Maintaining a national industry at the forefront in this area is an absolute priority.

For the broader field of sensitive data and communications, constraints must be set for the digital solutions used by states and critical operators. It is illusory to seek to meet all these needs with purely national solutions. Without fundamentally excluding foreign suppliers, this objective requires the local availability of a trusted industrial fabric capable of producing basic security building blocks but also of designing complex systems by integrating foreign building blocks. This implies that local operators must retain a sufficient level of competence to design security architectures that include the insertion of such bricks.

For the broader field of economic security of non-vital businesses and protection of citizens' digital uses, each state must preserve its ability to influence the digital choices of the actors concerned by identifying quality solutions without imposing them. To this end, labelling provisions should be gradually generalized to all digital solutions, in order to encourage the use of the best solutions. This scheme will gain economic relevance through its extension to the regional level. This three-pronged approach is fully applicable to the issue of the cloud. For example, for its classified data, states use exclusively an internal cloud.

On the other hand, for other public data and for the needs of enterprises, the qualification of clouds by security agencies will make it possible to identify offers (not necessarily national) that provide sufficient guarantees with regard to both technical (risk of computer attack) and legal risks (constraints on making data available to foreign authorities).

Finally, to encourage the deployment of digital infrastructures in states, it should be noted that no country can in fact become the simple user of goods and services, designed and produced elsewhere in the world. Several countries are still consumers of digital products and services and producers of data captured by major foreign players. It is difficult to ignore the failure of public policies conducted to date in this area. A country that consumes digital products has a balance of trade in computer, electronic and optical products (in millions of dollars). According to ExpertActions Group, this product category corresponds to the following categories: electronic components and cards; computers and peripheral equipment; telephones and communication equipment; consumer electronics; measuring, testing and navigation equipment; electro-medical diagnostic and treatment equipment; optical and photographic equipment and magnetic and optical media.

Like local reindustrialization, support for the emergence of a digital industry will enable the creation of added value to be repatriated from the states. If further proof of this need were needed, the measures adopted by the US government in the context of its trade war with China demonstrate the urgency of building up, where possible, an autonomous production capacity. One of the pillars of digital security is the existence of a sufficiently solid industrial base to enable the political entity to have a minimum of autonomy with regard to the infrastructure, equipment and software that enable it to intervene in cyberspace. If states do not have actors capable of producing the infrastructures, building the services, managing the first-level relationship with users and mastering the interfaces, they are likely to be vulnerable in terms of digital security.

A proactive policy in this area must pursue three directions if institutions and enterprises are to regain full digital security at all levels of cyberspace: deploy digital infrastructures on their territory; adopt a genuine industrial policy identifying the key technological sectors in which to invest their strengths; create a favourable ecosystem mobilizing human and financial resources to create national champions.

On the first point, despite the intangible nature of the web and "cyberspace," the Internet is still territorially anchored, giving public authorities a strong grip (the network depends on essential strategic physical assets that require considerable investment and are at least partly governed by national legal systems). But physical assets are not the only one's indispensable for the exercise of digital security. As we have seen, the importance of data makes it necessary to have gigantic databases, if only to stay in the race for artificial intelligence. However, this effort in favour of infrastructures must be at the service of a national digital security policy: it would indeed be paradoxical to finance the highways on which users who play with local laws and standards would travel.

Also, it should be noted that underwater cables, which carry 99% of intercontinental electronic communications, are the most important. According to ExpertActions Group, there are currently 405 cables deployed worldwide, representing 1.4 million kilometres of optical fibre. The fact that a country has a sufficient number of secure submarine cables is therefore an indispensable element of its digital security. It must be said that countries need to strengthen their attractiveness for investments of this type, through a provision introduced in the law to facilitate administrative procedures and another introduced in the finance law to explicitly exclude submarine cables for electronic communications from the scope of the preventive archaeology fee. The majority of states should continue to work on simplifying administrative procedures for the landing of underwater electronic communication cables, for example, by appointing a single point of contact for international investors.

In a logic of technological digital security, it is necessary to ensure that these infrastructures are not exclusively owned by foreign entities and cannot be damaged. On the first point, the Gafam offensive is worrying. Until a few years ago, these cables were in fact owned by consortia of enterprises mainly composed of telecommunications operators. They are now being carried by the American digital giants to ensure that the capacities of the submarine cables support the traffic generated by their activities and link their data centres.

This growing appetite has turned the sector into a true Wild West. Submarine cables are the only area of the Internet that is not regulated. The Gafams, like other players, can do what they want. Similarly, the law in force corresponds more to the secondary role played by the cables than to the fact that they are now indispensable. Thought should therefore be given to international regulation of these strategic infrastructures, which would allow states to impose certain rules, for both security and economic reasons (to guarantee the neutrality of the flows transported).

On the second point, any attack on a submarine cable could have disastrous economic effects. However, the public nature of their location makes them extremely vulnerable. It would therefore be appropriate to carry out a safety audit of these cables.

These cables may also be subject to state threats: for example, it is common knowledge that submarines and surface vessels have been spotted in their vicinity.

The landing and interconnection points of the cables are a strategic issue, allowing states to conduct espionage, piracy and intimidation operations. Some countries do not hesitate to exploit the physical dimension of the Internet from a strategic angle. This is a major digital security issue for states.

Another sensitive issue is the existence of a "digital divide" that undermines the potential of institutions and enterprises in terms of skills and innovation. This is reflected, on the one hand, by the existence of territories deprived of efficient access to digital technology and, on the other hand, by the distance of some citizens from digital technology ("illectronism" of enterprises.). It must be noted that, despite an improvement, digital coverage is still insufficient, both on fixed and mobile lines in several states. However, several countries have set up a plan to finance fixed infrastructures in the least dense areas of their territories. Lessons seem to have been learned from past mistakes.

The draft specifications for the allocation of the first 5G frequencies (in several countries) thus insist on the digital development of the territories (by providing that a quarter of the 5G sites to be deployed by 2025 will be located in rural areas). With regard to these terrestrial infrastructures, a paradox should once again be stressed: they are financed by local capital (public and private), they are accessible to all, but first and foremost they ensure the development of the Gafams, the first users of these information highways (who do not wish to be subject to the status of electronic communications operator).

With regard to increasing the attractiveness of the states for setting up data centres, it is estimated that 40% of data hosting capacity is now located in the United States. Having sufficient data hosting and processing capacity is one of the conditions for the digital security of institutions and enterprises. At the inauguration of a data centre last February, a Minister of Economy and Finance explained that if they do not have on their soil a sufficient number of data centres to host the algorithm data that are necessary (for the development of the autonomous vehicle, the data of automobiles and therefore security), then these data will be stored in other geographical areas and subject to the local legal regime. It is therefore a direct industrial risk, but also a direct security risk.

Data centres are therefore part of strategic digital infrastructures: they are industrial and technological "fortresses" responsible for storing, processing and transferring digital data. The first data centre was created in the United States in 1946, in the laboratories of the American army. Today, in order to control the management of their services and their users' data, the Gafams have chosen to develop their own data centres, rather than using an external service provider. Several states have chosen to change their tax systems to attract these infrastructures. Indeed, data centres are a valued asset for a territory that derives economic benefits (employment, construction, maintenance), tax revenues, investment and talent attraction.

They are also, and above all, a strategic infrastructure, which contributes to the digital security of a state and its citizens by guaranteeing the legal protection of data, the correlation between the number and/or surface area of data centres and the power of the digital industry, the control of services and the security of infrastructures. Finally, by their very nature, data can be hosted in any location, and the centre can be operated remotely: without tax incentives, it would therefore be more difficult for some states to attract these infrastructures.

Many countries are struggling to grasp what is at stake in this international competition. For example, other countries have announced their goals of becoming "a data centre nation". In order to be attractive, most of the states involved in this race, from the United States to Thailand, via the countries of the European Economic Area, are acting on energy taxation (electricity consumption can represent 30–50% of a centre's operating costs). These countries have also introduced a property tax exemption for production equipment and equipment for the installation of industrial sites (which indirectly means that most data centre equipment is exempt from property tax). The choices made by the states fall within their sovereign prerogatives and illustrate the values and priorities they wish to uphold. They also reflect the leeway they have. Taxation of data centres can therefore act as "a true indicator of digital security". This choice is also illustrated in the conditionality of tax incentives: a minimum of investment or jobs for American states and reduced or "green" energy consumption in certain European countries such as Sweden or the United Kingdom.

In Asia, the first tax incentive in favour of data centres should be included in the budget law recently. Digital data storage centres will be able to benefit from a reduced domestic tax rate on final electricity consumption, subject to a minimum consumption threshold depending on value added. Three elements supported the adoption of this new provision: making these countries more attractive and attracting the investments triggered by the entry into force of the Cloud Act, and participating in the plan for industrial transformation through digital technology. The tax system would not target data centres based on their economic benefits but on their energy consumption. The threshold of at least one gigawatt-hour would apply to the largest infrastructures. It would make sense to lower this threshold in favour of smaller facilities.

The environmental challenges posed by the intense energy consumption of these infrastructures should also be highlighted. The two issues are not incompatible, on the contrary. For example, the benefit of the energy tax reduction could be modulated according to the origin of the electricity (e.g. by providing a bonus for "green" electricity). It is important to continue efforts to promote digital infrastructures so that states can benefit, on their territories, from equipment that can defend their digital security and power.

Finally, it could be interesting and profitable for each country to publish a report on data centres. This report would present the fiscal and non-fiscal incentive measures put in place and envisaged; it would offer visibility to players in the sector, and it would constitute a first element in what could be called the "marketing" strategy of states as future data centre nations.

Also, the creation of massive databases must be encouraged. It is only at the price of greater access and better circulation of data (to benefit the public authorities, but also smaller economic players and public research) that it will be possible to rebalance the balance of power with the Gafams. These massive databases can be considered as an essential infrastructure (i.e. an indispensable input for a player to enter a market). It therefore seems necessary to think about ways of building databases that could benefit local economic players. Three levers appear to be complementary: the opening up of certain data, the imposition of a regulated right of access to the data and the encouragement of data sharing.

The "free flow of data" policy would address the issue of the circulation of non-personal data. States may not restrict the circulation of non-personal data except on grounds of public security. The non-personal data policy has for several years been based on the principle of open data with a view to encouraging the creation of new value-added services based on the reuse of data. The law should define a principle of openness for public data and certain private data. This edifice is to be completed by the revision of certain directives. Regarding private data, several countries favour a sectoral approach and various modalities by field of activity: this is the case in the energy sector, in transport, in the banking sector or in the health sector.

Let us take the example of the Health Data Hub or health data platform. Health is one of the priority sectors for the development of artificial intelligence. Consequently, there is a need to expand the existing national health data system. The Health Data Platform, set up as a public interest grouping in some countries, is responsible, among other things, for collecting, organizing and making health data available and promoting innovation in its use. This initiative makes it possible to make certain countries a leader in the use of health data (serving the common good, respecting patients' rights and in full transparency with civil society).

However, the openness of data comes up against several limits (the information industry grouping does not hesitate in some countries to describe it as an "unconscious denial of digital security"). Firstly, it is often seen as benefiting above all the digital giants, who alone have the expertise to quickly launch the exploitation of this data. Moreover, where they previously had to pay for the data, it is now (mostly) made available to them free of charge. However, proponents of open data point out that without open data, small innovative enterprises will never have the means to purchase this data. In other words, it is better to allow broad access to data so that everyone starts from the same starting line, rather than to maintain a situation where only digital giants have access to the data.

In any case, any opening up of private data should only be envisaged if there is a public interest reason, if this opening up does not disproportionately infringe on the freedom of enterprise and if its modalities are precisely framed (through a regulator or a dedicated administration). The public authority is being led to play the role of trusted third party in the management of the opening of data. Indeed, the degree of openness imposed on these data must take into account a set of factors, including the economic, financial and competitive impact on the enterprises concerned. Where the holding of databases constitutes a significant barrier to entry, a right of access to the data could be organized, under the supervision of a regulator who would be responsible for examining the terms and conditions (on the same basis as for infrastructure regulation: access under transparent, non-discriminatory and reasonable conditions), in order to promote competition and innovation.

Finally, if the first act of the "battle of AI" concerned personal data, this battle was won by the major platforms. The second act will focus on sector-specific data: it is on these data that states can differentiate themselves. The challenge is therefore for states to succeed in creating champions around professional and industrial data. This is why it is advisable to encourage private players to pool their data, to create "data commons" (here too, states may be called upon to play the role of trusted third parties).

Chapter 14
Governance Through the Development of Key Technologies and the Loss of Strategic Assets

A genuine industrial policy in favour of digital technology must constitute the framework for the new governance of states. Industrial policy is understood here in an all-encompassing sense, which takes into account the limits of the classical definition of industry. Industry is changing in nature and is now one with services. It is mass production, economies of scale, productivity gains and the application of technical progress that now define industry. It is important to ask: Are Apple, Google, Microsoft, IBM, Verizon, Facebook, Oracle and Amazon industrial enterprises or service enterprises?

Several countries need to prioritize the "emergence of champions" through a cross-cutting ecosystem policy. States cannot afford to be absent from a certain number of critical technologies (artificial intelligence, quantum computing, blockchain, semiconductors, etc.). Similarly, it is clear that without mastery of these technological breakthroughs, there is no political sovereignty. The identification of key technologies and the evaluation of the positioning of sectors on these technologies could make it possible to guide investment priorities and identify the technological bricks that are threatened (e.g. because of the financial fragility of certain enterprises, or their dependence on critical foreign suppliers).

Direct and vertical public intervention must be assumed. However, in order not to scatter resources, a graduated approach should be adopted. In short, while avoiding creating solutions ex nihilo, it is necessary to capitalize on existing successes and to focus, on the one hand, on solutions that are different and, on the other hand, on solutions for the future. Secure supplies and solutions used by sensitive sectors rather than creating ex nihilo solutions already dominated by dominant players. The technical and financial difficulties of creating solutions ex nihilo in already dominated markets are real.

In order to make up for the delay of certain countries in the development of certain structuring solutions for the current Internet, it is desirable for states to encourage the creation of solutions that compete with those proposed by the Gafams. This is particularly the case for the so-called sovereign operating system (which could

W. Amedzro St-Hilaire, *Digital Risk Governance*,
https://doi.org/10.1007/978-3-030-61386-0_14

also be called domestic). It is indeed necessary to develop these operating systems and local search engines in order to forge an operating system. To proceed without these tools is like waging war without tanks or guns for the states.

On the other hand, it would be desirable for states to place the responsibility for creating such an operating system in the hands of the private sector: private actors should be capable of an investment comparable to that made by Google, Microsoft or Apple. Let us not forget that it is the user who decides: there is no point in raising so much money if citizens ultimately prefer to use that of private American competitors. In the same way, such a system "would be little used."

On the possibility of creating a special police station, it must be said that, apart from the special case of China, few actors can hope to impose themselves on a field that is already occupied. It is therefore illusory to want to develop a sovereign SO beyond the strictly regalian sphere. Finally, developing a new system ex nihilo was nonsense from a technical point of view. It therefore seems unreasonable for states to drive the development of a solution from scratch. Such a programme would be too costly and would risk not finding its market in the face of the advance made by the duopoly formed by Google and Apple.

We can thus recall the failure of the sovereign cloud projects launched by certain states as part of future investment programmes. These states had invested in two rival "sovereign cloud" projects. The aim was to restore digital sovereignty by sheltering government and corporate data from foreign regulations. These projects were pursued by successive governments until they failed 10 years later (due to lack of market acceptance). These states would have lost an average of $56 million. Moreover, even Microsoft failed to develop an operating system that could compete with the duopoly in the sector.

It is therefore more appropriate to argue in favour of framing operating systems by rules which are specific to each state. Encryption of data and rules would constitute the two bricks of a nationalization of data (i.e. the creation of a sovereign common good protected by a border and administered by a common rule imposed on incoming actors). Thus, it may be too late to replicate digital giants, but it is not too late to achieve technological digital security in certain critical technological areas. In the face of the difficulties of creating solutions ex nihilo, technological solutions should nevertheless be developed for those activities that are directly relevant to digital security (i.e. the most regalian ministries of the state and possibly vital operators in the sense of defence codes).

In this respect, one example is the Clip OS operating system developed for the state and now open to sensitive sectors. Based on a Linux 2 kernel capable of managing information of several levels of sensitivity, Clip OS is now available in open source as part of a collaborative development project. The example of the Tchap application is also interesting. Instant messaging to ensure that data exchanged between public officials and ministerial or parliamentary offices does not wander around the world seemed indispensable.

In industrial sectors in which states have no production capacity, security of supply must be ensured. One example is the current dependence of several states in the world on the United States and certain Asian countries (Taiwan, South Korea) for the design and casting of advanced digital components. In the short and medium term, the acquisition of advanced foundry capacity for these countries would be too costly today (exceeding $10 billion on average) and would not be profitable in view of the market prospects of local producers. A diversity of suppliers should therefore be ensured in the short to medium term. Consideration should be given to identifying ways of limiting this dependence.

Finally, it is necessary to ensure the security of the solutions marketed in the countries by foreign enterprises. This is notably the choice made by several countries for 5G network equipment. It is therefore the question of securing fifth generation mobile networks that is addressed here. The fifth generation of mobile telecommunications standards promises a change of scale in network capacities (speeds multiplied by ten, latency time divided by ten, greater network flexibility, greater energy efficiency, etc.). Significant economic benefits are also expected ($250 billion per year in 2025 for operators in several countries), but above all the development of new uses that are particularly critical for the economic life of a country: "factory of the future," connected vehicles, Internet of Things, telesurgery, connected cities, etc.

A real 5G "race" is therefore underway worldwide. Governments intend to take part in it through the implementation of the 5G roadmap. However, the critical nature of the uses also makes it necessary to raise the level of requirements in terms of the security of these networks: this is the subject of several laws in the various countries aimed at safeguarding defence and national security interests in connection with the operation of mobile radio networks. Some countries have chosen not to ban a particular equipment manufacturer, despite the pressure exerted by the US Government (on its allies if Huawei brand equipment is allowed to be deployed). The law thus sets up in these countries a system of prior authorization for the operation of certain equipment considered "at risk" and listed by ministerial order. This authorization is granted after instructions from the Secretariats General for Defence and National Security and the National Agencies for Information Systems Security.

The aim is therefore to provide direct support for the development of technologies and tools that these countries must have technical mastery of. Some of these states are therefore opting for this strategy of direct support for research and digital enterprises based on the following logic:

- Building on what already exists to conquer new markets.
- In markets already dominated by the digital giants, only consider supporting a competitive solution if it is based on a strategy of differentiation.
- Invest in the markets of the future.

This strategy could be defined within the framework of the temporary institutional forum on digital technology and the law on the orientation and monitoring of digital security (which would make it possible to bring together all the driving forces of the digital sector). It would indeed be too risky to rely on a minister to identify technologies of the future or breakthrough technologies. It must be said that the typology at the heart of the digital economy represented on average per country 5.2% of GDP and 3.7% of employment. While most countries have some strengths in basic technologies and infrastructure, telecommunications services, computer applications and services, they are weaker in the net economy.

In terms of basic technologies and infrastructure, these countries have an industrial base of excellence that needs to be preserved and developed. This is particularly the case for optical fibre terrestrial cables (a market in which enterprises are either national or locally based in these countries). With regard to submarine cables, it must be said that some enterprises have both local production capacity (for both cables and optical terminals) and vessels capable of laying and maintaining cables, in particular optical terminals. It is crucial for these countries to preserve these skills locally.

In the field of electronic components, several countries also have advanced production capacities. Continued support for this sector through successive plans is essential. Components are at the heart of the digital economy, providing its engine and memory, and are integrated into most professional and consumer equipment. One of the priority areas for technological digital security, which is often overlooked, is the silicon, processor and component industry. Considering that the United States like China, Russia or Israel is also working to maintain or obtain their strategic autonomy in this area, it should be pointed out that China has announced an investment of 150 billion dollars to support its electronic components industry. It is therefore essential for other countries to continue public support for this sector.

When it comes to supercomputers, few local enterprises are still able to design and manufacture them. These enterprises provide, among other things, the atomic energy calculator for their countries' deterrence programmes. It should be recalled how this sector is crucial to digital security in many countries, especially since the majority of components are foreign (like the processors for which American enterprises have a virtual monopoly) and local initiatives should be supported. The processors used by supercomputers around the world are mainly American, Taiwanese and South Korean. The industry in most countries exists but is very far from making the processors specific to supercomputers. Some states have ended up releasing millions of dollars in purely local or regional processor development programs.

Although not enough, it is a start. To be effective and to face international competition, this funding must be concentrated on a small number of players. The success of these programmes, which are essential to the technological independence of these countries, must be ensured.

In the software, programming, consulting and computer services sectors, many states also have highly successful enterprises, whether in software publishing, consulting in computer activities, cyber security activities or video games. Even if these countries are not leaders, the success of some of the countries that are players in the "net economy" is worth noting. These successes must be valued and supported, particularly in their internationalization.

All these centres of excellence must be encouraged so as not to reproduce the difficulties experienced by the telecommunications equipment sector in some countries during the 2000s. Finally, with a view to preserving their economic base, the standards relating to foreign investment subject to prior authorization should be welcomed, which incorporate many aspects of digital technology, such as cyber security (and, under certain conditions, semiconductors or artificial intelligence), into the control system for foreign investment in several countries. However, it is important not to systematically (and in all digital sectors) equate foreign financing with the loss of strategic assets.

For the Cloud, a strategy based on differentiation would be the norm. Indeed, replicating existing technologies in an area where the Americans enjoy a dominant position seems to be possible only by adopting a strategy of differentiation in the proposed offer, either through innovation or a breakthrough technology, to establish a competitive advantage. This means, in particular, encouraging solutions that are in line with local values, i.e. respectful of users' privacy, and that incorporate a principle of "privacy by design," in other words, respect for privacy from the design stage.

This strategy has been adopted by several players:

1. Certain search engines, which are trying to carve out a place for themselves on this market through a model that protects user privacy and which benefit from the financial support of the Deposit and Consignment Banks.
2. Certain marketplaces, which differentiate themselves from data brokers by ensuring compliance with the regulations in force depending on the territory in which the data is produced and used and whose global data exchange projects are supported by several players.
3. Secure social and collaborative network platforms.

To date, governments seem to be focusing their efforts on two sectors in particular: the cloud and artificial intelligence. The "cloud of trust" is a welcome initiative but one that is slow to materialize. The global cloud market is dominated by four American players: Amazon Web Services (AWS), Microsoft, Google and IBM, with the exception of China where Chinese enterprises (Baidu, Alibaba, Tencent, Huawei) dominate each of the cloud market segments. Other countries have several champions on the infrastructure layers of the cloud that rely on a fast-growing domestic market to attack the international market. While these countries are competitive in some markets despite the strong growth in market share of US players, the application services market (SaaS or Software as a Service) is dominated by the Americans, relegating competitors far behind.

To remedy this situation, the General Management of Enterprises in several countries is leading work aimed at facilitating the emergence of a trusted cloud market, i.e. to offer enterprises and public authorities diversified, high-performance and secure offerings. The aim of this work is to promote local cloud offers that are differentiated by their level of trust. Unlike the "sovereign cloud" project already mentioned, the initiative aims, in a market that has now reached a good level of maturity, to rely on suppliers and offers already exposed to the market, if necessary, by adjusting these offers to meet the need. It is important to stress the relevance of pooling trusted cloud needs, as this will provide sufficient critical mass to guarantee the relevance of a national offer. Such mutualization could be envisaged for software needs, such as collaborative suites. This approach would extend the labelling of the cloud solutions implemented.

The objective of governments is now to "have the first proposals for setting up a secure cloud quickly." However, the initiative seems to be difficult to read and is slow to be put in place. It is necessary to underline the need for greater transparency in the cloud market: any call for tenders (public or private) should include a clause on the location of the stored data and the law applicable to it, which is not the case today. In addition, it is necessary to underline the need to anticipate the major change to come for the storage of computer data (i.e. the move from 80% of data stored in the cloud to 80% of data stored in edge computing) due to the exponential development of connected objects (such as watches, connected speakers and assistants or autonomous vehicles). States must now adopt a clear strategy on this subject. When it comes to artificial intelligence strategy, it also corresponds to a form of differentiation based on the ethical aspect. However, it is taking far too long to be put in place. It may therefore be thought, in view of the speed of innovation in this field, that these delays are far too long.

Moreover, the financial resources allocated by countries appear limited compared to those made available by the United States and China. Large American enterprises invest 30–40 billion dollars each year, as do Chinese enterprises and the Chinese State. The average amount invested by other countries as a whole is only $4–5 billion. On the artificial intelligence initiative, countries are continuing to think. In the majority of countries, it is divided into three main areas:

- To develop local AI champions, particularly in key sectors such as environment, health and safety, through AI Challenges ($5 million) and the major challenges financed by the Innovation and Industry Fund ($100 million in total) – medical diagnostics, transparency and auditability of autonomous systems based on artificial intelligence and automation of cyber security.
- Stimulating demand by supporting the spread of AI in all sectors and throughout their territory: an average of 250 million dollars has been mobilized through the Investment Programs for the Future to finance structuring projects dedicated to AI; the Directorate General for Enterprises, in consultation with local institutional and economic players, is supporting the standardization process in the field of AI.
- Laying the foundations for a genuine data economy via the call for projects aimed at co-financing data pooling initiatives and the Health Data Hub already mentioned.

The mastery of artificial intelligence and its development are crucial for all sectors of activity. This is, for example, the case of the automotive sector, which will have to master this technology in order to take advantage of the evolution of the market towards the autonomous vehicle. It should be noted that these countries have not yet reached a sufficient level of preparedness in several areas. For this reason, a national strategy dedicated to the autonomous vehicle will have to be published. Also, it is essential to develop the technologies of the future: quantum computer and blockchain. An industrial strategy must also invest in the sectors of the future where, for the time being, no player is permanently established. Several governments have apparently already identified two key technologies: the blockchain and, in the longer term, quantum technologies.

Hence the question of whether the blockchain is a tool of the future to defend our digital security? The development of the blockchain could respond to many of the challenges to digital security, whether collective, individual or state security. Several observatory forums are, for example, working on digital identity, an essential prerequisite for completing the digital single market. A long-term objective of the eIDAS Regulation is to enable legal and natural persons to identify themselves by revealing only the data necessary for authentication. The regulation also covers the prerequisites for the reliability of electronic signatures and electronic documents.

These three elements are particularly conducive to the development of a block chain and the maintenance of a decentralized register. These forums indeed promise a so-called self-sovereign identity (SSI) approach: users can manage their digital identities and use them according to their needs. States retain their sovereign prerogatives since they can provide an "official identity" and information that is both managed by the person concerned and provides guarantees to third parties. Although these countries are still far from having the necessary underlying technologies, they must anticipate these future developments, both so as not to let private enterprises develop and control them, without being able to regulate them, and so as not to fall behind other states.

New service proposals, based on the blockchain, are constantly emerging. This is the case, for example, of the experiment conducted by customs and certain national enterprises in several countries to record monitoring information in a forgery-proof manner. Customs has drawn an initial positive assessment of this experiment.

The blockchain also opens up prospects in terms of financing innovation, a difficulty that many local start-ups are stumbling over. Financing through token fundraising would make it possible to circumvent both investment constraints and the reluctance of certain banking institutions. For this reason, the Pact laws have decided, in an unprecedented move at the global level, to regulate the raising of funds in tokens (ICOs for initial coin offerings): the AMF will be able to grant an optional visa to enterprises wishing to carry out such an operation. The first visas have been granted and provide a guarantee to investors (who may be more inclined to finance innovative projects in the digital field).

Attracting these investments requires a favourable ecosystem. The local champions of fundraising on the block were small towns, whose businesses raised more funds through this than any other. Nicknamed "Crypto Valley," these cities were able to build an ecosystem favourable to the installation of these enterprises: a regulatory framework set by the financial market authority, a single portal for newcomers, advantageous taxation for young enterprises and development of the uses of cryptoactives, including for everyday purchases.

Finally, the blockchain offers prospects for all sectors of the economy: establishment of smart contracts, more transparent and decentralized corporate governance, lower transaction costs and support for the transfer of a number of goods and services (works of art, copyright, computer storage space, personal data, etc.). This is why the blockchain is a tool that has become so important today in the digital world. It should be explained that creating a favourable environment for blockchain entrepreneurs is a way to fight against the monopolistic situation of some digital giants: entering the race of quantum technologies.

Also, quantum technologies are likely, through their use, to revolutionize whole areas of industry and defence, from molecular medicine to CO2 storage, including cryptanalysis, prospecting and GPS-free navigation, thus giving the players who master them a strategic advantage. Among these, quantum computing will theoretically make it possible to solve problems so complex that even the most powerful supercomputers could never have handled them. Several enterprises are positioning themselves in this sector, through the marketing of the first quantum simulators.

Several countries have announced investments of billions of dollars over 10 years in this field. Visionary countries should adopt a strategy dedicated to the development of these technologies. There is a window of opportunity in a still immature field such as quantum and its various applications. Such a strategy could prove to be all the more urgent since Google has published, apparently mistakenly, a study in which its researchers claim to have built a quantum processor capable of carrying out a certain type of operation in 3 min and 20 sec (where it would take more than 10,000 years for the most advanced of today's supercomputers).

The Ministries of the Economy, the Armed Forces and Research have sent experts to several countries to lead discussions on a national strategy enabling these countries to capitalize on the excellence of their research (in order to become an industrial champion of quantum technologies).

Chapter 15
Optimize the Levers of Industrial Policy to Mobilize Financial and Human Capital

All the tools of industrial policy must be mobilized both to support strategic sectors (so-called "vertical" industrial policy) and to create favourable ecosystems for private actors (so-called "horizontal" industrial policy). State public support for enterprises is essential in a context where their trading partners, first and foremost the United States and China, are not or no longer playing the game of free and undistorted competition. The tools of a vertical industrial policy are numerous, from subsidies (especially upstream of product development) to public procurement and equity participation... Three points in particular should be stressed.

1. The philosophy of international competition policy should be changed, so as to avoid that it is detrimental to local industrial initiatives at world level. Indeed, the disproportionate attention paid by the authorities to competition and short-term consumer benefit (to the detriment of the formation of large digital enterprises) should be highlighted.

Conversely, countries must encourage closer links between major national groups in order to mobilize investment in sectors that are particularly capital intensive and ensure the emergence of an industrial policy that must now be aligned with competition policy. It is in this logic that ex post rather than ex ante merger control should be allowed (to prevent a merger only if the anti-competitive effects are proven).

2. It is necessary to improve the state aid regime, a peculiarity of several countries which, as it stands, complicates and lengthens the procedure for granting public support compared to practices observed in third countries. It is therefore appropriate to shorten the time limits for examining aid, to take better account of public aid paid by third countries and to develop important projects of national interest.
3. The leverage of public procurement is essential to promote national enterprises. For it is clear that choosing an American or Chinese player has serious consequences both in terms of data protection and for the entire ecosystem of the

W. Amedzro St-Hilaire, *Digital Risk Governance*,
https://doi.org/10.1007/978-3-030-61386-0_15

digital sector. If national preference is a concept that is absent from the law in some countries, it is a concrete reality in other states.

Public administrations could also consider the use of free software to ensure that they have control over their data and to better conduct, potentially at lower cost, the public policies for which they are responsible. Indeed, states, their administrations and public services produce, collect, manage and disseminate digital data in ever-increasing quantities.

They concern individuals, equipment, territories, research results, administrative or judicial decisions, procedural elements, etc. In their day-to-day management of this information, as far as personal data is concerned, they have an obligation to guarantee its confidentiality. Thus, when administrations use software purchased from private enterprises, they must ensure that access to this information is secure and that it is impossible for the supplier to collect and use it.

It must be said that states, in their procurement policies for computer hardware and software, have a general doctrine for integrating this essential dimension of data security into their calls for tenders. In order to ensure compliance with specifications that would incorporate this requirement, they would have to acquire the means to analyse the proposed solutions (which most departments seem to lack). It must be said that the total readability of the source codes of computer programs should be one of the essential conditions for the digital security of states.

As for the free software used by states, it is not very secure. Moreover, the full cost (taking into account maintenance costs) of OSS is not that far from that of proprietary software. There should be no dogma in either direction. Governments should constantly strive for interoperability of their forces in this area. It should be borne in mind that several other countries were using source codes from the same company, which was a difficulty and slowed down the development of the use of free software.

However, it is understandable that FOSS is an asset for small nations: in particular because the user (who has access to the source code) can understand how it works and can modify it (which is likely to preserve his freedom and foster his confidence in the digital solution).

These states should avoid ending the partnerships their governments have entered into (with the American digital giants) by encouraging open source software, for example, through tenders, or by supporting contributions from public officials. There are therefore two reasons why they should be given priority in the public procurement of small nations: (a) FOSS enables administrations to better adapt their public services by developing their own solutions while being interoperable and to better control them by allowing continuous auditing and correction of security flaws; (b) FOSS would be cheaper overall.

In order to meet this requirement, but also in order to achieve, as far as possible, savings in terms of acquisition, management, maintenance and training, several administrations have chosen to develop their own IT solutions based on software whose source codes are public. This is the case of the police services of some small countries, which have equipped the 80,000 computer stations of their services with open source software solutions. This strategy has enabled them to regain their independence and digital security from private publishers. It would be very useful to quickly take stock of this unique experience and assess the possibilities of extending it to other public administrations in these countries.

States should also strengthen the position of their stakeholders in Internet standardization and governance bodies. The active equipment and protocols used for data communication or encryption comply with technical standards negotiated in international forums such as the Internet Engineering Task Force (IETF) or the World Wide Web Consortium (W3C).

The large number of digital standardization bodies (a few hundred worldwide) and their thematic diversity mean that the influence of certain countries in these fora or consortia varies considerably. It must be said that the national standardization players are in a real race to be able to propose, before others, the opening of work in the international standardization bodies in certain fields. Beyond the web, the issue is all the more crucial today for artificial intelligence.

Some of these states are fortunate enough to host on their territories Telecommunication Standardization Institutes, which are world leaders in telecommunication and digital standardization. These players, the majority within the 3GPP, the international consortium setting standards for 5G in particular and having a strong influence on standards for machine-to-machine communications and the Internet of things through its oneM2M project, hosts more than 100 national players out of a total of around 900 members. These countries should thus be able to influence:

- The definition of strategic priorities for standardization (5G, cyber security, Internet of things, etc.)
- The mobilization of national stakeholders in the standardization process, in particular through various calls for projects under the Framework Programme for Research and Innovation (SMEs, academics and researchers can now benefit from European funding to take part in standardization work)
- The defence of the anchoring of a national agency in the field so that it can be a place for the development of technical specifications as a relay to political initiatives and in application of their regulations in the field of radiocommunications or security (while ensuring that it is open to the world, since digital standards are intended to be global)
- Decisions aimed at preserving the national interest in the governance of information and communication technology standardization policy in the face of the entry of large global enterprises

Strengthening the influence of states also involves enhancing and promoting their positions in international discussions related to the standardization of information and communication technologies, as well as implementing a strategy to promote local standards internationally. However, it seems that some states have not yet fully grasped what is at stake. Furthermore, the effort to multilateralize ICANN should be pursued in order to move towards global Internet governance. The reform of ICANN in 2016 has led to undeniable progress such as better accountability of the decision-making bodies, more sophisticated appeal mechanisms against the decisions of the Board of Directors and, above all, the end of the direct contractual link between the US administration and the organization.

However, the current situation does not seem conducive to further improving the governance of the organization: most non-governmental actors (private sector, technical community) as well as a number of governments, including the United States but also a good part of European countries, now favour the status quo. The priority today is therefore no longer to relaunch a reform of ICANN. Rather, the priority now is to identify the priority subjects over which ICANN has power and over which the players could lead it to evolve. For the countries, it is also necessary to maintain a constant link between the authorities and the major actors on the one hand and the ICANN staff members on the other.

Finally, states should set up a grant for volunteers (associations, academics, retired people, etc.) who get involved in working groups with a potential impact on the actors.

One very important thing to know is that there can be no fight for the digital security of states without mobilizing the necessary weapons. It is therefore necessary to insist on the need to adopt a more offensive approach (including to mobilize more financial and human capital). Without this capital, countries will not have the actors that will enable them to be sovereign.

Progress has been made in this area, and some announcements by several governments are moving in the right direction (such as the launch of the Innovation and Industry Fund in some countries, one-third of the income of which will be devoted to financing deep-tech start-ups, carrying advanced, riskier technologies with longer returns on investment). The fund is expected to be endowed with an average of $10 billion from asset sales and equity inflows and is expected to generate $250 million per year in some countries. In addition, these deep-tech start-ups benefit from financing from the Tech Seed fund, which is financed by the Future Investment Program in other countries.

However, there is still much progress to be made. Thus, to remain at the forefront of digital innovation, the emergence of technological nuggets and national unicorns must be encouraged and financed. In order to improve the venture capital and research tax credit schemes for financing technology nuggets, it is necessary to look more closely at two observations frequently put forward to explain why some countries are lagging behind: (1) start-ups in these countries would come up against a glass ceiling that would prevent them from growing and lead them to export their ideas, talent and funds, particularly to the United States; (2) start-ups and innovative enterprises in these countries would frequently be bought out by American or Asian funds, which would be detrimental to digital security. These findings need to be qualified. Reasonable optimism is possible.

This glass ceiling would originate in a shallower venture capital market than in other countries. What do the numbers tell us? Private equity players raised $18.7 billion over 1 year and supported an average of 2218 enterprises. However, in terms of amounts invested, several countries still lag far behind the rich countries. These data show that start-ups and enterprises from the big powers, while fewer of them benefit from the funds invested through venture capital, nevertheless obtain more resources when they are chosen by a private equity fund. The same is true for innovation capital.

Among this innovation capital, IT and digital is the largest beneficiary sector, both in terms of amount ($836 million or 51.6%) and number of enterprises (374 or 42.6%). Moreover, according to a recent study by ExpertActions Group, the proportion of funds exceeding the 8% return mark, which is a guarantee of capital appreciation for executives, is roughly the same in Southeast Asia (32%) and Europe (29%) as in the United States (28%), which is the world's leading market for venture capital. The situation is slightly less favourable if only the funds raised for start-ups are taken into account: Asia is in the first place.

These figures show that the situation in several countries is not out of step with that of their main partners. However, at the international level, the situation in these countries is less enviable. Fundraising by European start-ups, for example, accounted for only 10% of global funding, compared with 53% for the United States and 27% for China. Of the 392 unicorns registered in July 2019, 182 are American, 94 Chinese and 45 European. There is no denying the progress made by several countries. They are good at creating start-ups, they are good at research, especially fundamental research and innovation, but they do not have the means to make them grow.

To do this, the funds must reach a critical size to attract the largest foreign funds, in search of big tickets, and to allow the enterprises they support to change dimension. So, it is less a problem of capital than a problem of finding project leaders with hundreds of millions of dollars worth of tickets, without which you cannot create digital giants. In addition, there are many mechanisms for financing innovation and supporting innovative enterprises. Explanations of the difficulties that start-ups may encounter in obtaining financing can therefore be found elsewhere.

Firstly, in terms of maturity, these financing frameworks are very fragmented: they intervene either very upstream, at the level of academic research, or very downstream, for example, within competitiveness clusters. There is no overarching framework that makes it possible, for the same project, to carry out upstream research, bring products to maturity and finally help them to be marketed. To respond to the initiatives of the digital giants, but also of the United States and China, particularly on quantum or embedded artificial intelligence, other states would benefit from developing such a framework.

It must be admitted that it is not conceivable, at least in the short and medium term, to want to compete with the giants of the world. This is a common sense position, based first of all on a simple observation: the risk capital market is structurally narrower, with the risk of old age being managed differently. However, two gaps in the private financing of start-ups in several countries should be highlighted: at the beginning of the chain, with a smaller number of business angels; at the end of the chain, with growth capital having difficulty in meeting the financing needs of innovative enterprises. However, this is a major handicap to the defence of their digital security since in the international competition between innovative start-ups, the amount of funds raised is a fundamental determinant of the ability to succeed in the innovation process: carrying a technological project through to the industrialization phase or the speed of acquisition of market share in a digital innovation project. There are two possible approaches:

1. To address late-stage funding shortfalls (i.e. fundraising in excess of $30–40 million and $100 million to achieve unicorn status). Create ten late-stage funds managing at least $1 billion each. Another solution here is to act with constant legislation, to move millions of dollars to these innovative enterprises. One question remains: how? A first path is outlined with the establishment of a Tech Investment Label, based in particular on employee savings. Raising such funds would then enable start-ups to be floated on the stock market, a necessary step: all the world's technology leaders today, particularly American and Chinese, have been backed by venture capital funds until maturity, then floated on the stock market.
2. Stimulate shareholder demand for shares in start-ups or other innovative enterprises. The emergence of global-tech funds, such as those that exist on the Nasdaq, should be advocated here. These funds are managed by experts in the new technologies and business models carried by these innovative enterprises. The emergence of these funds therefore requires both financial resources and human skills. The objective is ambitious: to launch five to ten funds averaging 10 billion dollars in total within 3 years. The financing would rely here more largely on institutional investors (8 billion dollars) with, once again, a work of conviction, this time carried out with individuals, to make national-Tech a new category of investment established and recognized.

Also, the research tax credit remains highly appreciated by businesses to finance their R&D efforts. However, the RTC should be better adapted to the digital sector. Innovations in the digital field are based less on technological innovations than on innovations in use. However, the eligibility criteria of the EIF should be clarified so that young digital enterprises know very precisely whether and how much they can benefit from it. How do the knowledge creation criteria apply to the creation of an algorithm, iterations and software development? This simplification of the rules would also benefit enterprises in the start-up phase, which here too do not always have sufficient human resources to conduct and understand the cumbersome procedures involved in qualifying for this tax credit.

On the buyout of technology nuggets and the financing of innovation, there are fairly strong differences of opinion on this subject between those who consider that the vast majority of technology nuggets are bought out and integrated by large groups and those who defend the opposite and show a certain optimism. It has to be said that there is room for progress here, without falling into alarmist rhetoric about some kind of "exodus" of entrepreneurs and patents. In this respect, initiatives must be taken through the strategic information and economic security services of states to protect structuring start-ups from takeovers by finding national enterprises capable of buying their technologies. We must therefore take advantage of big data and artificial intelligence to detect threats to French economic interests.

The major digital enterprises, whether Facebook, Google or Cisco, have invested heavily in the countries, through innovation laboratories, funding for training programmes or even through start-up support programmes. We should not be naive enough to believe that these investments are disinterested. However, they also support ecosystems that sometimes struggle to find the funds needed for their growth. This is a strategy encouraged by the public authorities, who consider that the development of these start-ups is a national issue.

It would thus be detrimental to automatically oppose "foreign" funds and digital security, especially since this would be to misunderstand the strategies of these players, especially Americans. When it comes to takeovers, enterprises established on the digital market sometimes prefer to work with start-ups. This so-called give and take strategy works like this: in exchange for commercial support, enterprises gain access to state-of-the-art products and solutions. Furthermore, to consider that enterprises, particularly American ones, opt for exclusively predatory strategies would be to forget that the managers of start-ups or innovative enterprises have their own interests. Behind entrepreneurs, there are funds and investment strategies that need to increase their profitability and reap the benefits of their investments.

In other words, foreign funding should not be confused with the loss of assets, whether tangible or intangible. The example of Israel is striking in this regard: in order to develop its innovations and enterprises, Israel encourages foreign funds to invest through domestic funds so that they comply with national regulations and Israeli economic and sovereign interests are not threatened. Moreover, only a minority share of tech enterprises are actually bought out by American players. What gives the impression of a massive takeover is simply the fact that they are focusing on acquisitions of fast-growing enterprises with much higher valuations. This should therefore encourage the states to improve the tools for identifying and defending the most promising start-ups.

In addition, the consideration of complex technical subjects (economic mechanisms, legal constraints, financial circuits, technological and scientific developments, etc.) also means that recruitment and training must be constantly adapted to ensure understanding of the issues at stake, the relevance of sensor orientation and the quality of analysis in the production of services.

This observation, which applies to intelligence services, applies to all state administrations. Indeed, the subject of human resources is undoubtedly one of the most difficult when it comes to defending the digital security of states. To sum up, without qualified people, there can be no digital security. Independent authorities and public administrations are finding it increasingly difficult to recruit digital experts, computer scientists, mathematicians or engineers. In this context, how can we compete with the attractive salaries offered by these enterprises? How to keep a talent pool "in-house"?

While it may seem difficult to fight against enterprises offering salaries at least three to four times higher than those of the public service, this battle was far from being lost by the states. Administrations certainly have limited room for manoeuvre on remuneration: no free negotiation (e.g. making a counter-offer to a private sector proposal), no arrangements similar to participation or profit sharing and no benefits in kind linked to functions, but they must play on the elements they can control:

career progression, flexibility of working conditions and framework, creation of major future projects, etc.

Moreover, it seems that a sense of public action and pride in working on projects of national interest and future projects for digital security and for the nation remain a factor in attracting young talent and more experienced professionals. Organizations can also adopt more original solutions to retain their talent: one strategy would be to offer their staff, for example, to create their own start-ups by providing them with an incubation system and the possibility of forming industrial partnerships.

A Pact law should thus include provisions to encourage researchers to move more to the private sector, in particular by making it easier for them to participate in the conduct of a project in enterprises or to set up their own enterprises. The procedures should be flexible: authorization given by the institution employing the researcher, the possibility for the researcher to retain a share of his or her company after reintegration into a public body and the possibility of devoting up to 50% of working time to the enterprise.

Funds should also be devoted to the training of researchers in entrepreneurship by supporting training programmes and granting public support to winners of innovation competitions so that they can bring their products to the market more quickly. However, these factors of optimism are fragile, and without additional effort on the part of governments, the public sectors could quickly lose their pull.

There is also a civic issue here: the higher education system in several countries is financed through taxation. How can we ensure that the students who are trained there do not go directly to work for the digital giants, specialists in tax optimization? At least by creating attractive opportunities to capture this talent, through major innovation projects and by being aware of the strategies employed by the digital giants. For example, the latter are forging partnerships with schools to take on large contingents of trainees within their entities: this is a way for them to identify the most promising talent and retain this workforce, with the promise of recruitment after graduation.

In the absence of in-house skills, the use of contract workers is increasingly common for these highly qualified and specialized professions. Until now, two conditions had to be met to recruit a contract worker, for a fixed-term contract of 3 years renewable in some countries:

(a) Where there was no corps of officials capable of performing the corresponding functions
(b) When the nature of the functions or the needs of the services justified it for category A posts

With the aim of making contract posts more attractive, a circular should facilitate the use of contracts of indefinite duration, when this proves to be a sufficient motivating factor and when the public employer has demonstrated the long-term employability of the profile sought. However, this is far from sufficient: for highly qualified staff with such sought-after profiles, this contract is not necessarily the first entry criterion. If states are not able to attract the best talent, there will be no digital security. We need to change managerial practices, make the flow of information more fluid and involve staff in decision-making through digital solutions. This is a change in managerial paradigm.

Rather optimistic about state funding tools, it should be considered that the next two essential steps in the development of an ecosystem favourable to start-ups and digital enterprises will be (i) to get research and industry to work together more and (ii) to support the transformation of the production system through innovation by encouraging partnerships between start-ups and traditional enterprises.

Despite repeated efforts by governments to increase the porosity between the academic and industrial worlds, it is forced to note the failure of this public policy in many countries. Bridging this gap is nevertheless a key issue if states wish to develop breakthrough innovations and control technologies that will enable them to preserve their digital security. Weak links between research and business are not a "national evil": at the level of technically advanced countries, these vertical chains are being set up much more quickly. In most countries, the process seems to be more "artisanal" and is usually based on historical and trusting relationships between a research centre and a company.

In view of these observations, without going back on the high level of recruitment requirements for the managers of structures aimed at promoting research partnerships, two proposals should be supported to improve the governance of innovation and the links between public research establishments and enterprises: a better involvement of enterprises within public research establishments, to better take into account their expectations and thus facilitate collaborative projects, for example, through a steering committee; and the creation of a single point of contact for enterprises within each establishment and an Internet portal for everything concerning interactions between enterprises and public research.

It may seem surprising, when talking about digital security, to see the importance of the efforts made by some foreign enterprises to support training and research programmes. Thus, they accompany the training in digital professions and uses of digital technology of several hundred thousand people, at all ages of training. Here again, enterprises, including foreign enterprises, benefit from this. A system that is highly appreciated by enterprises should be that of doctoral students (Industrial Agreements for Training through Research).

It aims to develop public-private partnership research: the project is defined by the enterprise, the public establishment oversees the partnership, the enterprise recruits the doctoral student, and part of his or her remuneration is provided by the state. This framework could be extended to post-doctoral researchers and made more flexible (e.g. the 3-year period is sometimes too long in view of the enterprise's strategy). In order to defend digital security, rapid action is needed in all fields where states today find themselves weakened, bypassed and competing. This is the aim of this book.

Chapter 16
Conclusion

At the end of this book on the governance of digital risks, some will say it is "too much"; others will find it "too precise" and, finally, "utopian" or "excessively technical," according to readers with opposing but also critical opinions. But today, faced with the scale and complexity of the digital risk, the author regrets putting an end to this book when so many other ideas come to him.

To start with, this one: the digital risk, once analysed, can be an opportunity for creative approaches with significant spin-offs. It is on this condition that the risk can avoid becoming a danger. But this prerequisite for understanding, which is the only way to grasp the digital tool properly, requires new attitudes on the part of everyone, in both their private and social lives, including their professional life, possibly within enterprises, especially those considered to be of vital importance.

Until now, humanity has believed that it is putting digital technology at its service. Today, digital developments are such that a shift has begun to take place: digital technology is shaping a different humanity, hyper-connected but even more fragile, relying on protections whose apparent power is in danger of disappointing. This is why it was necessary to test the theoretical potential for solidity, resistance and resilience of the particularly sensitive cogs of modern societies, namely the very special enterprises that make up the vitally important operators, focusing first on two sectors, telecommunications and energy.

This examination has revealed the extreme interweaving of these operators in the social fabric and the impossibility of reinforcing digital security only around them, while at the same time they are the lifeblood of society, of which they illustrate only the most obvious fragility. It has also been observed that digital security is not simply to be expected from various hardware, software, antivirus or firewalls in the face of other hardware, software, etc., since the major vulnerabilities lie in people. The most successful digital attacks are based on the weakness of this technological link.

Therefore, to reduce the digital risk, it is a question of education, awareness raising, acquisition of reflexes and knowledge of how to behave in the face of the digital world rather than a digital science or technology imposing its binary logic. In order

W. Amedzro St-Hilaire, *Digital Risk Governance*,
https://doi.org/10.1007/978-3-030-61386-0_16

to be in control of himself, the digital man, who is at the same time increased and decreased, 1 then 0 in turn, must question himself on his relationship to the world, on the digital security from which he can expect protection and initiatives at an accelerated pace compared to previous societal evolutions.

These questions must be thought out on the basis of analyses from multiple horizons and filtered through new, original, multidisciplinary discussion forums. Some are already in place. Such a dialogue has been modestly sketched out in recent research on the issue. It must now be actively pursued, particularly in the worlds of education and business.

For your information, at the beginning of the investigations to write this book, it appeared that security flaws, related to hardware, attacks and also behaviour, could not be totally dissociated from their environment and only drew attention to the identical but even more gaping flaws, existing in subsidiaries, subcontractors and customers of strategic enterprises for the states (not to mention the daily users of digital technology who are the staff of enterprises).

In any case, it seems obvious that the omnipresence of digital technology in today's social and individual life makes its security a major issue. The interweaving of digital networks, their impact and their vulnerabilities make it necessary to have a global understanding of the requirements of digital security. This is why the strategies below present an a priori complex architecture, which is the only one capable of rising to the changing challenges to be met in record time.

This construction will allow a different understanding of the concept of digital security, identify its limits, introduce confidence and propose ways to give economic extensions to the innovative ideas that are essential to implement. In addition, after a first series of general and rather political strategies, a vademecum of digital security strategies for enterprises is proposed.

(I) Developing a digital culture: massive computer training and information for all age groups in all social environments

Digital education within the education system, from nursery school to higher education, throughout life – including through continuing education, particularly in vocational fields:

- Training to understand what digital is rather than just learning to use digital tools
- Teaching digital symbols, the basics of coding and programming and the principles of encryption

Educating about security:

- Teaching computer science at school: including computer security through computer hygiene rules and training in digital risk.
- Higher education curricula: strengthen the means of university training in cybersecurity and introduce training modules in computer security including computer hygiene, including the validation of diploma courses in this discipline.
- Promote other types of training, including experimental training.
- Create a research centre with European ambitions in the field of civil cybersecurity, in addition to the military centres.

- Initial and continuing training of civil servants and magistrates in the field of justice and civil security: include raising awareness of digital risk and digital security.

Introduce a licence for the ability to use digital technology in complete security in enterprises – a kind of digital driving licence, ensuring that its holders are regularly upgraded to cope with the very rapid changes in this sector (possible economic spin-offs).

- Carry out prevention campaigns on the theme of computer security aimed at the general public and professionals alike:
- Broadcasting digital security awareness programmes on radio, television and at prime time and ensuring their presence on the Internet.
- Raise awareness among users and managers, using platforms for demonstrating computer attacks and resistance tests (possible economic spin-offs).

(II) Ensuring the conditions for digital independence to preserve digital security

- Develop computer attack detection equipment (benefiting from funding from the Future Investment Program) and high-security laboratories (possible economic spin-offs).
- Define circles of confidence appropriate to digital security.
- Develop a French cybersecurity doctrine for use by businesses.
- Establish a unified framework conducive to the security of citizens' data.
- Create the equivalent of a sovereign Google just like China, India and Russia, which are currently developing their own Internets (for questions of languages and alphabets, etc.).
- To subject to national laws enterprises managing servers on the national territory and the clients of enterprises managing servers outside the national territory.
- Insofar as the law does not allow solutions to be found to the problems encountered, for example, in the case of widespread espionage by French diplomats and industrialists, authorize specialized laboratories, both civilian and military, to carry out offensive research in the dual domain of cyber security.
- Strengthen teams working on computer cryptology and virology and give them, including in university laboratories, the ability to unblock operating systems, unlock, disassemble software, check computer flows and reverse engineer to better understand the nature of threats in order to give them the means to trace flows carrying malicious software.

(III) Providing the means for digital security through better cooperation between stakeholders

- Create a forum for digital exchange bringing together engineers, politicians and administrators to develop a digital culture within the political and administrative sphere.
- Establish cooperation between industrialists, the defence community and the academic world to develop and implement a medium- and long-term national cyber security strategy to deal with attacks.

- Broaden the powers of security agencies by giving them regulatory and injunctive powers.
- Encourage, on all national territories, the development of trusted actors specialized in computer security (possible economic spin-offs).

(IV) Building a digital right based on virtuous national provisions and practices

- Amend the public procurement code so that responses to calls for tenders do not reveal a company's entire information system (possible economic spin-offs).
- Better organize the preservation of evidence of a digital crime.
- Reform states legislation so as to impose the level of protection and the security reference system of strategic enterprises on the small- and medium-sized enterprises (SMEs) linked to them (subsidiaries, suppliers, subcontractors) – possible economic spin-offs.
- Imagine a data right, after a broad citizen consultation, to:
  - Impose on the Internet the respect of the presumption of innocence and of the contradictory
  - Regulate the right to dereferencing and to oblivion for personal data
  - Extend the duration of prescriptions related to computer crimes where the damage continues
  - Set the starting date of the statute of limitations for computer crimes at the date of discovery of the crime by the victim

(V) Parliamentary assemblies, local and regional authorities and administrations

- Raise the awareness of local and regional authorities and administrations about IT security.
- Make parliaments in the countries an exemplary place of awareness of digital vulnerabilities.

(VI) For business use

A company's digital security depends only on itself: it is the result of a thoughtful and evolutionary construction and cannot automatically result from external service providers, the purchase or installation of equipment.

This construction can be ordered around the following ten aspects:

1. The prerequisites for the digital security of the enterprise
2. The general principles to be respected in order to ensure the enterprise's digital security
3. The construction of the enterprise's digital security
4. Continuous critical appraisal of the digital security structure
5. The enterprise's computer equipment
6. The distinctions between:
   - Digital for personal use and digital for professional use
   - The enterprise's permanent staff and other digital users
   - The distinction between digital use within the enterprise or outside

7. The principles specific to the use of each digital network or equipment, including cloud computing
8. The digital security reflexes to be acquired
9. The assessment of the enterprise's digital security
10. Building business resilience after a digital attack

Some of the above ten aspects need to be strengthened for vital operators and their partners.

1. The prerequisites for digital security:

   - Classify data according to its confidentiality in order to apply an appropriate security regime; encrypt sensitive data, especially on nomadic stations or equipment that may be lost. Encryption products for the entire system (full or disk encryption) or a subset (partition encryption). Full disk encryption mechanisms are the most effective and do not require identification of the files to be encrypted.
   - Base IT security on a comprehensive, in-depth approach (rather than perimeter protection), using a stack of security bricks, and on social engineering.
   - Consider, on a case-by-case basis, the best technical means to be used for the transmission of information according to its degree of confidentiality and urgency (new profession).
   - Give priority to digital security over continuous connection or immediate recharging.
   - Adopt behaviour adapted to the level of security of equipment and networks.

2. The construction of the enterprise's digital security:

   - Review company organization charts so as to ensure that digital security managers have direct access to the enterprise's management and therefore the power to impose the necessary security standards or habits. Identify the position of IT systems security manager as high in a career path.
   - Raise the awareness of decision-makers about IT security, in particular the need to use only secure mobile phones or even to set up meeting rooms that are opaque to the airwaves (Faraday's cage principle).
   - Set up a permanent alert and reaction chain known to all parties involved, including one or more reference contacts trained in reaction.
   - Train managers and staff, subcontractors, suppliers and customers in IT security.
   - Communicate with other strategic enterprises on digital risk.
   - Establish a global security plan (for management and industrial IT and the applications used) and extend compliance to subsidiaries and subcontractors.
   - Set up, from their conception, a controlled partitioning of internal IT networks. Create a subnetwork protected by a specific connection gateway for

workstations or servers containing information important to the life of the enterprise.

- Prohibit all access to the Internet from administration accounts by equipping administrators with two separate positions.
- Verify the watertightness of so-called closed networks.
- Systematically use secure applications and protocols and therefore ban unsecure protocols (telnet, FTP, POP, SMTP, HTTP) and use only their secure equivalents (SSH, SFTP, POPS, SMTPS, HTTPS, etc.).
- Multiply data storage sites.
- Have rights management of user and administrator profiles on workstations and, above all, on company services that is described in the enterprise's security policy.
- Reserve administrator rights only to authorized persons, including on mobile phones, devices such as 3D printers and connected objects.
- Never give users administrative privileges – regardless of their hierarchical position in the enterprise.
- Identify by name each person with access to the system and remove generic and anonymous accounts and access.
- Establish a comprehensive inventory of privileged and generic accounts and keep it up to date.
- Separate the administration network from the users' work network (physical network partitioning or, failing that, logical cryptographic partitioning or, at the very least, logical partitioning by VLAN) and keep the administration workstations up to date.
- Centralize in a single controllable access point the enterprise's Internet access and interconnections with a minimum number of partner networks, the use of Wi-Fi and telephone (control, monitoring and analysis of logs).
- Introduce mandatory mapping of Supervisory Control and Data Acquisition (SCADA).
- Disconnect SCADA systems from the Internet, which means that the direct updating of systems via the Internet will not be necessary but will be carried out by means of an isolated and controlled server after the update has been downloaded.
- Use various antivirus software in order to ensure a kind of biodiversity of protection.
- Offer SMEs "All-in-One" digital security solutions.
- Study the possibility of insuring digital risk as well as possible.
- Continuous critical appraisal of the digital structure put in place.
- Set up an operational security centre carrying out permanent monitoring and including detection systems in the networks, crisis cells and own intervention teams.
- Working alongside the information systems managers, have an operational line attached to the IT production teams.

- Draw up the mapping (IP addresses, domain names, machine names, software, network interfaces, etc.) of the IT installation, keep it up to date as part of a systems deployment policy and do not store it on the network.
- Map the risks of its information systems and the network of its subcontractors, suppliers, customers and staff in order to assess the degree of IT vulnerability of its activities.
- Frequently audit or have audited the configuration of the central directory (Active Directory, Windows or LDAP), in particular to check whether the access rights to data of the enterprise's key people are correctly positioned.
- Install probes on the network in order to assess, in real time, what is happening and have the attack detection probes managed by qualified service providers.
- Within the framework of system and network supervision, concretely define the events triggering an alert to be processed within 24 hours (connection of a user outside his usual hours or declared presence massive data transfer outside the enterprise, etc.).
- Define the frequency, analysis methods and consequences (alerts) of events in the enterprise's logs.

3. The enterprise's computer equipment:

- Investing in the security of information systems (possible economic spin-offs).
- Set up a homogeneous level of security for the entire computer population (deactivate unnecessary services, etc.).
- Use an IT asset management tool for the deployment of security policies and equipment updates.
- Purchase only hardware and use only suppliers referenced by the ANSSI (possible economic benefits).
- Set up procedures for the destruction or recycling of IT media at the end of their life.

4. Computer hardware

- Integrate digital security into the design of hardware and applications and conduct risk assessments of hardware (potential economic impact).
- Always match technical security with security in use.
- Subject equipment manufacturers to specific security obligations.
- Quickly certify locally distributed critical software and equipment (possible economic benefits).
- Correct faulty software.
- Prohibit remote data capture.
- Connected objects: define protocols for their manufacture and use, including information for their users on the possibility of disconnecting them, and promote research into the security of these objects.

5. The three sets of distinctions to be made between digital for personal use and digital for professional use:

    • Do not use personal digital tools for professional use – not even USB sticks, but rather give professional phones for incidental personal use.
    • Prohibit any loading of non-professional software on workstations (USB keys, external disks, etc.).
    • When using workstations at home, guarantee them a level of security that does not compromise the security of the enterprise.

6. Between the enterprise's permanent staff and other digital users:

    • It is essential to use robust mechanisms for access to the enterprise's premises.
    • Develop and apply procedures for the arrival and departure of information system users (staff, trainees, suppliers, customers, etc.).
    • Do not leave any internal network access sockets or cable ducts accessible in areas open to the public (waiting rooms, corridors, cupboards where printers, display screens, surveillance cameras, telephones, network sockets, etc. are connected).
    • Rigorously protect keys and badges allowing access to the premises and alarm codes (keys and badges to be retrieved, alarm codes to be changed, keys and codes never to be given to outside service providers).

7. Between the use of digital in the enterprise and outside:

    • Check that no network equipment (industrial or supervision equipment, network switches, routers, servers, printers, etc.) has an administration interface accessible from the Internet.
    • Secure interconnection gateways to the Internet so as to ensure a separation between Internet access, the service area and the internal network.
    • Prohibit, wherever possible, remote connections on client workstations and, otherwise, apply the security recommendations relating to remote assistance available on the ANSSI website.
    • If the enterprise's Intranet is used from the outside, implement secure access via Virtual Private Networks (VPN).
    • Authorize remote access to the enterprise network, including for the network administrator, only from company workstations equipped with strong authentication mechanisms protecting the integrity and confidentiality of exchanges.

8. Principles specific to the use of each network or digital equipment:

    • Avoid the use of wireless infrastructure (Wi-Fi). At the very least, partition the Wi-Fi access network from the rest of the information system (a controlled gateway providing interconnection with the main network) and encrypt the Wi-Fi network.
    • Encrypt Wi-Fi networks using WPA Enterprise (Secure Wi-Fi).

• Proscribe protection mechanisms based on a shared key.
• Avoid the use of powerline carrier technologies (PLC).
• Define a security policy for updating software components and workstations and strictly apply it to the entire fleet.
• Update software securely to resist viruses from their publisher's site; keep informed of vulnerabilities and updates; if a component cannot be updated, it should not be used.
• Define rules for the management and use of personal messaging.
• Technically prohibit the connection of removable media.
• Manage nomadic terminals according to a security policy at least as strict as that applicable to fixed workstations. This often requires the reinforcement of certain security functions (disk encryption, reinforced authentication, etc.).
• Leave mobile phones outside rooms where confidential meetings are held in enterprises that do not have a security policy for mobiles in guest mode, which not all administration software can do today; ban all Internet connections in these rooms and consider the creation of secure rooms (Faraday cages).
• Define rules for the use of printers and photocopiers: physical presence of the applicant to start printing, destruction of documents forgotten on printers or photocopiers and shredding of documents rather than throwing them in the bin.

9. Digital security reflexes to be acquired:

• Remind users, at least every year, of the basic rules of IT hygiene: information, which is sensitive by nature, requires exemplary behaviour (compliance with the security policy, systematic locking of sessions not in immediate use, non-connection of personal equipment, non-disclosure and non-reuse of passwords to third parties, reporting of suspicious events, arranging visits) (possible economic spin-offs).
• Signature of a charter for the use of IT resources by each user.

10. Digital identity:

• Carry out a digital identity project based on the SIM card.
• Promote the development of RFID chips, barcodes and other identification, referencing and classification devices, to bring about the emergence of an open and abundant market for devices for the recognition and security of objects, transactions and uses (possible economic spin-offs).
• Immediately carry out all updates of antivirus, firewalls, etc. to ensure the security of your data.
• Passwords:

– Define rules for choosing and sizing passwords according to the degree of sensitivity of the accesses to be protected.

  - Do not store passwords in clear text on computer systems or use automatic password backup mechanisms.
  - Change passwords every 6 months and block accounts until this rule is effectively enforced.
  - Systematically renew the default authentication elements on devices.
  - Give preference to smart card authentication requiring a PIN code.

- Digital clouds:

  - Prefer its own data storage centres (possible economic spin-offs).
  - Only store in digital clouds data that is not very confidential.

- Diversify data storage locations (potential economic benefits).
- Move from the concept of a digital safe, which does not offer sufficient security guarantees to entrust all your assets to it, to active risk management by keeping the current backup procedures, since it has become impossible to control the tool.
- Assess the reliability of a cloud based on three criteria: availability, integrity and confidentiality.
- Store only in clouds that allow data authentication and encryption.
- Create and promote a European label for data storage (possible economic spin-offs).
- Develop controlled clouds with French suppliers (possible economic spin-offs).
- Create secure, encrypted and processed national messaging offers (possible economic spin-offs).
- Location in one's own country may allow on-site monitoring by the regulator (possible economic spin-offs).
- Reduce dependence on clouds, thanks to French or European tools based on the dynamics of open source (possible economic spin-offs).
- Favour clouds using European routers and consider the manufacture of European processors (possible economic spin-offs).
- Digital security can be facilitated by equipment, qualified services and national redundancies (possible economic spin-offs).
- Take out an insurance policy in the event of the use of the digital cloud (possible economic benefits).

11. Assessing the digital security of the enterprise.

    - Conduct intrusion tests including local engineering. Consequently, update the IT security policy (possible economic spin-offs).
    - Carry out regular IT crisis exercises.
    - Carry out regular security audits of IT rules (possible economic spin-offs).

- The annual audit of information system security must be accompanied by an action plan, frequent meetings to monitor this plan and a dashboard of the progress of the actions of this plan taken into account at the highest level.
- Have the possibility of having the risk taken assessed using commercially available equipment.
- Training in hacking.

12. Building business resilience after a digital attack:

    - In the event of an attack on the enterprise's site, always have the name of the developer, access keys, passwords and how to obtain logs available.
    - Set up an incident transmission network to inform the authorities of strategic intentions and other parties at the same level of the attacks suffered.
    - Record all logs and place them on a separate backup in order to make them available in the event of an attack, including for mobile phones and connected objects (possible economic repercussions).
    - Anticipate the loss of archives by classifying them by backup hierarchy (current, intermediate, definitive archives, distinguishing sensitive archives in each category) and ensuring their readability over time by reading devices (possible economic spin-offs).

13. The use of the digital cloud to store archives does not exempt from this precaution.

    – Complement this approach by simulating the loss of archives and exercises to restore them (possible economic benefits).
    – Have an up-to-date IT business continuity and recovery plan in place to safeguard critical business data.
    – Periodically and automatically back up sensitive corporate data in a separate location from the servers in operation.
    – Fully address the infection of a machine (How did the malicious code get there? How many workstations are compromised? What information has been disclosed?) including feedback and capitalization.
    – Take the following immediate measures: isolate the infected machines from the network, do not electrically shut them down, copy the memories and hard disks and completely reinstall the machine after copying the disks.

14. Computer incidents:

    - Provide the information system with an administration structure capable of protecting it from a chain reaction in the event of an attack.
    - Define a procedure for small- and medium-sized enterprises, local authorities and individuals to follow in order to inform them of the local actors to turn to in the event of an incident (possible economic repercussions).
    - Train users to analyse and respond to antivirus incidents.
    - React to a virus in less than 24 h.

• Build French tools for analysing computer incidents (possible economic repercussions). Encourage the development of these tools at national level by young innovative enterprises and mid-sized enterprises. The IT security market is in full development, and countries have a network of enterprises that are well placed to become major players, thanks to schools of mathematics and computer science.

• Encourage the experiences of police and justice services to be taken into account.

Glossary

Access control Certifying that only authorized access is given to assets (both physical and electronic). For physical assets, access control may be required for a facility or restricted area (e.g., screening visitors and materials at entry points, escorting visitors). For IT assets, access controls may be required for networks, systems, and information (e.g., restricting users on specific systems, limiting account privileges).

Accountable COMSEC material COMSEC material requiring control and accountability within the National COMSEC Material Control System (NCMCS) as directed by its Accounting Legend Code (ALC). Control and accountability is required because transfer or disclosure of this material could be detrimental to Canada's national interest. Also known as ACM.

Administrative privileges The permissions that allow a user to perform certain functions on a system or network, such as installing software and changing configuration settings.

Advanced persistent threat (APT) An advanced persistent threat is deployed by cyber-criminals who have a high level of expertise and important resources to infiltrate a network. They usually use this type of attack to target large organizations seeking to retrieve economic or financial information. In some cases, they might even try to use this form of attack to stop or block a company's program or agenda. Since an advanced persistent threat is executed over long periods of time, it is difficult to be detected and blocked by average users and requires a specialized security program or a team of experts to find a solution.

Adware Adware is a type of software that delivers ads on your system. Usually, these pop-up ads appear while visiting sites, like annoying pop-up ads or banners. They come in "bundle" versions with other applications. Most types of adware are not dangerous, maybe a bit annoying since they deliver pop-up ads while visiting a website, but there is another dangerous form of adware that delivers spyware, which can track down your activity and retrieve sensitive information. For this reason, users must not download an application from unsafe websites

W. Amedzro St-Hilaire, *Digital Risk Governance*,
https://doi.org/10.1007/978-3-030-61386-0

and pay attention to software that comes bundled. Less serious issues caused by adware can be slow down problems or too many annoying pop-up ads that can fill your computer screen. Not to mention the stability issues which could affect your system. To remove malicious adware or spyware from the system, check online for specialized tools like Malwarebytes or Spybot.

Angler Exploit Kit Angler emerged in 2013 and now is one of the most famous and sophisticated exploit kits in the cybercriminal community. It features aggressive tactics to avoid being detected by security products and it's capable of exploiting a vast array of software vulnerabilities in order to infect unsuspecting victims with malware. Because it's usually spread through drive-by downloads, Angler is extremely difficult to detect and can infect users without any interaction. It also features fileless infection capabilities, and it's able to deliver a variety of payloads, from ransomware, to Trojans, rootkits and backdoor Trojans. Its prevalence is also consolidated by the fact that cyber criminals don't need advanced technical skills to use it and the fact that it's a constantly evolving threat.

Anomaly-based detection Anomaly-based intrusion detection is a new technology that protects systems or networks against malicious and cyber-criminal activities using a heuristics-based detection, and less the classic signature-based methods. This detection type is still new and delivers a high number of false positives. The problem is that a system must recognize abnormal activities and flag them as dangerous, but it is yet difficult to instruct a computer on what exactly a normal usage of the system is.

Anonymizing proxy An anonymizing proxy is a way to hide your online activity and/or make it really difficult to be disclosed by third parties, like countries that apply Internet censorship. These proxy servers act like an intermediary connection between your computer and the final target. From an outsider's point of view, they access those web locations and hide your computer's IP from further identification. Usually, they are used to access freely Internet content under strict censorship.

Anti-malware The general usage of this term—anti-malware—refers to a number of software programs and applications that are capable to detect and remove malware from individual systems or from larger networks. Though the term is usually used in connection with classic antivirus products, the anti-malware abilities can include anti-spyware, anti-phishing, or anti-spam solutions. Lately, the term has spread to name specialized software that fights data stealing malware delivered by online criminals.

Anti-spam Anti-spam, or better said the anti-spam techniques, is employed by special software programs that fight spam, which is unsolicited e-mail. The spam problem needs to be solved not only at the individual level of each user but at an even greater level, that of system administrators that need to secure thousands of computers from spam. Spamming attempts become a greater problem for everybody because this is one of the main ways to deliver the most dangerous malware in the wild and additional phishing threats.

Anti-spoofing Anti-spoofing techniques are used in order to stop the DDoS (Distributed Denial-of-Service) attacks that affect so many websites. To deliver these attacks, hackers are "spoofing" IP addresses, from where they send a great number of requests. When the website server attempts to reply to the requests, it gets stalled by waiting to access servers that actually do not exist. In this case again, it is difficult to detect the source of the attacks; therefore, the only available solution is to use a software that can detect these fake IP addresses and refuse the connection.

Antispyware software Anti-spyware technology is used in detecting and blocking spyware attempts. Spyware is a type of software that allows advertisers or online criminals to discover personal data from a computer, without the user's permission. Spyware can infect your computer if you visit certain websites by pop-up messages that ask you to download an application or program. If such a software gets on your computer, it will attempt to track down your online activity and send that information to third parties. Usually, spyware is detected when it starts using system resources, finally affecting the overall stability.

Antivirus software Antivirus software, sometimes called an anti-malware program, appeared a few years ago to protect computers from viruses and other threats that affected the initial modern computers. Nowadays, antivirus programs protect users from more advanced online dangers, like ransomware, rootkits, Trojans, spyware, phishing attacks, or botnets. Nevertheless, the name "antivirus" was preserved for these software solutions that protect computers from a large number of threats.

Artificial intelligence A subfield of computer science that develops intelligent computer programs to behave in a way that would be considered intelligent if observed in a human (e.g., solve problems, learn from experience, understand language, interpret visual scenes).

Asymmetric key Two related keys (a public key and a private key) that perform complementary operations, such as encrypt and decrypt or generate signatures.

Atmos Atmos is a form of financial malware emerged from Citadel (which, in turn, is based on the ZeuS leaked code). Atmos has been active since late 2015, but there was no serious uptick in activity until April 2016.

Attack (online) Online attacks come in many forms and target average individuals and large corporations alike. They usually attempt to steal financial and commercial information and disclose important data, and sometimes they are delivered to simply destroy data or block access to a server. One of the most famous online attacks have been deployed in 2014 against Sony Pictures, but many others have made the news ever since.

Attack signature An attack signature is a unique piece of information that is used to identify a particular cyberattack aimed at exploiting a known computer system or a software vulnerability. Attack signatures include certain paths used by cyber criminals in their malicious compromise attempts. These paths can define a certain piece of malicious software or an entire class of malware.

Authentication A process or measure used to verify a user's identity.

Authentication The process of authentication (or identification) of an individual is usually based on a username and a password. This process is used to allow access to an online location or resource to the right individual by validating the identification.

Authorization Access privileges granted to a user, program, or process.

Autorun worm Autorun worms are malware programs that use the Windows AutoRun feature to launch automatically when the device, usually a USB drive, is plugged into a PC. AutoPlay, a similar technology, has been used recently to deliver the infamous Conficker worm. Microsoft has set on new systems the AutoRun setting to off, so this issue should disappear in the future.

Availability The ability for the right people to access the right information or systems when needed. Availability is applied to information assets, software, and hardware (infrastructure and its components). Implied in its definition is that availability includes the protection of assets from unauthorized access and compromise.

Backdoor Trojan A backdoor Trojan is a way to take control of a system without permission. Usually, a backdoor Trojan poses as a legitimate program spreading though phishing campaigns and fooling users into clicking a malicious link or accessing malware on a website. Once the system is infected, the Trojan can access sensitive files, send and receive data online, and track the browsing history. To avoid this type of infection, you should keep the system up-to-date with the latest patches and have strong anti-malware protection.

Backdoor An undocumented, private, or less-detectible way of gaining remote access to a computer, bypassing authentication measures, and obtaining access to plaintext.

Backup A backup is an exact copy of your files, your system files, or any other system resources you need to protect. This precaution is necessary for all types of unpredictable events, like a system crash or when you remove or lose those files. The backup is supposed to be independent from your system and be used only when necessary. There are also cases when the system or those files become infected and you need to recover them. Or when the system is blocked by a ransomware.

Baseline security controls The minimum mandatory protective mechanisms outlined by the Treasury Board of Canada Secretariat policy instruments to be used in interdepartmental IT security functions and information systems.

Baseline security An IT security baseline check is a set of basic measures and objectives that any service or network system should be able to meet. This baseline methodology is usually a set of security steps that are implemented and imposed in an organization's IT security level.

Beaconing A common technique in which a threat actor uses malware to connect infrastructure to another system or network, bypassing firewall restrictions on incoming traffic.

Black list An access control list used to deny specific items (e.g., applications, email addresses, domain names, IP addresses) known to be harmful.

Blackhat hacker Skilled computer users with malicious intents, they seek to compromise the security of a person or organization for personal gain. Blackhat hackers frequently specialize, for example, in malware development, spam delivery, exploit discovery, DDoS attacks, and more. Not all blackhat hackers use the malware they developed or the exploits they discover. Some just find them and sell the know-how to the highest bidder. Their favorite targets are financial information (such as credit card data or bank accounts), personal information (like email accounts and passwords), as well as sensitive company data (such as employee/client databases).

Blacklisting To blacklist in IT security means to organize a list of senders that have developed malicious activities, like phishing or spam. At the same time, a blacklist can contain a number of applications or programs that should not be launched on a system. For a firewall solution, blacklisting refers to a number of IP addresses that have been blocked and to which the system cannot connect for safety reasons.

Blended threat A blended threat is a widely used term that describes an online attack that spreads by using a combination of methods, usually a combination of worms, Trojans, viruses, and other malware. This combination of malware elements that uses multiple attack vectors increases the damage and makes individual systems and networks difficult to defend.

Blockchain A blockchain is a write-only database, dispersed over a network of interconnected computers, that uses cryptography to create a tamperproof public record of transactions. Because blockchain technology is transparent, secure, and decentralized, a central actor cannot alter the public record.

Boot sector malware A boot sector malware is capable of replicating the original boot sector of the system so that at the following system boot-up the malware may become active. This way, the bootkit in the boot sector manages to hide its presence before the operating system can load up. This is a clear advantage for the malware, which is loaded before the system and the anti-malware solution. Since it loads before the security solution, it can even disable it and make it useless against it. This type of infection is usually difficult to clean.

Bot Internet bots or web bots are software programs that perform automated tasks and specific operations. Though some bots serve harmless purposes in video games or online locations, there are a number of bots that can be employed in large networks, from where they can deliver malicious ads on popular sites or launch distributed online attacks against a number of designated targets.

Botnet A botnet is a network of infected computers that communicate with each other in order to perform the same malicious actions, like launching spam campaigns or distributed denial-of-service attacks. The network can be controlled remotely by online criminals to serve their interests, and, at the same time, this allows the hackers to avoid detection or legal actions by law agencies.

Boundary interface A network-layer interface between two zone interface points (ZIPs).

Browser hijacking Browser hijacking is the process of changing the default homepage or search engine in your web browser by a malicious program without your permission. The user can notice that the affected changes cannot be reversed and a security tool needs to be used against this type of software. It is not considered a serious threat to the overall system security, but it needs to be addressed fast since web browsing is affected.

Browser-based exploitation A misuse of legitimate browser components to execute malicious code. Simply visiting a website with hidden malicious code can result in exploitation.

Brute force attack A brute force attack is a technique used by hackers in which a high number of keywords or password combinations are tested in order to gain access to a site or a network. This is one of the main reasons users should set strong passwords.

Buffer overflow A buffer overflow takes place when a program or an application tries to store excess data in a temporary storage area (a buffer) and that extra information overflows into other parts of a computer's memory. This is something hackers took advantage from, and these types of attacks can lead to unauthorized code running or system crashes.

Bug A bug is a software flaw that produces an unexpected result that may affect the system's performance. Usually, a bug may cause system crashing or freezing. The main security issue that could appear is that bugs allow hackers to bypass access privileges or retrieve sensitive data from a network.

Bulk encryption Bulk encryption is a set of security protocols that provide the necessary means to encrypt and decrypt data transmissions in order to offer protection from security breaches and online theft.

Business Impact Analysis (BIA) Business Impact Analysis is an important key element of an organization's business continuity plan that detects vulnerabilities and analyzes their operational and financial impact on the overall business plan. According to the analysis, strategies are planned to minimize the detected risks.

BYOD BYOD (acronym for Bring Your Own Device) is a company policy by which employees are allowed to bring their own devices (laptops, smartphones, tablets, etc.) to work. This type of flexibility increases the number of vulnerabilities in a company's environment, since the devices are managed and secured individually.

Cache cramming Cache cramming is a technique to trick a browser into running malicious Java code from the local disk, instead of the Internet. The execution of local code (which runs with less permissions) enables online criminals access the target computer.

Cache A cache is a technology to store data and allow future requests to be served at a higher speed. This high-speed storage method is usually used for web pages and online documents, like HTML pages and images, to increase the loading speed and avoid unwanted lag.

Catfishing The process of creating a fake online profile in order to trick people into believing they are someone else. Catfishing is frequently done for financial gain. The impersonator fools the victim into believing there is a genuine relationship between the two, carried out through text or phone but never in person. At some point, the impersonator will ask for a large favor, usually monetary, with an attached promise that after this the two will finally meet face to face. Even after the favor is completed, the impersonator still finds reasons to not meet and will keep trying to extract money from the victim until he/she gives up.

Chargeware This form of scamming is usually associated with online porn. It is a method to manipulate the user into signing for unclear terms and conditions that overcharge the credit card and makes it difficult to unsubscribe.

Chief Information Officer (CIO) The Chief Information Officer is the title name of the person that is responsible for the information technology system in a company. The job responsibilities include planning the technology architecture, align corporate network to the business developed, and develop a secure financial management system for the company.

Ciphertext A cryptography term for encrypted information.

CISO CISO (acronym for Chief Information Security Officer) is a senior-level executive job in a company, in the IT, or cybersecurity department. A CISO's responsibilities include ensuring and maintaining adequate protection for the company's assets and technology, in terms of both strategy and development, to mitigate and manage cybersecurity risks. CSO (Chief Security Officer) is another name used for the same job.

Citadel Citadel is a form of financial malware which emerged in 2012, after the source code for the infamous ZeuS malware was leaked online. Because the code was open source, cyber criminals started improving it to get newer, more sophisticated, and stealthier malware types. Just like ZeuS/Zbot, Citadel aims to retrieve confidential information, especially banking and financial information, from the victim. On top of financial fraud, Citadel can also run different types of malware, such as ransomware or scareware, which makes it an advanced toolkit for cyber criminals.

Classified Information A Government of Canada label for specific types of sensitive data that, if compromised, could cause harm to the national interest (e.g., national defense, relationships with other countries, economic interests).

Clearing Applying logical techniques to sanitize data in all user-addressable storage locations to protect against simple ways of recovering data. This is done by overwriting data with a new value, or if overwriting is not supported, by using a menu option to reset the device to factory settings.

Cloud computing The use of remote servers hosted on the Internet. Cloud computing allows users to access a shared pool of computing resources (such as networks, servers, applications, or services) on demand and from anywhere. Users access these resources via a computer network instead of storing and maintaining all resources on their local computer.

Code injection The code injection technique is usually used by online attackers to change the course of execution of a computer program. This method is used by online criminals to spread malicious software by infecting legitimate websites with malicious code.

Command and control center A command and control center (C&C) is a network server that controls a large network of compromised systems. The malicious server is used by hackers to send and receive commands from and to the infected computers. Using this type of network, hackers can launch distributed denial-of-service attacks by instructing the computers to perform the same action.

Compromise The intentional or unintentional disclosure of information, which adversely impacts its confidentiality, integrity, or availability.

Compromising emanations Unintentional signals that, if intercepted and analyzed, would disclose the information emanating from any information processing system or equipment.

Computer abuse Computer abuse is the unethical use of a computer to launch online attacks, like phishing and malware delivery campaigns, sabotage, and cyberwar activities.

Computer forensics Computer forensics is connected to digital forensic science and is the practice by which digital data is collected and analyzed for legal purposes. The main goal is to identify, analyze, and present facts about digital information. The conclusions can be used in fight against cybercrime or for civil proceedings.

Computer Incident Response Team (CIRT) The Computer Incident Response Team investigates network security incidents that occur when unauthorized access takes place to network resources or protected data. Their job is to analyze how the incident took place and provide a response by discovering how the breach occurred and what information has been lost.

COMSEC account custodian The person responsible for the receipt, storage, access, distribution, accounting, disposal, and destruction of all COMSEC material charged to the COMSEC account. The custodian is appointed by the organization's COMSEC authority.

COMSEC incident An occurrence that threatens, or potentially threatens, the security of classified or protected Government of Canada information as it is being stored, processed, transmitted, or received.

COMSEC material An item designed to secure or authenticate telecommunications information (e.g., cryptographic keys, equipment, modules, devices, documents, hardware, firmware, or software the includes or describe cryptographic logic and other items that perform COMSEC functions).

COMSEC Communications security (COMSEC) is the discipline of preventing unauthorized access to telecommunications information in readable form, while still delivering the information to the intended recipients. COMSEC is comprised of multiple disciplines such as Cryptographic Security, EMSEC (Emission Security), Transmission Security, and Physical Security.

Confidentiality Confidentiality represents a set of rules or an agreement that limits access or restricts that access to certain types of information. When such an agreement is in place, information is disclosed to only those who are authorized to view it.

Controlled cryptographic item An unclassified secure telecommunications or information system, or any associated cryptographic component, governed by a set of control requirements in the National COMSEC Material Control System (NCMCS). The type of item is labelled in the NCMCS as a "controlled cryptographic item" or "CCI."

Cookie A cookie is a small text file which is placed on your computer when you visit a website. This cookie allows the website to keep track of your visit details and store your preferences. These cookies were designed to be helpful and increase the website speed the next time you access that location. At the same time, they are very useful for advertisers who can match the ads to your interests after they see your browsing history. Usually, cookies and temporary files may affect your privacy since they disclose your online habits, but it is possible to modify your web browser preferences and set a limit.

CoreBOT CoreBOT is a modular Trojan from the infostealer category. As the name says, CoreBOT was initially designed to collect and loot information from the infected computer or network. In time, CoreBOT quickly evolved and went to add other capabilities, such as browser-based web injects, real-time form-grabbing, man-in-the-middle attacks, etc. Now, its structure and tactics are similar to infamous financial malware strains, such as Dyreza or Neverquest. Its modular character makes CoreBOT appealing to cyber criminals because they can pack it with other types of malware and use it in complex cyberattacks.

Crimeware Crimeware is distinct from adware or spyware, and it's created for identity theft operations that use social engineering schemes to gain access to a user's online accounts. Crimeware is a growing issue for networks' security, as numerous types of malware look to steal valuable data from the systems. The retrieved information may be sent to other interested parties for a certain price.

Critical infrastructure Processes, systems, facilities, technologies, networks, assets, and services essential to the health, safety, security, or economic well-being of Canadians and the effective functioning of government. Critical infrastructure can be stand-alone or interconnected and interdependent within and across provinces, territories, and national borders. Disruptions of critical infrastructure could result in catastrophic loss of life, adverse economic effects, and significant harm to public confidence.

Cross-site scripting (XSS) Cross-site scripting (XSS) is a software vulnerability usually found in Web applications. This XSS allows online criminals to inject client-side script into pages that other users view. The cross-site scripting vulnerability can be employed at the same time by attackers to overwrite access controls. This issue can become a significant security risk unless the network administrator or the website owner doesn't take the necessary security means.

Cryptographic key A numerical value used in cryptographic processes, such as encryption, decryption, signature generation, and signature verification.

Cryptographic material All material, including documents, devices, and equipment, that contain cryptographic information and is essential to encrypting, decrypting, or authenticating communications.

Cryptography The study of techniques used to make plain information unreadable, as well as to convert it back to a readable form.

CryptoLocker CryptoLocker is a type of ransomware which emerged in 2013 and whose objective is to infect victims using PCs with Microsoft Windows installed. As is the case with most ransomware, the main distribution method is spam emails with a malicious attachment. CryptoLocker relies on external infrastructure (a botnet) to launch its attacks and, when activated, encrypts the files and data stored on the local device, but also those in cloud storage accounts, if, for example, the Dropbox account is synced locally on the affected PC. CryptoLocker then displays a message so the victims can know that paying a ransom in Bitcoins is necessary if they want to get the decryption key (which is stored on the servers controlled by the cyber criminals).

CryptoWall CryptoWall is a ransomware Trojan which emerged as a CryptoLocker variant. Like most data-stealing ransomware, CryptoWall spreads mainly through phishing and spam campaigns that invite users to click a malicious link or download and execute an email attachment. Moreover, in order to increase distribution, cyber criminals included CryptoWall code in websites ads. The ransomware, once executed, encrypts all the data on the victim's PC and any other PC tied to the first affected computer by the same network. The victim is then prompted to pay the ransom in Bitcoins so they can get the decryption key and regain access to their data. CryptoWall has already reached its fourth iteration, and there is reason to believe that this won't be the last one.

CSO CSO (acronym for Chief Security Officer) is a top-level executive in charge of ensuring the security of a company's personnel, financial, physical and digital assets. A CSO has both security and business-oriented objectives, as they are responsible for aligning cyber protection with the company's business goals. All security strategies, tactics, and programs have to be directed and approved by the CSO. CISO (acronym for Chief Information Security Officer) is another name used for the same job.

CTB Locker CTB Locker is a type of file-encrypting ransomware that emerged in 2014. Its name is an acronym and comes from Curve-Tor-Bitcoin Locker: Curve stands for its persistent cryptography based on elliptic curves, which encrypts the affected files with a unique RSA key; Tor comes from the malicious server placed in onion-domain (TOR), which is very difficult to take down; and Bitcoin refers to the possibility to pay the ransom in Bitcoins, avoiding normal payment systems that can lead back to online criminals. CTB Locker achieved very high infection rates because of its capabilities and multilingual adaptations, but most of because it employed an affiliate model to recruit malicious actors that could spread the infection further in return for a percentage of the profits. CTB Locker is delivered through aggressive spam campaigns and achieves a large volume of infections based on this affiliate business model.

Cyberattack A cyberattack is considered to be any type of offensive action used by an individual or an organized group that targets computer networks, information systems, or a large IT infrastructure by using various means to deploy malicious code for the purpose of stealing, altering, or taking any advantage from this type of action. A cyberattack can appear under different names, from cyber-campaign, cyber-warfare to cyber-terrorism or online attack. In recent years, the software deployed in online attacks seems to have become more and more sophisticated and law enforcement agencies around the world have a hard time trying to keep up with this global menace.

Cyber incident A cyber incident takes place when there is a violation of a security policy imposed on computer networks and the direct results affect an entire information system. Any unauthorized attempt, whether successful or not, to gain access to, modify, destroy, delete, or render unavailable any computer network or system resource.

Cybersecurity Cybersecurity is a general term that refers to the possibility of organizing a defensive strategy against online criminals and their malicious actions. A complete cybersecurity strategy includes multiple tools and methods to protect an operating system from classical viruses and Trojans, spyware, and financial and data stealing malware. At the same time, online security is important and needs to be protected with other means, like VNP software and backup solutions.

Cyber threat A threat actor, using the Internet, who takes advantage of a known vulnerability in a product for the purposes of exploiting a network and the information the network carries.

Cyber-weapon The term "cyber-weapon" refers to an advanced and sophisticated piece of code that can be employed for military or intelligence purposes. The term has recently emerged from the military area to name malicious software that can be used to access enemy computer networks.

Dark web The dark web refers to websites and online content that exists outside the reach of traditional search engines and browsers. This content is hidden by encryption methods (in most cases, these sites use the Tor encryption tool to hide their identity and location) and can only be accessed with specific software, configuration settings, or pending approval from their admins. The dark web is known for being a hub for illegal activities (drug and crime transactions, dark hat hacking and so on).

Data asset A data asset is a piece of information that contains valuable records. It can be a database, a document, or any type of information that is managed as a single entity. Like any asset, the information involved contains financial value that is directly connected to the number of people that have access to that data, and for this reason it needs to be protected accordingly.

Data integrity Data integrity refers to information property that has not been altered or modified by an unauthorized person. The term is used to refer to information quality in a database, data warehouse, or other online locations.

Data leakage Data leakage describes a data loss of sensitive information, usually from a corporation or large company, that results in unauthorized personnel access to valuable data assets. The sensitive data can be company information, financial details, or other forms of data that puts the company name or its financial situation at risk.

Data loss Data loss is a process in which information is destroyed by failure or neglect in transmission and processing or sometimes by cybercriminal hands. To prevent data loss, IT teams install backup and recovery equipment to avoid losing important information.

Data theft Data theft describes illegal operations in which private information is retrieved from a company or an individual. Usually, the stolen data includes credentials for online accounts and banking sites, credit card details, or valuable corporate information. In the last years, these types of operations have increased, and it has now become necessary to protect data by additional security means.

Declassify An administrative process to remove classification markings, security designations, and handling conditions when information is no longer considered to be sensitive.

Deep web The deep web is a concept similar to the dark web, but has a less shady nature. The world wide web content which is not indexed by traditional search engines is known as the deep web and preferred by certain groups for its increased privacy levels. However, unlike the dark web, the deep web doesn't require its users to be particularly tech-savvy and is not hidden by sophisticated methods; all you need is to know is the address of the website you want to access.

Defence-in-depth An IT security concept (also known as the Castle Approach) in which multiple layers of security are used to protect the integrity of information. These layers can include antivirus and antispyware software, firewalls, hierarchical passwords, intrusion detection, and biometric identification.

Demilitarized zone (DMZ) Also referred to as a perimeter network, the (demilitarized zone) DMZ is a less-secure portion of a network which is located between any two policy-enforcing components of the network (e.g., between the Internet and internal networks). An organization uses a DMZ to host its own Internet services without risking unauthorized access to its private network.

Denial of service attack (DDoS) This type of online attack is used to prevent normal users from accessing an online location. In this case, a cybercriminal can prevent legitimate users from accessing a website by targeting its network resources and flooding the website with a huge number of information requests. Any activity that makes a service unavailable for use by legitimate users or delays system operations and functions.

Departmental security control profile A set of security controls that establishes an organization's minimum mandatory IT security requirements.

Departmental security officer The individual responsible for a department's or organization's security program.

Departmental security requirement Any security requirements prescribed by senior officials of a department that applies generally to its information systems.

Detection The monitoring and analyzing of system events in order to identify unauthorized attempts to access system resources.

Dialer A dialer in the information security world is a spyware device or program that is used to maliciously redirect online communication. Such a software disconnects the legitimate phone connection and reconnects to a premium rate number, which results in an expensive phone bill received by the user. It usually installs itself on the user's system.

Digital signature A digital signature is a technique used to encrypt and validate the authenticity and integrity of a message, software or digital document. The digital signature is difficult to duplicate by a hacker, that's why it is important in information security. A cryptologic mechanism used to validate an item's (e.g., document, software) authenticity and integrity.

Disaster recovery plan (DRP) A recovery plan is a set of procedures that are meant to protect or limit potential loss in a business IT infrastructure in case of an online attack or major hardware or software failure. A recovery plan should be developed during the business impact analysis process.

Distributed denial-of-service attack An attack in which multiple compromised systems are used to attack a single target. The flood of incoming messages to the target system forces it to shut down and denies service to legitimate users.

DNS cache poisoning DNS cache poisoning is a method used by online criminals to launch online attacks. This method supposes the domain name system's modification, which results in returning an incorrect IP address. The purpose is to divert traffic to a malicious server, which is controlled by hackers. That's why the DNS is considered poisoned and it should be taken down by the authorities.

DNS hijacking DNS hijacking or DNS redirection is an online attack that overrides a computer's TCP/IP settings to direct communication to a malicious server controlled by cybercriminals.

Document malware Document malware takes advantage of vulnerabilities in applications that let users read or edit documents.

Domain generation algorithm (DGA) Domain generation algorithm (DGA) is a computer program used by various malware families to generate a large number of domains by creating slightly different variations of a certain domain name. The generated domains are used to hide traffic transmitted between the infected machines/networks and the command and control servers. This way, cyber criminals can cover their tracks and keep their anonymity from law enforcement and private cybersecurity organizations. For example, DGA domains are heavily used to hide botnets and the attacks they help launch.

Domain shadowing Domain shadowing is a malicious tactic used by cyber criminals to build their infrastructure and launch attacks while remaining undetected. First, attackers steal and gather credentials for domain accounts. Using these stolen credentials, they log into the domain account and create subdomains which redirect traffic towards malicious servers, without the domain owner having any knowledge of this. Domain shadowing allows cyber attackers to bypass reputation-based filters and pass their malicious traffic as safe.

Dormant code Modern, advanced malware often has modular structure, including multiple components. One of them is dormant code, which means that the malware needs specific triggers to execute the task it was created for. This type of behavior is coded into the malware so it can bypass signature-based detection in products such as traditional antivirus and anti-malware solutions. There is also another reason for using dormant code: since advanced malware, such as ransomware or financial malware, usually rely on extern infrastructure to download components for infection, the malware can remain dormant and undetected if it can't reach its Control and Command servers to execute further.

Dridex Dridex is a strain of financial malware that uses Microsoft Office macros to infect information systems. Dridex is engineered to collect and steal banking credentials and additional personal information, and its fundamental objective is banking fraud.

Drive-by attack A drive-by attack is the unintentional download of a virus or malicious software (malware) onto your system. A drive-by attack will usually take advantage of (or "exploit") a browser, app, or operating system that is out of date and has a security flaw.

Due diligence Due diligence compels organizations to develop and deploy a cybersecurity plan to prevent fraud, abuse, and deploy means to detect them if they occur, in order to maintain confidential business data safe.

Dumpster diving Dumpster diving is the illegal method of obtaining passwords and corporate directories by searching through discarded media.

Dyreza/Dyre Dyreza (also called Dyre) is a banking Trojan (financial malware) that appeared in 2014, whose behavior is similar to the ZeuS family, although there is no connection between Dyreza and ZeuS. The malware hides in popular web browsers that millions of users employ to access the web and aims to retrieve sensitive financial information every time the victim connects to a banking website. Dyreza is capable of key-logging, circumventing SSL mechanisms and two-factor authentication, and is usually spread through phishing emails.

Eavesdropping attack Network eavesdropping or network sniffing is an attack that aims to capture information transmitted over a network by other computers. The objective is to acquire sensitive information like passwords, session tokens, or any kind of confidential information.

Edge interface A network-layer service interface point that attaches an end system, internal boundary system, or zone interface point to a zone internetwork.

Email malware distribution Although outdated, some malware families still use email attachments as a mean of spreading malware and infecting users' computers. This type of infection relies on the user double clicking on the attachment. A current method that uses email as a dispersion mechanism is inserting links to malicious websites.

Emission security The measures taken to reduce the risk of unauthorized interception of unintentional emissions from information technology equipment that processes classified data.

Encrypted network A network on which messages are encrypted using a special algorithm in order to prevent unauthorized people from reading them.

Encryption Converting information from one form to another to hide its content and prevent unauthorized access. Encryption is a process that uses cryptographic means to turn accessible data or information into an unintelligible code that cannot be read or understood by normal means.

End system A network connected computer that, for a communication, is the end source or destination of a communication.

End-to-end encryption This process involves using communications encryption to make information unavailable to third parties. When being passed through a networking, the information will only be available to the sender and the receiver, preventing ISPs or application service providers to discover or tamper with the content of the communication.

End-to-end encryption A confidentiality service provided by encrypting data at the source end system, with corresponding decryption occurring only at the destination End-System.

End-to-end security The way of ensuring that data transmitted through an information system stays secure and safe from origin point to destination.

End-user systems End systems for human use, such as a desktop with a personal computer (display, keyboard, mouse, and operating system).

Enterprise risk management The methods and processes that organizations use to identify and manage cybersecurity risks that could endanger its corporate mission. As part of this plan, the organization will also establish a plan to protect its assets and a plan to react in case a cybersecurity risk becomes reality.

Equipment emanation An electric field radiation that comes from the equipment as a result of processing or generating information.

Exfiltration The unauthorized removal of data or files from a system by an intruder.

Exploit kit Exploit kits (EKs) are computer programs designed to find flaws, weaknesses, or mistakes in software apps (commonly known as vulnerabilities) and use them to gain access into a system or a network. They are used in the first stages of a cyberattack, because they have the ability to download malicious files and feed the attacked system with malicious code after infiltrating it.

Exploit kits-as-a-service Exploit kits as-a-service are a relatively recent business model employed by cyber criminals in which they create, manage, and sell or rent exploit kits which are accessible and easy to use in cyberattacks. Exploit kits-as-a-service don't require much technical expertise to be used, they are cheaper (especially if rented), they're flexible and can be packed with different types of malware, offer broader reach, are usually difficult to detect, and can be used to exploit a wide range of vulnerabilities. This business model makes it very profitable for exploit kit makers to sell their malicious code and increase their revenues.

Exploit A piece of software, a chunk of data, or a sequence of commands that take advantage of a bug, a glitch, or a vulnerability in software in order to penetrate a user's system with malicious intentions. These malicious intentions may include gaining control of a computer system, allowing privilege escalation, or launching a denial-of-service attack.

External security testing Security testing conducted from outside the organization's security perimeter.

Fail-safe A fail-safe security system or device is an automatic protection system that intervenes when a hardware or software failure is detected.

Fake antivirus malware Rogue antivirus or rogue security is a form of computer malware that simulates a system infection that needs to be removed. The users are asked for money in return for removal of malware, but it is nothing but a form of ransomware.

False positive A false positive is identified when a security solution detects a potential cyber threat which is, in fact, a harmless piece of software or a benign software behavior. For example, your antivirus could inform you that there's a malware threat on your PC, but it could happen that the program it's blocking is safe.

File binder File binders are applications used by online criminals to connect multiple files together in one executable that can be used in launching malware attacks.

Fileless malware Fileless malware is a type of malicious code used in cyberattacks that don't use files to launch the attack and carry on the infection on the affected device or network. The infection is run in the RAM memory of the device, so traditional antivirus and antimalware solutions can't detect it at all. Malicious hackers use fileless malware to achieve stealth, privilege escalation, to gather sensitive information, and achieve persistence in the system, so the malware infection can continue to carry on its effect for a longer period of time.

Financial malware Financial malware is a category of specialized malicious software designed to harvest financial information and use it to extract money from victims' accounts. Because it is a rather new type of malware, it is also very sophisticated and it can easily bypass traditional security measures, such as antivirus. Financial malware is capable of persisting in the affected system for a long time, until it gathers the information associated with financial transactions and it can start to leak money from the targeted account. Banking fraud cybercrimes are one of the most serious cyber threats in the current risk landscape.

Firewall A firewall is a network security system designed to prevent unauthorized access to public or private networks. Its purpose is to control incoming and outgoing communication based on a set of rules. A security barrier placed between two networks that controls the amount and kinds of traffic that may pass between the two. This protects local system resources from being accessed from the outside.

Flip button In the malware world, a flip button appears when spyware or adware solutions trick users into following various actions and installing malicious software on the system.

Flooding Flooding is a security attack used by hackers against a number of servers or web locations. Flooding is the process of sending a large amount of information to such a location in order to block its processing power and stop its proper operation.

Forensic specialist A forensic specialist in IT security is a professional who identifies and analyzes online traffic and data transfer in order to reach a conclusion based on the discovered information.

Form-grabbing malware This type of malware can harvest your confidential data when you're filling a web form, before the data is sent over the Internet, to a secure server. By doing this, the malware can avoid the security ensured by an HTTPS connection. Unfortunately, using a virtual keyboard, autofill or copy/paste won't protect your from this threat. What's more, the malware can categorize data according to type (username, password, etc.) and even grab the URL where you were inputting your information.

Gateway An intermediate system that is the interface between two computer networks. A gateway can be a server, firewall, router, or other device that enables data to flow through a network.

Greyhat hacker Greyhat hackers have a more ambiguous mode of operation compared to blackhat and whitehat hackers. For instance, they may use illegal means to detect a vulnerability but then disclose it to the targeted organization. Another perspective on greyhat hackers focuses on those that find exploits and then sell the know-how to governments but only after receiving a payment. Greyhat hackers distinguish themselves from blackhat hackers on a single important criterion: they don't use or sell the exploit for criminal gain.

Guard A gateway that is placed between two networks, computers, or other information systems that operate at different security levels. The guard mediates all information transfers between the two levels so that no sensitive information from the higher security level is disclosed to the lower level. It also protects the integrity of data on the higher level.

Hacker A hacker is generally regarded as a person who manages to gain unauthorized access to a computer system in order to cause damage. But keep in mind that there are two types of hackers: whitehat hackers, who do penetration testing and reveal their results to help create more secure systems and software, and blackhat hackers, who use their skills for malicious purposes. Someone who uses computers and the Internet to access computers and servers without permission.

Hacktivism Hacktivism is the activity of using hacking techniques to protest against or fight for political and social objectives. One of the most well-known hacktivist groups in the world is Anonymous.

Heartbleed vulnerability Heartbleed is a security bug that appeared in 2014, which exposed information that was usually protected by SSL/TLS encryption. Because of a serious vulnerability that affected the OpenSSL library, attackers could steal data that was kept confidential by a type of encryption used to secure the Internet. This bug caused around 500.000 web servers (17% of all severs on the Internet) to be exposed to potential data theft.

Hoax A hoax is a false computer virus warning. You may receive such hoaxes via email, instant messaging, or social media. Before acting on it, be sure to go online and check the validity of the claim. Also, when you have proof that it's fake, it's a good idea to inform the sender as well. Remember that such hoaxes can lead to malicious websites which can infect your devices with malware.

Honeymonkey This is an automated system designed to simulate the actions of a user who's browsing websites on the Internet. The purpose of the system is to identify malicious websites that try to exploit vulnerabilities that the browser might have. Another name for this is Honey Client.

Honeypot This a program used for security purposes which is able to simulate one or more network services that look like a computer's ports. When an attacker tries to infiltrate, the honeypot will make the target system appear vulnerable. In the background, it will log access attempts to the ports, which can even include data like the attacker's keystrokes. The data collected by a honeypot can then be used to anticipate incoming attacks and improve security in companies.

HTTPS scanning This is another name of a man-in-the-middle attack. Scanning HTTPS (Hypertext Transfer Protocol Secure) content allows the attackers to decrypt, analyze, and re-encrypt content between websites that use SSL (Secure Sockets Layer) for security and a user's browser. This type of attack is usually used to snoop in on information exchanges and steal confidential data.

Hybrid attack A hybrid attack makes a dictionary attack (used to crack passwords) even stronger by adding numerals and symbols, so credentials can be hacked even faster.

Identity theft Identity theft refers to the process of stealing someone's personal identification data and using it online in order to pose as that person. Hackers can make use of a person's name, photos, papers, social security number, and so on to gain financial advantage at this person's expense (by obtaining credit or by blackmailing) or as a means of damaging the person's reputation, etc.

Inadvertent disclosure This type of security incident involves accidentally exposing information to an individual who doesn't have access to that particular data.

Incremental backups Incremental backups are extremely important for keeping information safe and up-to-date. This type of backup will only back up the files that you've modified since performing the last backup. This means the backup is faster and you can ensure that you'll always have all your worked backed up safely.

Information assurance (IA) This is a set of measures designed to protect and defend data and information systems by ensuring that they are always available, that their integrity is safe, that they're confidential and authentic (nonrepudiation principle). These measures include having a data backup to restore information in case of an unfortunate event, having cybersecurity safeguards in place, and ensuring that detection and reaction capabilities are featured.

Information flow control This is an important safeguard in companies, created to ensure that data transfers in an information system comply with the security policy and are as safe as possible.

Information security policy A must-have for any company, this includes up the directives, regulations, rules, and practices that define how an organization should manage, protect, and distribute information.

Information security risk A risk in this category can be evaluated according to how and how much it threatens a company's operations (including mission, functions, brand, reputation) or assets, employees, partners, etc. A risk is based on the potential for cyber criminals to gain unauthorized access and use it to collect confidential data, disclose it to the public or to unauthorized parties, modify it, or destroy it, thus disrupting the organization's activity.

Information security The tactics, tools, measures, and actions taken to protect data and information systems against unauthorized access, use, disclosure, disruption, modification, or destruction. Its purpose is to ensure the confidentiality, integrity, and availability of the data and information systems.

Information system resilience A resilient information system is a system that can continue to work even while under attack, even if becomes degraded of weakened. Moreover, it has to be able to recover from a successful attack fast and regain operational capabilities, at least for the core functions.

Information systems security (INFOSEC) One of the most used terms in cybersecurity, INFOSEC is the protection of information systems against unauthorized access or attempts to compromise and modify data, whether it's stored data, processed data, or data that's being transmitted. The necessary measures to detect, document, and counter these threats are also included in INFOSEC.

Injury level The severity of an injury, which is defined in five levels: very low, low, medium, high, very high.

Injury The damage to the national interests and nonnational interests that business activities serve resulting from the compromise of IT assets.

Inside threat The insider threat usually refers to employees or other people with authorized access who can potentially harm an information system by destroying it or parts of it, by disclosing or modifying confidential information, and by causing denial of service.

Integrity The ability to protect information from being modified or deleted unintentionally or when it's not supposed to be. Integrity helps determine that information is what it claims to be. Integrity also applies to business processes, software application logic, hardware, and personnel. This is one of the core principles in cybersecurity, and it refers to the fact that we must ensure that information has not been changed (deliberately or unwillingly) and that the data is accurate and complete.

Intellectual property Legal rights that result from intellectual activity in the industrial, scientific, literary, and artistic fields. Examples of types of intellectual property include an author's copyright, trademark, and patents. This refers to useful artistic, technical, or industrial information, concepts, ideas, or knowledge that clearly show that they're owned by someone who has control over them, either in physical form or in representation.

Interface A boundary across which two systems communicate. An interface might be a hardware connector used to link to other devices, or it might be a convention used to allow communication between two software systems.

Internal security testing This type of testing is conducted from inside an organization, to examine the resilience and strength of a company's security perimeter and defenses.

Internet worm Internet worms were created by researchers in the 1980s to find a reliable way of growing the Internet through self-replicating programs that can distribute themselves automatically through the network. An Internet worm does exactly that: it distributes itself across the web by using the computers' Internet connection to reproduce.

Internet-of-Things The network of everyday web-enabled devices that are capable of connecting and exchanging information between each other.

Intrusion detection systems (IDS) This is a security management system set up to actively protect computer and networks. It works by analyzing information from various areas of a computer/network o spot potential security breaches.

These breaches can be either caused by intrusions (external attacks) and misuse (insider attacks).

Intrusion detection A security service that monitors and analyzes network or system events to warn of unauthorized access attempts. The findings are provided in real-time (or near real-time).Intrusion: In cybersecurity, intrusion refers to the act of getting around a system's security mechanisms to gain unauthorized access.

IP flood This is a denial of service attack which aims to send a host an avalanche of pings (echo request packages) that the protocol implementation cannot manage. This causes a system to fail and send a denial of service error.

IP spoofing This is a tactic used by cyber criminals to supply a false IP address that masquerades a legitimate IP. This helps the attacker gain an unfair advantage and trick the user or a cybersecurity solution that's in place.

IT asset The components of an information system, including business applications, data, hardware, and software.

IT threat Any potential event or act (deliberate or accidental) or natural hazard that could compromise IT assets.

Key management The procedures and mechanisms for generating, disseminating, replacing, storing, archiving, and destroying cryptographic key.

Keylogging Through keylogging, cyber criminals can use malicious software to record the keystrokes on a user's keyboard, without the victim realizing it. This way, cyber criminals can collect information such as passwords, usernames, PIN codes, and other confidential data.

Keystroke logger Software or hardware designed to capture a user's keystrokes on a compromised system. The keystrokes are stored or transmitted so that they may be used to collect valued information.

Kovter Kovter is a Trojan whose primary objective is performing click-fraud operations on the PC it compromises. However, in 2015, Kovter incorporated new cloaking tricks in order to evade detection, which is why cyber criminals started using it to deliver other types of malware, such as ransomware, or to recruit PCs into botnets.

Least privilege The principle of giving an individual only the set of privileges that are essential to performing authorized tasks. This principle limits the damage that can result from the accidental, incorrect, or unauthorized use of an information system.

Level of concern This is the rating which indicates which protection tactics and processes should be applied to an information system to keep it safe and operating at an optimum level. A level of concern can be basic, medium or high.

Likelihood of occurrence This defines the probability of a specific threats to exploit a given vulnerability, based on a subjective analysis.

Locky Locky is a type of encrypting malware (also known as ransomware) distributed through Microsoft Office macros and targeting Windows-running PCs. The name comes from the fact that once the victim's PC is infected, the ransomware will scramble and encrypt all the data on that PC, setting every file extension to Locky. Locky is spread through spam email campaigns, which make heavy use of spoofing, the same as the cyber criminals behind Dridex operate. In order to get the data decrypted, Locky creators ask for a ransom, which, if not paid, will leave the data useless if the victim doesn't have a backup.

Logic bomb This is a piece of code that a miscreant can insert into software to trigger a malicious function when a set of defined conditions are met.

Low impact This level of impact of a cyber threat or cyberattack on an organization shows that there could be a loss of confidentiality, integrity, or availability, but with limited consequences. This includes reducing the capabilities of the organization, while still retaining the ability to function, but also other minor damages, financial loss, or harm to people.

Macro virus This type of virus attaches itself to documents and uses macro programming options in a document application (such as Microsoft Word or Excel) to execute malicious code or propagate itself.

Malicious Applet This is a small application that is automatically downloaded and executed, being capable of performing an unauthorized action/function on an information system.

Malicious code This is a type of software camouflaged to seem useful and suitable for a task but which actually obtains unauthorized access to system resources or fools a user into executing other malicious actions.

Malvertisement This is an online ad infected with malicious code that can even be injected into a safe, legitimate website, without the website owner's knowledge. This is short for "malware advertisement."

Malvertising This is also called "malicious advertising," and it refers to how malware is distributed through online advertising networks. This type of technique is widely used to spread financial malware, data-stealing malware, ransomware, and other cyber threats.

Malware Malicious software designed to infiltrate or damage a computer system, without the owner's consent. Common forms of malware include computer viruses, worms, Trojans, spyware, and adware. This is a short version for "malicious software," and it works as an umbrella term that refers to software that is defined by malicious intent. This type of ill-intentioned software can disrupt normal computer operations, harvest confidential information, obtain unauthorized access to computer systems, display unwanted advertising, and more.

Malware-as-a-service This type of malware is developed by cyber criminals to require little or no expertise in hacking, to be flexible, polymorphic, offer a broader reach and often comes packed with ready-coded targets. Malware-as-a-service can be bought or rented on the deep web and in cybercriminal communities and sometimes can even include technical support from its makers and their team, which they run as a business. The main purpose behind it is making as much money as possible.

Management security control A security control that focuses on the management of IT security and IT security risks.

Man-in-the-middle attack (MitM) Through this attack, cyber criminals can change the victim's web traffic and interpose themselves between the victim and a web-based service the victim is trying to reach. At that point, the attacker can either harvest the information that's being transmitted via the web or alter it. This type of attack is often abbreviated to MITM, MitM, MIM, MiM, or MITMA.

Maximum tolerable downtime This refers to the maximum amount of time that organizational processes and activities can be disrupted without causing severe consequences for the organization's mission.

Mazar BOT Mazar BOT is a strain of malware-targeting Android devices which first emerged in February 2016. The malware spreads through SMSs sent to random numbers, which include a link shortened through a URL shortner service (such as bit.ly). Once clicked, the link installs the Mazar BOT malware on the affected device, gaining the ability to write, send, receive, and read SMS, access Internet connections, call phones, erase the phone it's installed on, and many more. Mazar BOT doesn't run on smartphones running Android with the Russian language option. Spoofing has also been observed in Mazar BOT attacks.

Mobile code This is a type of software that can be transferred between systems (across a network) and which can also be executed on a local system, such as a computer, without the recipient's explicit consent. Here are some examples of mobile code that you may come across: JavaScript, VBScript, Flash animations, Shockwave movies, Java applets, ActiveX controls, and even macros embedded in Microsoft Office or Excel documents.

Mobile phone malware This type of malware targets mobile phones, tablets, and other mobile devices, and it aims to disrupt their normal functions and cause system damage or data leakage and/or data loss.

Moderate impact When this type of impact is estimated or observed on an information system, it means that confidentiality, integrity, or availability have suffered a significant blow. The organization may record barely working primary functions and significant damage to its assets, finances, and individuals.

Multifactor authentication This type of authentication uses two or more factors to achieve authentication. These factors can include: something the user knows (a password or a PIN), something the user has (an authentication token, an SMS with a code or a code generator on the phone/tablet), and/or something the user is (biometric authentication methods, such as fingerprints or retina scans).

Netiquette Netiquette (short for network etiquette) is a collection of best practices and things to avoid when using the Internet, especially in communities such as forums or online groups. This is more of a set of social conventions that aim to make online interactions constructive, positive, and useful. Examples include: posting off-topic, insulting people, sending or posting spam, etc.

Network security zone A networking environment with a well-defined boundary, a network security zone authority, and a standard level of weakness to network threats. Types of zones are distinguished by security requirements for interfaces, traffic control, data protection, host configuration control, and network configuration control.

Network sniffing This is a technique that uses a software program to monitor and analyze network traffic. This can be used legitimately, to detect problems and keep an efficient data flow. But it can also be used maliciously, to harvest data that's transmitted over a network.

Neutrino Neutrino is a famous exploit kit which has been constantly evolving since it first appeared in 2013. This exploit kit rose to fame because of its user friendly features and low entry barrier to using it. Neutrino includes a user-friendly control panel, continuous monitoring of antivirus detection rates, infostealer capabilities, recommendations of which exploits to use and more. Neutrino is a tool often used to compromise PCs and deliver different types of malware and is itself delivered through malvertising campaigns and web injects. Neutrino is also available through the exploit kit-as-a-service model, where attackers can rent the exploit kit and increase their profits with smaller investments.

Node A connection point that can receive, create, store, or send data along distributed network routes. Each network node, whether it's an endpoint for data transmissions or a redistribution point, has either a programmed or engineered capability to recognize, process, and forward transmissions to other network nodes.

Nonrepudiation This refers to a system's ability to prove that a specific user (and that user alone) sent a message and that the message hasn't been modified in any way.

Nuclear Exploit Kit Nuclear is a highly effective exploit kit which appeared in 2010 and gave cyber criminals the opportunity to exploit a wide range of software vulnerabilities in applications such as Flash, Silverlight, PDF reader, Internet Explorer, and more. Polymorphic in nature, Nuclear advanced over the years into a notorious tool used for launching zero-day attacks, spreading ransomware or for data exfiltration operations. Nuclear was often used in high-volume compromises and gave attackers the possibility to customize their attacks to specific locations and computer configurations. This constantly evolving exploit kit features various obfuscation tactics in order to avoid being detected by traditional anti-virus and anti-malware solutions.

Obfuscation In cybersecurity, obfuscation is a tactic used to make computer code obscure or unclear so that humans or certain security programs (such as traditional antivirus) can't understand it. By using obfuscated code, cyber criminals make it more difficult for cybersecurity specialists to read, analyze, and reverse engineer their malware, preventing them for finding a way to block the malware and suppress the threat.

Offline Attack This type of attack can happen when an attacker manages to gain access to data through offline means, such as eavesdropping, by penetrating a system and stealing confidential information, or looking over someone's shoulder and obtaining credentials to secret data.

Operation Tovar Operation Tovar was an international, collaborative effort undertaken by law enforcement agencies and private security companies from multiple countries. The operation's main objective was to take down the Zeus GameOver botnet, which was believed to be used for distributing the CryptoLocker ransomware. Heimdal Security was also involved in this effort, alongside the US Department of Justice, Europol, the FBI, Microsoft, Symantec, Sophos, Trend Micro, and more.

Operational security control A security control primarily implemented and executed by people and typically supported by the use of technology (e.g., supporting software).

Outside threat This refers to an unauthorized person from outside the company's security perimeter who has the capacity to harm an information system by destroying it, modifying or stealing data from it and disclosing it to unauthorized recipients, and/or causing denial of service.

Overwrite To write or copy new data over existing data. The data that was overwritten cannot be retrieved.

Packet sniffer This is a type of software designed to monitor and record traffic on a network. It can be used for good, to run diagnostic tests and troubleshoot potential problems. But it can also be used for malicious purposes, to snoop in on your private data exchanges. This includes: your web browsing history, your downloads, the people you send emails to, etc.

Parasitic viruses A type of virus that's capable of associating itself with a file or inserting itself into a file. To remain undetected, this virus will give control back to the software it infected. When the operating system looks at the infected software, it will continue to give it rights to run as usual. This means that the virus will be able to copy itself, install itself into memory or make other malicious changes to the infected PC. Although this type of virus appeared early on in the history of computer infections, it's now making a comeback.

Passive attack This is a type of attack during which cyber criminals try to gain unauthorized access to confidential information. It's called passive because the attacker only extracts information without changing the data, so it's more difficult to detect as a result.

Password sniffing This is a tactic used by cyber criminals to harvest passwords. They do this through monitoring and snooping in on network traffic to retrieve password data. If the password is sent over an unencrypted connection (for example, you put in a password on a website that isn't protected by a security certificate – doesn't start with https), it's even easier for attackers to get their hands on your passwords.

Patch management This refers to the activity of getting, testing, and installing software patches for a network and the systems in it. Patch management includes applying patches both for security purposes and for improving the software programs used in the network and the systems within it.

Patch A patch is a small software update released by manufacturers to fix or improve a software program. A patch can fix security vulnerabilities or other bugs or enhance the software in terms of features, usability, and performance.

Patching The act of applying a patch, which is designed to fix or enhance a software program. This includes both security-related updates and improvements in terms of software features and user experience.

Payload In cybersecurity, the payload is the data cargo transported by a piece of malware onto the affected device or network. The payload contains the fundamental objective of the transmission, which is why the payload is actually the element of the malware that performs the malicious action (i.e., stealing financial information, destroying data, encrypting data on the affected device/network). When you consider a malware's damaging consequences, that's when you can talk about the payload.

Penetration testing This is a type of attack launched a network or computer system in order to identify security vulnerabilities that can be used to gain unauthorized access to the network's/system's features and data. Penetration testing is used to help companies better protect themselves against cyberattacks.

Penetration In cybersecurity, penetration occurs when a malicious attacker manages to bypass a system's defenses and acquire confidential data from that system.

Perimeter The boundary between two network security zones through which traffic is routed.

Personal firewall This is a type of firewall that's installed and runs on personal computers. A firewall is a network security system designed to prevent unauthorized access to public or private networks. Its purpose is to control incoming and outgoing communication based on a set of rules.

Pharming This is a type of online scam aimed at extracting information such as passwords, usernames, and more from the victim. Pharming means redirecting Internet traffic from a legitimate website to a fake one, so victims can put in their confidential information and attackers can collect it. This type of attacks usually targets banking and ecommerce websites. What makes it difficult to detect is that even if the victim types in the right URL, the redirect will still take the user to the fake website, operated by IT criminals.

Phishing Phishing is a malicious technique used by cyber criminals to gather sensitive information (credit card data, usernames and passwords, etc.) from users. The attackers pretend to be a trustworthy entity to bait the victims into trusting them and revealing their confidential data. The data gathered through phishing can be used for financial theft, identity theft, to gain unauthorized access to the victim's accounts or to accounts they have access to, to blackmail the victim, and more. An attempt by a third party to solicit confidential information from an individual, group, or organization by mimicking or spoofing, a specific, usually well-known brand, usually for financial gain. Phishers attempt to trick users into disclosing personal data, such as credit card numbers, online banking credentials, and other sensitive information, which they may then use to commit fraudulent acts.

Plaintext This is how ordinary text is called before it's encrypted or after being decrypted. When someone says that your passwords are stored in plaintext, it means that they can be read by anyone snooping into your private information, because the passwords aren't encrypted. This is a big lapse in cybersecurity, so watch out for it. Unencrypted information.

Point of presence An access point, location, or facility at which two or more different networks or communication devices connect with each other and the Internet. Also referred to as PoP.

Polymorphic code Polymorphic code is capable of mutating and changing while maintaining the initial algorithm. Each time it runs, the code morphs but keeps its function. This tactic is usually used by malware creators to keep their attacks covert and undetected by reactive security solutions.

Polymorphic engine A polymorphic engine is used to generate polymorphic malware. This is a computer program capable of transforming a program in derivative versions (different versions of code) but which perform the same function. Polymorphic engines rely on encryption and obfuscation to work and are used almost exclusively by malware creators and other cyber criminals. Using this type of engine, malicious hackers can create malware types that can't be detected by antivirus engines or have a very low detection rate.

Polymorphic malware Polymorphic malware is capable of transforming itself into various derivative versions that perform the same function and have the same objective. By using obfuscated code and constantly changing their code, polymorphic malware strains can infect information systems without being detected by solutions such as traditional malware, which is a key asset in the perspective of cyber criminals.

Polymorphic packer This is a software tool used for bundling up different types of malware in a single package (e.g., in an email attachment). Malicious actors use polymorphic packers because they're able to transform over time, so they can remain undetected by traditional security solutions for longer periods of time.

Pop-up ad Pop-up ads are windows used in advertising. They appear on top of your browser window when you're on a website, and they're often annoying because they are intrusive. While they're not malicious by nature, sometimes they can become infected with malware, if a cyber attacker compromises the advertising networks serving the pop-up.

Potential impact When a cybersecurity risk is assessed, the loss of the three essential factors is considered: confidentiality, integrity, and availability. If a risk becomes a cyberattack, it can have low, moderate, or high impact.

Potentially unwanted application (PUA) There are applications you might install on your devices which contain adware, which may install toolbars or have confusing purposes. These applications can be nonmalicious by nature, but they come with the risk of potentially becoming malicious. Users must seriously consider the risks before they install this type of applications.

Poweliks Poweliks is a Trojan designed to perform click-fraud operations on the affected PC. Its specific character is given by the fact that it's a type of fileless malware, which makes it very difficult to be detected by traditional, signature-based anti-malware and antivirus solutions. Poweliks installs itself in the Windows registry, where it can inject itself into essential Windows functions. This also helps Poweliks achieve persistence on the infected PC. This malware can be used to also download other threats onto the victim's PC, such as ransomware delivered through malvertising.

Power virus This type of computer virus is capable of executing a specific code that triggers maximum CPU power dissipation (heat generated by the central processing units). Consequently, the computer's cooling ability would be impaired and the virus could cause the system to overheat. One of the potential effects is permanent physical damage to the hardware. Power viruses are used both by good actors, to test components, but can also be used by cyber criminals.

Proprietary information (PROPIN) Proprietary information is made of all the data that is unique to a company and ensures its ability to stay competitive. This can include customer details, technical information, costs, and trade secrets. If cyber criminals compromise or reveal this information, the impact on the company can be quite severe, as we've seen in major data breaches.

Proxy server A proxy server is a go-between a computer and the Internet. Proxies are used to enhance cyber safety because they prevent attackers from invading a computer/a private network directly.

Quantum computing A quantum computer can process a vast number of calculations simultaneously. Whereas a classical computer works with ones and zeros, a quantum computer will have the advantage of using ones, zeros, and "superpositions" of ones and zeros. Certain difficult tasks that have long been thought impossible for classical computers will be achieved quickly and efficiently by a quantum computer.

Ransomware Ransomware is a type of malware (malicious software) which encrypts all the data on a PC or mobile device, blocking the data owner's access to it. After the infection happens, the victim receives a message that tells him/her that a certain amount of money must be paid (usually in Bitcoins) in order to get the decryption key. Usually, there is also a time limit for the ransom to be paid. There is no guarantee that if the victim pays the ransom, he/she will get the decryption key. The most reliable solution is to back up your data in at least three different places (for redundancy) and keep those backups up-to-date, so you don't lose important progress.

Real-time reaction This is a type of immediate reaction and response to a spotted compromise attempt. This is done in due time so the victim can ensure protection against unauthorized network access.

Reconnaissance Activity conducted by a threat actor to obtain information and identify vulnerabilities to facilitate future compromise(s).

Redaction A form of data sanitization for selected data-file elements (not to be confused with media sanitization, which addresses all data on media).

Remote access Trojan (RAT) Remote access Trojans (RATs) use the victim's access permissions and infect computers to give cyber attackers unlimited access to the data on the PC. Cyber criminals can use RATs to exfiltrate confidential information. RATs include backdoors into the computer system and can enlist the PC into a botnet, while also spreading to other devices. Current RATs can bypass strong authentication and can access sensitive applications, which are later used to exfiltrate information to cybercriminal-controlled servers and websites.

Remote access This happens when someone uses a dedicated program to access a computer from a remote location. This is a norm for people who travel a lot and need access to their company's network. But cyber criminals can also use remote access to control a computer they've previously hacked into.

Remote diagnostics/maintenance This is a maintenance service carried on by authorized companies/individuals who use the Internet to communicate with the company's network.

Remote exploitation Exploitation of a victim machine by sending specially crafted commands from a remote network to a service running on that machine to manipulate it for the purpose of gaining access or information.

Replay attacks This type of attack uses authentication data that cyber criminals have previously gathered to retransmit this confidential information. The purpose is to gain unauthorized access or produce other malicious effects.

Residual risk assessment An assessment, which is performed at the end of the system development lifecycle, to determine the remaining likelihood and impact of a threat.

Residual risk level The degree of residual risk (e.g., high, medium, low).

Residual risk The likelihood and impact of a threat that remains after security controls are implemented.

Residual risk This is a type of risk that remains after all available security measures and tactics have been applied. Because there is no such thing as 100% cybersecurity, a residual risk remains for each identifiable cyber threat.

Resilience This is an organization's or system's ability to restore its ability to function and achieve its objectives during and after a cyberattack or other transformations. Resilience includes ensuring contingency plans, doing constant risk management, and planning for every crisis scenario.

Reverse engineering This is a technique heavily used by cybersecurity researchers who constantly take malware apart to analyze it. This way, they can understand and observe how the malware works and can devise security solutions that can protect users against that type of malware and its tactics. This is one of the most valuable activities in cybersecurity intelligence gathering.

Risk assessment This is a risk analysis process that defines an organization's cybersecurity risks and their potential impact. Security measures are then suited to match the importance and potential impact of the risks identified as a result of the risk assessment.

Risk level The degree of risk (e.g., high, medium, low).

Risk management This is the process by which an organization manages its cybersecurity risks to decrease their potential impact and take the adequate measures to avoid cyberattacks. Doing a risk assessment is also part of the process as well as the risk mitigation strategy and all the procedures that must be applied in order to ensure proper defenses against cyber threats. This is a continuous process and should be viewed as a cycle.

Risk mitigation This is the process by which risks are evaluated, prioritized, and managed through mitigation tactics and measures. Since any company has a dynamic environment, a periodical revision should be a defining characteristic of the risk mitigation process.

Rogue security software Rogue security software (usually antivirus) is a common Internet scam used by cyber criminals to mislead victims and infect their PCs with malware. Malicious actors could also use fake antivirus to trick victims into paying money or extort them (like ransomware does) into paying for having the rogue software removed. So please only buy security software from trusted vendors or from the software makers themselves.

Rogueware This is a type of deceitful malware which claims to be a trusted and harmless software program (such as antivirus). Cyber criminals use rogueware to harvest data from their victims or to trick them intro paying money. Often, rogueware also includes adware functions, which adds a burden and a potential risk to the infected PC.

Root cause analysis This is the process used to identify the root causes for certain security risks in an organization. This must be done with utmost attention to detail and by maintaining an objective perspective.

Rootkit A rootkit is a type of malicious software (but not always) which gives the attackers privileged access to a computer and is activated before the operating system boots up. Rookits are created to conceal the existence of other programs or processes from being spotted by traditional detection methods. For example, rookit malware is capable of covering up the fact that a PC has been compromised. By gaining administrator rights on the affected PC (through exploits or social engineering), attackers can maintain the infection for a long time and are notoriously difficult to remove.

Safeguards This refers to a set of protection measures that have to meet an information system's core security requirements, in order to ensure confidentiality, integrity, and availability. This includes everything from employee security to ensuring the safety of physical structures and devices, to management limitations, and more.

Sanitize Sanitization is a process through which data is irreversibly removed from media. The storage media is left in a reusable condition in accordance with IT security policy, but the data that was previously on it cannot be recovered or accessed.

Scareware This is a type of malware (or rogueware) that employs social engineering to intimidate and confuse the victims through shock, anxiety, fear, and time restrictions. The objective is to maliciously persuade the victims into buying unwanted software. The software could be rogue security software, ransomware, or other type of malware. For example, malicious actors often try to manipulate users that their computer is infected with a virus and that the only way to get rid of it is to pay for, download, and install a fake antivirus, which, of course, turns out to be the malware itself.

Scavenging This is the action of trying to find confidential or sensitive data by searching through a system's data residue.

Secure destruction The destruction of information assets through one or more approved methods, carried out alone or in combination with erasing, to ensure that information cannot be retrieved.

Secure erasure A digital sanitization process that uses tools and industry-standard commands (e.g., ATA security erase) to erase all accessible memory locations of a data storage device.

Security control A management, operational, or technical high-level security requirement needed for an information system to protect the confidentiality, integrity, and availability of its IT assets. Security controls can be applied by using a variety of security solutions that can include security products, security policies, security practices, and security procedures. This is a set of safeguards designed to avoid and mitigate the impact of cybersecurity risks that an organization has.

Security impact analysis An organization should always conduct a security impact analysis to determine if certain changes to the information systems have influenced and impacted its security state.

Security requirements Security requirements are derived from multiple sources and make up for the security necessities of an information system, in order to ensure confidentiality, integrity, and availability of the information that's managed, transmitted, or stored in the system. The sources for security requirements can be legislation, directives, policies, standards, best practices, regulations, procedures, or other business necessities.

Sensitive information This type of information is defined by the fact that not everyone can access it. Sensitive information is data that is confidential for a certain category of users, who can view, access, and use this data. This type of information is protected for reasons either related to legal aspects or ethical ones. Examples include: personal identification numbers, health information, education records, trade secrets, credit card information, etc.

Separation of duties A security principle stating that sensitive or critical responsibilities should be shared by multiple entities (e.g., staff or processes), rather than a single entity, to prevent a security breach.

Shylock Shylock is a banking malware created to steal users' banking credentials for fraudulent purposes. Shylock is based on the leaked ZeuS code and acts similar to Zeus GameOver (created based on the same malicious code), because it uses a (DGA) Domain generation algorithm to hide its traffic and remain undetected by traditional antivirus and anti-malware solutions. Shylock is delivered mainly through drive-by downloads on compromised websites which are hit by malvertising, but also through malicious JavaScript injects.

Signature In cybersecurity, a signature is an identifiable, differentiating pattern associated with a type of malware, an attack, or a set of keystrokes which were used to gain unauthorized access to a system. For example, traditional antivirus solutions can spot, block, and remove malware based on their signature, when the AV sees that a piece of software on your PC matched the signature of a malicious software stored in their database.

Skimming Skimming happens when a malicious actor uses a tag reader in an unauthorized manner, in order to collect information about a person's tag. The victim never knows or accepts to be skimmed. For example, card skimming is an illegal practice which consists of the illegal collection of data from a card's magnetic stripe. This information can then be copied onto a blank card's magnetic stripe and used by malicious actors to make purchases and withdraw cash in the name of the victim.

Sniffer A sniffer is a tool used to monitor traffic over a network. It can be used legitimately, to detect issues with the data flow. But it can also be used by malicious actors, to harvest data that's transmitted over a network.

Social engineering In information security, social engineering if a form of psychological manipulation used to persuade people to perform certain actions or give away sensitive information. Manipulation tactics include lies, psychological tricks, bribes, extortion, impersonation, and other type of threats. Social engineering is often used to extract data and gain unauthorized access to information systems, either of a single, private user or which belong to organizations.

Spam filtering software This is a type of program which can analyze emails and other types of messages (i.e., instant messages) to weed out spam. If spam filtering software decides to categorize a message as spam, it'll probably move that message to a dedicated folder.

Spam Spam is made up of unsolicited emails or other types of messages sent over the Internet. Spam is often used to spread malware and phishing, which is why you should never open, reply to, or download attachments from spam messages. Spam cam come your way in the form of emails, instant messages, comments, etc.

Spear phishing Spear phishing is a cyberattack that aims to extract sensitive data from a victim using a very specific and personalized message. This message is usually sent to individuals or companies, and it's extremely effective, because it's very well planned. Attackers invest time and resources into gathering information about the victim (interests, activities, personal history, etc.) in order to create the spear phishing message (which is usually an email). Spear phishing uses the sense of urgency and familiarity (appears to come from someone you know) to manipulate the victim, so the target doesn't have time to double check the information. The use of spoofed emails to persuade people within an organization to reveal their usernames or passwords. Unlike phishing, which involves mass mailing, spear phishing is small-scale and well targeted.

Spillage Information spillage happen when data is moved from a safe, protected system to another system, which is less secure. This can happen to all types of data, from health information to financial or personal data. If the system the data is moved to is less secure, people who should not have access to this information may be able to access it.

Spoofing (Email) This is a compromise attempt during which an unauthorized individual tries to gain access to an information system by impersonating an authorized user. For example, email spoofing is when cyber attackers send phishing emails using a forged sender address. You might believe that you're receiving an email from a trusted entity, which causes you to click on the links in the email, but the link may end up infecting your PC with malware.

Spy-phishing This is a type of malware that employs tactics found in both phishing and spyware. By combining these cyber threats, spy-phishing is capable of downloading applications that can run silently on the victim's system. When the victims open a specific URL, the malware will collect the data the victim puts into that website and send it to a malicious location (like a web server). This technique is used to extend the duration of the phishing attack, even after the phishing website has been taken down.

Spyware Spyware is a type of malware designed to collect and steal the victim's sensitive information, without the victim's knowledge. Trojans, adware and system monitors and are different types of spyware. Spyware monitors and stores the victim's Internet activity (keystrokes, browser history, etc.) and can also harvest usernames, passwords, financial information, and more. It can also send this confidential data to servers operated by cyber criminals, so it can be used in consequent cyberattacks.

SQL injection This is a tactic that used code injection to attack applications which are data-driven. The maliciously injected SQL code can perform several actions, including dumping all the data in a database in a location controlled by the attacker. Through this attack, malicious hackers can spoof identities, modify data or tamper with it, disclose confidential data, delete and destroy the data, or make it unavailable. They can also take control of the database completely.

Secure Sockets Layer (SSL) SSL comes from Secure Sockets Layer, which is an encryption method to ensure the safety of the data sent and received from a user to a specific website and back. Encrypting this data transfer ensures that no one can snoop on the transmission and gain access to confidential information, such as card details in the case of online shopping. Legitimate websites use SSL (start with https) and users should avoid inputting their data in websites that don't use SSL.

Stealware This is a type of malware which is capable of transferring data or money to a third, malicious party. This type of malware usually targets affiliate transactions. It then uses an HTTP cookie to redirect the commission earned by an affiliate marketer to an unauthorized third party.

Strong authentication This is a specific requirement that calls for employing multiple authentication factors from different categories and sophisticated technology to verify an entity's identity. Dynamic passwords, digital certificates, protocols, and other authentication elements are part of strong authentication standards. This is especially applied in banking and financial services, where access to an account has to be tied to a real person or an organization.

Supply chain attack This type of attack aims to inflict damage upon an organization by leveraging vulnerabilities in its supply network. Cyber criminals often manipulate with hardware or software during the manufacturing stage to implant rootkits or tie in hardware-based spying elements. Attackers can later use these implants to attack the organization they're after.

Suppression measure This can be any action or device used to reduce the security risks in an information system. This is part of the risk mitigation process, aimed at minimizing the security risks of an organization or information system.

Suspicious files and behavior Suspicious behavior is identified when files exhibit an unusual behavior pattern. For example, if files start copying themselves to a system folder, this might be a sign that those files have been compromised by malware. Traditional antivirus solutions incorporate this type of detection to spot and block malware.

Symmetric key A cryptographic key used to perform the cryptographic operation and its inverse operation (e.g., encrypt and decrypt, create a message authentication code and verify the code).

System administrator/Sysadmin The sysadmin, how it's also called, is a person in charge of all the technical aspects of an information system. This includes aspects related to configuration, maintenance, ensuring reliability, and the necessary resources for the system to run at optimal parameters while respecting a budget and more.

System integrity This state defines an information system which is able to perform its dedicated functions at optimal parameters, without intrusion or manipulation (either intended or not).

Tampering The intentional activity of modifying the way an information system works, in order to force it to execute unauthorized actions.

Targeted threat Targeted threats are singled out because of their focus: they are usually directed at a specific organization or industry. These threats are also designed to extract sensitive information from the target, so cyber criminals take a long time to prepare these threats. They are carefully documented, so the chances for successful compromise can be as big as possible. Targeted threats are delivered via email (phishing, vishing, etc.), they employ zero days and other vulnerabilities to penetrate an information system, and many more. Government and financial organizations are the most frequent targets for this type of cyber threats.

Tempest The name for specifications and standards for limiting the strength of electromagnetic emanations from electrical and electronic equipment which lead to reduced vulnerability to eavesdropping. This term originated in the US Department of Defense.

TeslaCrypt TeslaCrypt is a ransomware Trojan, which was first designed to target computers that have specific computer games installed. However, in the past months, this strain of cryptoware had broadened its reach to affect all users (mainly Windows users), not just gamers. As with every other ransomware, TeslaCrypt creators use spam to distribute the infection, and once they get into the victim's PC, all the data on the device will be encrypted and held hostage. The ransom can vary between $150 and $1000 worth of bitcoins, which the victim has to pay in order to get the decryption key. In March 2016, TeslaCrypt 4.0 emerged, featuring unbreakable encryption and rendering any available TeslaCrypt decoders useless.

Threat analysis This refers to the process of examining the sources of cyber threats and evaluating them in relation to the information system's vulnerabilities. The objective of the analysis is to identify the threats that endanger a particular information system in a specific environment.

Threat and risk assessment A process of identifying system assets and how these assets can be compromised, assessing the level of risk that threats pose to assets, and recommending security measures to mitigate threats. During a threat assessment, cyber threats against an organization are categorized in types, so they can be managed, prioritized and mitigated more easily.

Threat event An actual incident in which a threat agent exploits a vulnerability of an IT asset of value.

Threat event In cybersecurity, a threat event is defined as a potentially harmful situation for an information system that can have unwanted consequences.

Threat monitoring During this process, security audits and other information in this category are gathered, analyzed, and reviewed to see if certain events in the information system could endanger the system's security. This is a continuous process.

Threat scenario A threat scenario draws information from all available resources and focuses on three key elements: vulnerabilities, threats, and impact. This helps associate a specific cyber threats to one or more threat sources and establish priorities.

Threat shifting This is the process of adapting protection measures in response to cyber attackers' ever-changing tactics. Countermeasures must be constantly updated to meet the challenges posed by polymorphic malware.

Threat source This refers to the objective and method used by cyber attackers to exploit a security vulnerability or a certain context in order to compromise an information system. Triggering a system vulnerability may happen accidentally or on purpose.

Threat In cybersecurity, a threat is a possible security violation that can become certainty if the right context, capabilities, actions, and events unfold. If a threat becomes reality, it can cause a security breach or additional damages.

Time bomb This is a type of malware that stays dormant on the system for a definite amount of time, until a specific event triggers it. This type of behavior is present in malware to make detection by security software more difficult.

Time-dependent password This type of password can be either valid for a limited amount of time or it can be valid for use during a specific interval in a day. Time-dependent passwords are most often generated by an application and are part of the two-factor or multi-factor authentication mechanisms.

Token In security, a token is a physical electronic device used to validate a user's identity. Tokens are usually part of the two-factor or multi-factor authentication mechanisms. Tokens can also replace passwords in some cases and can be found under the form of a key fob, a USB, an ID card, or a smart card.

Tracking cookie This type of cookies are places on users' computers during web browsing sessions. Their purpose is to collect data about the user's browsing preferences on a specific website, so they can then deliver targeted advertising, or to improve the user's experience on that website by delivering customized information.

Traffic analysis During this process, the traffic on a network is intercepted, examined, and reviewed in order to determine traffic patterns and volumes and extract relevant statistics about it. This data is necessary to improve the network's performance, security, and general management.

Traffic Encryption Key (TEK) This is a term specific to network security, which depicts the key used to encrypt the traffic within a network.

Trojan (Trojan horse) Probably one of the most notorious terms in cybersecurity, a Trojan horse is a type of malware that acts according to the Greek legend: it camouflages itself as a legitimate file or program to trick unsuspecting users into installing it on their PCs. Upon doing this, users will unknowingly give unauthorized, remote access to the cyber attackers who created and run the Trojan. Trojans can be used to spy on a user's activity (web browsing, computer activity, etc.), to collect and harvest sensitive data, to delete files, to download more malware onto the PC, and more. A malicious program that is disguised as or embedded within legitimate software.

Two-factor authentication A type of multi-factor authentication used to confirm the identity of a user. Authentication is validated by using a combination of two different factors including: something you know (e.g., a password), something you have (e.g., a physical token), or something you are (a biometric).

Two-step verification A process requiring two different authentication methods, which are applied one after the other, to access a specific device or system. Unlike two-factor authentication, two-step verification can be of the same type (e.g., two passwords, two physical keys, or two biometrics). Also known as two-step authentication.

Typhoid adware This is a cybersecurity threat that employs a man-in-the-middle attack in order to inject advertising into certain web pages a user visits while using a public network, like a public, nonencrypted Wi-Fi hotspot. In this case, the computer being used doesn't need to have adware on it, so installing a traditional antivirus can't counteract the threat. While the ads themselves can be nonmalicious, they can expose users to other threats. For example, the ads could promote a fake antivirus that is actually malware or a phishing attack.

Unauthorized access When someone gains unauthorized access, it means that they've illegally or illegitimately accessed protected or sensitive information without permission.

Unauthorized disclosure This happens when sensitive, private information is communicated or exposed to parties who are not authorized to access the data.

Unpatched application A supported application that does not have the latest security updates and/or patches installed.

URL injection A URL (or link) injection is when a cybercriminal created new pages on a website owned by someone else, that contain spammy words or links. Sometimes, these pages also contain malicious code that redirects your users to other web pages or makes the website's web server contribute to a DDoS attack. URL injection usually happens because of vulnerabilities in server directories or software used to operate the website, such as an outdated WordPress or plugins.

Vaccine In cybersecurity, a vaccine is a digital solution that focuses on neutralizing attacks once they gain unauthorized access into an information system. Cyber vaccines exploit flaws in the way some malware strains work and spread, so their distribution and effects can be blocked. A cyber vaccine could train an information system to detect and stop cyberattacks after they've penetrated the system/PC just before the attacker can do any actual damage. Cyber vaccines are a new concept, so there is a lot of work to be done for their advancement. They can potentially be used to stop ransomware, block data exfiltration, intercept phishing attacks, block zero-day exploits, and more.

Vawtrak/Neverquest Vawtrak (or Neverquest) is a classic infostealer malware, which aims to mainly steal login credentials for banking portals, either stored on the local device or transmitted from the affected PC, but it can also harvest other financial institutions. Vawtrak uses the stolen credentials to gain unauthorized access to bank account and commit financial fraud. The infostealer has other capabilities too, such as taking screenshots of the infected device, capturing videos, and launching man-in-the-middle attacks. Vawtrak is delivered through drive-by downloads in compromised websites or by injecting malicious code on legitimate websites, but it also spreads through phishing campaigns in social media networks and spam.

Virtual private network (VPN) A VPN, uses the Internet public infrastructure to connect to a private network. VPNs are usually created and owned by corporations. By using encryption and other security means, a VPN will hide your online activity from attackers and offer extra shield when you want to safely navigate online. A private communications network usually used within a company or by several different enterprises or organizations to communicate over a wider network. VPN communications are typically encrypted or encoded to protect the traffic from other users on the public network carrying the VPN.

Virus hoax A computer virus hoax is a message that warns about a nonexistent computer virus threat. This is usually transmitted via email and tells the recipients to forward it to everyone they know. Computer hoaxes are usually harmless, but their intent is not innocent, since they exploit lack of knowledge, concern, or ability to investigate before taking the action described in the hoax.

Virus A computer program that can spread by making copies of itself. Computer viruses spread from one computer to another, usually without the knowledge of the user. Viruses can have harmful effects, ranging from displaying irritating messages to stealing data or giving other users control over the infected computer. A computer virus is a type of malicious software capable of self-replication. A virus needs human intervention to be ran, and it can copy itself into other computer programs, data files, or in certain sections of your computer, such as the boot sector of the hard drive. Once this happens, these elements will become infected. Computer viruses are designed to harm computers and information systems and can spread through the Internet, through malicious downloads, infected email attachments, malicious programs, files, or documents. Viruses can steal data, destroy information, log keystrokes, and more.

Vishing Vishing (short for voice over IP phishing) is a form of phishing performed over the telephone or voice over IP (VoIP) technology, such as Skype. Unsuspecting victims are duped into revealing sensitive or personal information via telephone calls, VoIP calls, or even voice mail.

Vulnerability assessment A process to determine existing weaknesses or gaps in an information system's protection efforts.

Vulnerability A flaw or weakness in the design or implementation of an information system or its environment that could be exploited to adversely affect an organization's assets or operations. A vulnerability is a hole in computer security that leaves the system open to damages caused by cyber attackers. Vulnerabilities have to be solved as soon as they are discovered, before a cybercriminal takes advantage and exploits them.

Wabbits A wabbit is one of four main classes of malware, among viruses, worms, and Trojan horses. It's a form of computer program that repeatedly replicates on the local system. Wabbits can be programmed to have malicious side effects. A fork bomb is an example of a wabbit: it's a form of DoS attack against a computer that uses the fork function. A fork bomb quickly creates a large number of processes, eventually crashing the system. Wabbits don't attempt to spread to other computers across network.

Watering Hole Watering Hole is the name of a computer attack strategy that was detected as early as 2009 and 2010. The victim is a particular, very targeted group, such as a company, organization, agency, industry, etc. The attacker spends time to gain strategic information about the target: observes which legitimate websites are more often visited by the members of the group. Then the attacker exploits a vulnerability and infects one of those trusted websites with malware, without the knowledge of the site's owner. Eventually, someone from that organization will fall into the trap and get their computer infected. This way, the attacker gains access to the target's entire network. These attacks work because of the constant vulnerabilities in website technologies, even with the most popular systems, such as WordPress, making it easier than ever to stealthily compromise websites.

Web bug A web bug, also called a web beacon or pixel tag, is a small, transparent GIF image, usually not bigger than 1 pixel. It's embedded in an email or webpage and is usually used in connection with cookies. Web bugs are designed to monitor your activity, and they load when you open an email or visit a website. Most common uses are marketing related: for email tracking (to see if readers are opening the emails they receive, when they open them), web analytics (to see how many people visited a website), advertisement statistics (to find out how often an ad appears or is being viewed), IP addresses gathering, type of browser used.

Web content filtering software A web content filtering software is a program that will screen an incoming web page and restrict or control its content. It is used by governments that can apply them for censorship, by ISPs to block copyright infringement, by employers to sometimes block personal email clients or social media networks, by a school, by parents, etc. This software can block pages that include copyright infringement material, pornographic content, social networks, etc.

Webattacker Webattacker is a do-it-yourself malware creation kit that demands minimal technical knowledge to be manipulated and used. It includes scripts that simplify the task of infecting computers and spam-sending techniques.

Whaling Whaling is a form of sophisticated phishing whose objective is to collect sensitive data about a target. What's different from phishing is that whaling goes after high-profile, famous, and wealthy targets, such as celebrities, CEOs, top-level management, and other powerful or rich individuals. By using the phished information, fraudsters and cyber criminals can trick victims into revealing even more confidential or personal data or they can be extorted and suffer from financial fraud.

White list An access control list that identifies who or what is allowed access, in order to provide protection from harm.

Whitehat hacker Also known as ethical hackers, these are usually cybersecurity specialists, researchers, or just skilled techies who find security vulnerabilities for companies and then notify them to issue a fix. Unlike blackhat hackers, they do not use the vulnerabilities except for demonstration purposes. Companies often hire whitehat hackers to test their security systems (known as "penetration testing"). As their expertise has grown to be more in demand and sought after, whitehat hackers started to collect rewards for their work, ranging from 500$ all the way to 100,000$.

Whitelist A whitelist is a list of email addresses or IP addresses that are considered to be spam-free. It's the opposite of a blacklist, which usually includes a list of blocked users. Spam filters have both whitelists and blacklists of senders and also keywords to look for in emails, which enable them to help detect a spam email.

Worm A computer worm is one of the most common types of malware. It's similar to a virus but it spreads differently: worms have the ability to spread independently and self-replicate automatically by exploiting operating system vulnerabilities, while viruses rely on human activity in order to spread. It's usually "caught" via mass emails that contain infected attachments. Worms may also include "payloads" that damage host computers, commonly designed to steal data, delete files, send documents via email, or install backdoors. A malicious program that executes independently and self-replicates, usually through network connections, to cause damage (e.g., deleting files, sending documents via email, or taking up bandwidth).

Zero-day virus/malware A zero-day virus, also known as zero-day malware, is a computer virus, Trojan horse, or other malware, previously unknown by the software maker or by traditional antivirus producers. This means the vulnerability is also undisclosed publicly, though it might be known and quietly exploited by cyber attackers. Because it's not known yet, this means patches and antivirus software signatures are not yet available for it and there is little protection against an attack.

Zero day A zero-day or zero-hour attack is an attack that uses vulnerabilities in computer software that cyber criminals have discovered and software makers have not patched (because they weren't aware that those vulnerabilities existed). These are often exploited by cyber attackers before the software or security companies become aware of them. Sometimes, Zero Days are discovered by security vendors or researchers and kept private until the company patches the vulnerabilities.

Zero-day attack A zero-day (or zero-hour or day-zero) attack or threat is a computer threat that tries to exploit computer application vulnerabilities that are unknown to others or undisclosed to the software developer. Zero-day exploits (actual code that can use a security hole to carry out an attack) are used or shared by attackers before the software developer finds out about the vulnerability.

Zero-day vulnerability A zero-day vulnerability is a software vulnerability that is not yet known by the vendor and therefore has not been mitigated. A zero-day exploit is an attack directed at a zero-day vulnerability.

ZeuS/Zbot Zeus, also known as Zbot, is a notorious banking Trojan which infects Windows users and tries to retrieve confidential information from the infected computers. Once installed, it also tries to download configuration files and updates from the Internet. Its purpose is to steal private data from the victims, such as system information, passwords, banking credentials, or other financial details. Zeus could be customized to gather banking details in specific countries by using a vast array of methods. Using the retrieved information, cyber criminals could log into banking accounts and make unauthorized money transfers through a complex network of computers, thus leading to severe banking fraud. Operation Tovar, carried out in 2014, took down the ZeuS network of control and command servers, as it had done millions of dollars in damages and spread very quickly.

Zeus GameOver/Zeus P2P Zeus GameOver is a variant of the ZeuS/Zbot family – the infamous financial stealing malware – which relied on a peer-to-peer botnet infrastructure to work. Zeus GameOver was used by cyber criminals to collect financial information (credentials, credit card numbers, passwords, etc.) and any other personal information which could be used to access the victim's online banking accounts. GameOver Zeus is estimated to have infected 1 million users around the world, and it was taken down in mid-2014 through Operation Tovar.

Zip bomb A zip bomb, also known as zip of death or decompression bomb, is a malicious archive file. When uncompressed, it expands dangerously, requiring large amounts of time, disk space and memory, causing the system to crash. Usually it's a small file, only up to a few hundred kilobytes, in the form of a loop, which will continuously unpack itself until all system resources are exhausted. It's designed in order to disable the antivirus software so that a more traditional virus sent afterwards could get into the system without being detected.

Zombie A zombie computer is one connected to the Internet, that in appearance is performing normally, but can be controlled by a hacker who has remote access to it and sends commands through an open port. Zombies are mostly used to perform malicious tasks, such as spreading spam or other infected data to other computers or launch of DoS (Denial of Service) attacks, with the owner being unaware of it.

References

Abrath B, Coppens B, Volckaert S, De Sutter B (2015) Obfuscating windows dlls. In: 2015 IEEE/ACM 1st international workshop on software protection, pp 24–30. IEEE. https://doi.org/10.1109/spro.2015.13

Aho AV, Garey MR, Hwang FK (1977) Rectilinear steiner trees: efficient special-case algorithms. Networks 7(1):37–58. https://doi.org/10.1002/net.3230070104

Akl SG, Taylor PD (1983) Cryptographic solution to a problem of access control in a hierarchy. ACM Trans Comput Syst 1(3):239–248

Apon D, Huang Y, Katz J, Malozemoff AJ (2014) Implementing cryptographic program obfuscation. IACR Cryptol ePrint Arch

Arapinis M, Bursuc S, Ryan M (2013) Privacy-supporting cloud computing by in-browser key translation. J Comput Secur 21(6):847–880. https://doi.org/10.3233/JCS-130489

Arboit G (2002) A method for watermarking java programs via opaque predicates. In: The Fifth International Conference on Electronic Commerce Research

Atallah, MJ, Frikken KB, Blanton M (2005) Dynamic and efficient key management for access hierarchies. In: Proceedings of the 12th ACM conference on computer and communications security, CCS 2005, Alexandria, VA, USA, November 7–11, 2005, pp 190–202. https://doi.org/10.1145/1102120.1102147

Baker KA, Fishburn PC, Roberts FS (1972) Partial orders of dimension 2. Networks 2(1):11–28. https://doi.org/10.1002/net.3230020103

Balachandran V, Emmanuel S (2011) Software code obfuscation by hiding control flow information in stack. In: IEEE international workshop on information forensics and security. https://doi.org/10.1109/wifs.2011.6123121

Balakrishnan A, Schulze C (2005) Code obfuscation literature survey. CS701 Constr Compilers

Barak B (2016) Hopes, fears, and software obfuscation. Commun ACM. https://doi.org/10.1145/2757276

Barak B, Goldreich O, Impagliazzo R, Rudich S, Sahai A, Vadhan S, Yang K (2001) On the (im) possibility of obfuscating programs. In: Annual international cryptology conference. Springer. https://doi.org/10.1007/3-540-44647-8_1

Barr JK, Bradley BA, Hannigan BT, Alattar AM, Durst R (2012) Layered security in digital watermarking. Google Patents Patent 8, US:190,901

Barrantes EG, Ackley DH, Forrest S, Stefanović D (2005) Randomized instruction set emulation. ACM Trans Inf Syst Secur. https://doi.org/10.1145/1053283.1053286

Barrington DA (1986) Bounded-width polynomial-size branching programs recognize exactly those languages in NC1. In: STOC. https://doi.org/10.1145/12130.12131

Bhatkar S, DuVarney DC, Sekar R (2003) Address obfuscation: an efficient approach to combat a broad range of memory error exploits. In: USENIX Security Symposium

W. Amedzro St-Hilaire, *Digital Risk Governance*,
https://doi.org/10.1007/978-3-030-61386-0

Bichsel B, Raychev V, Tsankov P, Vechev M (2016) Statistical deobfuscation of android applications. In: CCS. https://doi.org/10.1145/2976749.2978422

Blundo C, Cimato S, Vimercati SDC, Santis AD, Foresti S, Paraboschi S, Samarati P (2010) Managing key hierarchies for access control enforcement: heuristic approaches. Comput Secur 29(5):533–547. https://doi.org/10.1016/j.cose.2009.12.006

Bohannon D, Holmes L (2017) Revoke-obfuscation: powerShell obfuscation detection using science. BlackHat

Cappaert J, Preneel B (2010) A general model for hiding control flow. In: ACM Workshop on Digital Rights Management. https://doi.org/10.1145/1866870.1866877

Chan J-T, Yang W (2004) Advanced obfuscation techniques for java bytecode. J Syst Softw. https://doi.org/10.1016/s0164-1212(02)00066-3

Chen H, Yuan L, Wu X, Zang B, Huang B, Yew P-C (2009) Control flow obfuscation with information flow tracking. In: The 42nd annual IEEE/ACM international symposium on microarchitecture. https://doi.org/10.1145/1669112.1669162

Cheng X, Lin Y, Gao D, Jia C (2019) Dynopvm: Vm-based software obfuscation with dynamic opcode mapping. In: International conference on applied cryptography and network security. Springer. https://doi.org/10.1007/978-3-030-21568-2_8

Chow S, Gu Y, Johnson H, Zakharov VA (2001) An approach to the obfuscation of control-flow of sequential computer programs. In: Information security. Springer. https://doi.org/10.1007/3-540-45439-x_10

Chow S, Eisen P, Johnson H, Van Oorschot PC (2002a) White-box cryptography and an AES implementation. In: International workshop on selected areas in cryptography. Springer. https://doi.org/10.1007/3-540-36492-7_17

Chow S, Eisen P, Johnson H, Van Oorschot PC (2002b) A white-box DES implementation for DRM applications. In: ACM workshop on digital rights management. https://doi.org/10.1007/978-3-540-44993-5_1

Collberg C, Thomborson C, Low D (1997) A taxonomy of obfuscating transformations, Technical report. The University of Auckland

Collberg C, Thomborson C, Low D (1998a) Manufacturing cheap, resilient, and stealthy opaque constructs. In: POPL. https://doi.org/10.1145/268946.268962

Collberg C, Thomborson C, Low D (1998b) Breaking abstractions and unstructuring data structures. In: IEEE international conference on computer languages. https://doi.org/10.1109/iccl.1998.674154

Collberg C, Davidson J, Giacobazzi R, Gu YX, Herzberg A, Wang F-Y (2011) Toward digital asset protection. IEEE Intell. Syst. https://doi.org/10.1109/mis.2011.106

Crane S, Homescu A, Brunthaler S, Larsen P, Franz M (2015a) Thwarting cache side-channel attacks through dynamic software diversity. In: NDSS. https://doi.org/10.14722/ndss.2015.23264

Crane SJ, Volckaert S, Schuster F, Liebchen C, Larsen P, Davi L, Sadeghi A-R, Holz T, De Sutter B, Franz M (2015b) It's a TRaP: table randomization and protection against function-reuse attacks. In: CCS. https://doi.org/10.1145/2810103.2813682

Dalla Preda M, Maggi F (2017) Testing android malware detectors against code obfuscation: a systematization of knowledge and unified methodology. J Comput Virol Hack Tech. https://doi.org/10.1007/s11416-016-0282-2

DexGuard (2018). https://www.guardsquare.com/dexguard. Accessed Aug 2018

DexProtector (2018). https://dexprotector.com/. Accessed Aug 2018

di Vimercati SDC, Foresti S, Jajodia S, Paraboschi S, Samarati P (2007) Over-encryption: management of access control evolution on outsourced data. In: Proceedings of the 33rd International Conference on Very Large Data Bases, University of Vienna, Austria, September 23–27, pp 123–134. http://www.vldb.org/conf/2007/papers/research/p123-decapitani.pdf

di Vimercati SDC, Foresti S, Samarati P (2008) Recent advances in access control. In: Handbook of database security - applications and trends, pp 1–26. https://doi.org/10.1007/978-0-387-48533-1_1

Dolan S (2013) mov is Turing-complete

Dolz D, Parra G (2008) Using exception handling to build opaque predicates in intermediate code obfuscation techniques. J Comput Sci Technol

Domas C (2015) The movfuscator: Turning 'move' into a soul-crushing RE nightmare. REcon

Drape S et al (2004) Obfuscation of abstract data types. Citeseer

Drape S et al (2009) Intellectual property protection using obfuscation. SAS

Ertaul L, Venkatesh S (2004) Jhide-a tool kit for code obfuscation. In: IASTED Conf. on Software Engineering and Applications

Ertaul L, Venkatesh S (2005) Novel obfuscation algorithms for software security. In: International conference on software engineering research and practice. Citeseer

FIPS 19 (2001) Advanced encryption standard. NIST. https://doi.org/10.6028/nist.fips.197

FIPS 46 (1999) The data encryption standard. NIST

Foket C, De Sutter B, Coppens B, De Bosschere K (2012) A novel obfuscation: class hierarchy flattening. In: International symposium on foundations and practice of security. Springer. https://doi.org/10.1007/978-3-642-37119-6_13

Forrest S, Somayaji A, Ackley DH (1997) Building diverse computer systems. In: The 6th IEEE workshop on hot topics in operating systems. https://doi.org/10.1109/hotos.1997.595185

Fukushima K, Tabata T, Sakurai K (2003) Evaluation of obfuscation scheme focusing on calling relationships of fields and methods in methods. Commun Netw Inf Secur

Fukushima K, Kiyomoto S, Tanaka T, Sakurai K (2008) Analysis of program obfuscation schemes with variable encoding technique. Trans Fundam Electron IEICE Commun Comput Sci. https://doi.org/10.1093/ietfec/e91-a.1.316

Garg S, Gentry C, Halevi S (2013a) Candidate multilinear maps from ideal lattices. In: Annual international conference on the theory and applications of cryptographic techniques. Springer. https://doi.org/10.1007/978-3-642-38348-9_1

Garg S, Gentry C, Halevi S, Raykova M, Sahai A, Waters B (2013b) Candidate indistinguishability obfuscation and functional encryption for all circuits. In: Proceedings of the 2013 IEEE 54th Annual Symposium on Foundations of Computer Science (FOCS). IEEE. https://doi.org/10.1109/focs.2013.13

Garg S, Gentry C, Halevi S, Raykova M, Sahai A, Waters B (2013c) Candidate indistinguishability obfuscation and functional encryption for all circuits (full version). In: Cryptology ePrint archive. https://doi.org/10.1109/focs.2013.13

Ge J, Chaudhuri S, Tyagi A (2005) Control flow based obfuscation. In: ACM Workshop on Digital Rights Management. https://doi.org/10.1145/1102546.1102561

Gonzalez C, Liñan E (2019) A software engineering methodology for developing secure obfuscated software. In: Future of information and communication conference. Springer. https://doi.org/10.1007/978-3-030-12385-7_72

Harrison WA, Magel KI (1981) A complexity measure based on nesting level. ACM SIGPLAN Not. https://doi.org/10.1145/947825.947829

Hassen HR, Lounes E (2017) A key management scheme evaluation using markov processes. Int J Inf Secur 16(3):271–280

Horváth, M, Buttyán L (2016) The birth of cryptographic obfuscation-a survey

Hosseinzadeh S, Rauti S, Laurén S, Mäkelä J-M, Holvitie J, Hyrynsalmi S, Leppänen V (2018) Diversification and obfuscation techniques for software security: a systematic literature review. Inf Softw Technol. https://doi.org/10.1016/j.infsof.2018.07.007

Hwang FK, Richards DS (1992) Steiner tree problems. Networks 22(1):55–89. https://doi.org/10.1002/net.3230220105

Information Assurance Technical Framework (IATF) (2002) Release 3.1. http://www.dtic.mil/docs/citations/ADA606355. Accessed Aug 2018

Junod P, Rinaldini J, Wehrli J, Michielin J (2015) Obfuscator-LLVM: software protection for the masses. https://doi.org/10.1109/spro.2015.10

Kilian J (1988) Founding cryptography on oblivious transfer. In: STOC. https://doi.org/10.1145/62212.62215

Kovacheva A (2013) Efficient code obfuscation for android. In: International conference on advances in information technology. Springer. https://doi.org/10.1007/978-3-319-03783-7_10

Kuang K, Tang Z, Gong X, Fang D, Chen X, Wang Z (2018) Enhance virtual-machine-based code obfuscation security through dynamic bytecode scheduling. Comput Secur. https://doi.org/10.1016/j.cose.2018.01.008

Kumar N, Mathuria A, Das ML (2015) Comparing the efficiency of key management hierarchies for access control in cloud. In: Security in computing and communications - third international symposium, SSCC 2015, Kochi, India, August 10–13, 2015. Proceedings, pp 36–44. Springer. https://doi.org/10.1007/978-3-319-22915-7_4

Kuzurin N, Shokurov A, Varnovsky N, Zakharov V (2007) On the concept of software obfuscation in computer security. In: Information security. Springer. https://doi.org/10.1007/978-3-540-75496-1_19

Landi W, Ryder BG (1991) Pointer-induced aliasing: a problem classification. In: POPL. https://doi.org/10.1145/99583.99599

Larsen P, Homescu A, Brunthaler S, Franz M (2014) Sok: automated software diversity. In: IEEE Symposium on Security and Privacy. https://doi.org/10.1109/sp.2014.25

László T, Kiss A (2009) Obfuscating c++ programs via control flow flattening. Annales Universitatis Scientarum Budapestinensis de Rolando Eötvös Nominatae, Sectio Computatorica

Lattner C, Adve V (2004) Llvm: a compilation framework for lifelong program analysis & transformation In: IEEE International Symposium on Code Generation and Optimization. https://doi.org/10.1109/cgo.2004.1281665

Lewi K, Malozemoff AJ, Apon D, Carmer B, Foltzer A, Wagner D, Archer DW, Boneh D, Katz J, Raykova M (2016) 5gen: a framework for prototyping applications using multilinear maps and matrix branching programs In: CCS. https://doi.org/10.1145/2976749.2978314

Lin Z, Riley RD, Xu D (2009) Polymorphing software by randomizing data structure layout. In: Detection of intrusions and malware, and vulnerability assessment. Springer. https://doi.org/10.1007/978-3-642-02918-9_7

Linn C, Debray S (2003) Obfuscation of executable code to improve resistance to static disassembly. In: CCS. https://doi.org/10.1145/948109.948149

Low D (1998) Protecting java code via code obfuscation. Crossroads. https://doi.org/10.1145/332084.332092

Majumdar A, Thomborson C (2006) Manufacturing opaque predicates in distributed systems for code obfuscation. In: The 29th Australasian computer science conference. Australian computer society

Majumdar A, Thomborson C, Drape S (2006) A survey of control-flow obfuscations. In: Information systems security. Springer. https://doi.org/10.1007/11961635_26

Marcelli A, Sanchez E, Squillerò G, Jamal MU, Imtiaz A, Machetti S, Mangani F, Monti P, Pola D, Salvato A, et al (2018) Defeating hardware trojan in microprocessor cores through software obfuscation. In: The 19th Latin-American test symposium. IEEE. https://doi.org/10.1109/latw.2018.8349680

Martín A, Menéndez HD, Camacho D (2017) MOCDroid: multi-objective evolutionary classifier for Android malware detection. Softw Comput. https://doi.org/10.1007/s00500-016-2283-y

McCabe TJ (1976) A complexity measure. IEEE Trans Softw Eng

Moser A, Kruegel C, Kirda E (2007) Limits of static analysis for malware detection. In: ACSAC. IEEE. https://doi.org/10.1109/acsac.2007.21

Norouzi M, Souri A, Samad Zamini M (2016) A data mining classification approach for behavioral malware detection. J Comput Netw Commun. https://doi.org/10.1155/2016/8069672

Ogiso T, Sakabe Y, Soshi M, Miyaji A (2003) Software obfuscation on a theoretical basis and its implementation. Trans Fundam Electron IEICE Commun Comput Sci

Palsberg J, Krishnaswamy S, Kwon M, Ma D, Shao Q, Zhang Y (2000) Experience with software watermarking. In: ACSAC. https://doi.org/10.1109/acsac.2000.898885

Pawlowski A, Contag M, Holz T (2016) Probfuscation: an obfuscation approach using probabilistic control flows. In: International conference on detection of intrusions and malware, and vulnerability assessment. Springer. https://doi.org/10.1007/978-3-319-40667-1_9
Popov IV, Debray SK, Andrews GR (2007) Binary obfuscation using signals. In: Usenix Security
ProGuard (2016). http://developer.android.com/tools/help/proguard.html. Accessed Aug 2018
Protsenko M, Muller T (2013) Pandora applies non-deterministic obfuscation randomly to android. In: The 8th international conference on malicious and unwanted software. IEEE. https://doi.org/10.1109/malware.2013.6703686
Raykova M, Zhao H, Bellovin SM (2012) Privacy enhanced access control for outsourced data sharing. In: Financial cryptography and data security - 16th international conference, FC 2012, Kralendijk, Bonaire, Februray 27–March 2, 2012, Revised Selected Papers, pp 223–238. Springer. https://doi.org/10.1007/978-3-642-32946-3_17
Rescorla E (2001) SSL and TLS: designing and building secure systems. Addison-Wesley, Reading
Rolles R (2009) Unpacking virtualization obfuscators. In: 3rd USENIX workshop on offensive technologies. WOOT
Rothvoß T (2011) Directed steiner tree and the lasserre hierarchy. CoRR abs/1111.5473. http://arxiv.org/abs/1111.54731111.5473
Roundy KA, Miller BP (2012) Binary-code obfuscations in prevalent packer tools. ACM Comput Surv. https://doi.org/10.1145/2522968.2522972
Sandhu RS, Samarati P (1994) Access control: principle and practice. Commun Mag 32(9):40–48. https://doi.org/10.1109/35.312842
Schrittwieser S, Katzenbeisser S (2011) Code obfuscation against static and dynamic reverse engineering. In: Information hiding. Springer. https://doi.org/10.1007/978-3-642-24178-9_19
Schrittwieser S, Katzenbeisser S, Kinder J, Merzdovnik G, Weippl E (2016) Protecting software through obfuscation: can it keep pace with progress in code analysis? ACM Comput Surv. https://doi.org/10.1145/2886012
Selman B, Mitchell DG, Levesque HJ (1996) Generating hard satisfiability problems. Artif Intell. https://doi.org/10.1016/0004-3702(95)00045-3
Sharif MI, Lanzi A, Giffin JT, Lee W (2008) Impeding malware analysis using conditional code obfuscation. In: NDSS
Simonyi C (1999) Hungarian notation. MSDN Libr
Sosonkin M, Naumovich G, Memon N (2003) Obfuscation of design intent in object-oriented applications. In: ACM workshop on digital rights management. https://doi.org/10.1145/947380.947399
Souri A, Hosseini R (2018) A state-of-the-art survey of malware detection approaches using data mining techniques. Human-centric Comput Inf Sci. https://doi.org/10.1186/s13673-018-0125-x
Suchý O (2016) On directed steiner trees with multiple roots In: Graph-Theoretic Concepts in Computer Science - 42nd International Workshop, WG 2016, Istanbul, Turkey, June 22–24, 2016, Revised Selected Papers, pp 257–268. https://doi.org/10.1007/978-3-662-53536-3_22
Tiella R, Ceccato M (2017) Automatic generation of opaque constants based on the k-clique problem for resilient data obfuscation. In: The 24th international conference on software analysis, evolution and reengineering. IEEE. https://doi.org/10.1109/saner.2017.7884620
Udupa SK, Debray SK, Madou M (2005) Deobfuscation: Reverse engineering obfuscated code in: The 12th IEEE working conference on reverse engineering. https://doi.org/10.1109/wcre.2005.13
Vimercati SDC, Foresti S, Jajodia S, Livraga G, Paraboschi S, Samarati P (2013) Enforcing dynamic write privileges in data outsourcing. Comput Secur 39:47–63
Wang C, Hill J, Knight J, Davidson J (2000) Software tamper resistance: obstructing static analysis of programs, Technical report. University of Virginia
Wang C, Davidson J, Hill J, Knight J (2001) Protection of software-based survivability mechanisms. In: DSN. https://doi.org/10.21236/ada466288

Wang W, Li Z, Owens R, Bhargava BK (2009) Secure and efficient access to outsourced data. In: Proceedings of the First ACM Cloud Computing Security Workshop, CCSW 2009, Chicago, IL, USA, November 13, 2009, pp 55–66. https://doi.org/10.1145/1655008.1655016

Wang Z, Ming J, Jia C, Gao D (2011) Linear obfuscation to combat symbolic execution. In: ESORICS. Springer. https://doi.org/10.1007/978-3-642-23822-2_12

Wang P, Wang S, Ming J, Jiang Y, Wu D (2016) Translingual obfuscation. https://doi.org/10.1109/eurosp.2016.21

Wang P, Bao Q, Wang L, Wang S, Chen Z, Wei T, Wu D (2018) Software protection on the go: a large-scale empirical study on mobile app obfuscation. In: ICSE. https://doi.org/10.1145/3180155.3180169

Wermke D, Huaman N, Acar Y, Reaves B, Traynor P, Fahl S (2018) A large scale investigation of obfuscation use in google play. arXiv preprint arXiv:1801.02742. https://doi.org/10.1145/3274694.3274726

Wroblewski G (2002) General method of program code obfuscation, PhD thesis. Wroclaw University of Technology

Xin Z, Chen H, Han H, Mao B, Xie L (2010) Misleading malware similarities analysis by automatic data structure obfuscation. In: Information security. Springer. https://doi.org/10.1007/978-3-642-18178-8_16

Xu H, Zhou Y, Lyu MR (2016) N-version obfuscation In: ACM International Workshop on Cyber-Physical System Security. https://doi.org/10.1145/2899015.2899026

Xu D, Ming J, Fu Y, Wu D (2018a) Vmhunt: a verifiable approach to partially-virtualized binary code simplification. In: Proceedings of the 2018 ACM SIGSAC Conference on Computer and Communications Security. https://doi.org/10.1145/3243734.3243827

Xu H, Su Y, Zhao Z, Zhou Y, Lyu MR, King I (2018b) Deepobfuscation: securing the structure of convolutional neural networks via knowledge distillation. arXiv preprint arXiv:1806.10313

Yildiz M, Abawajy J, Ercan T, Bernoth A (2009) A layered security approach for cloud computing infrastructure. In: International symposium on pervasive systems, algorithms, and networks. IEEE. https://doi.org/10.1109/i-span.2009.157

You I, Yim K (2010) Malware obfuscation techniques: a brief survey. In: International conference on broadband, Wireless Computing, Communication and Applications. https://doi.org/10.1109/bwcca.2010.85

Zhang X, He F, Zuo W (2010) Theory and practice of program obfuscation. INTECH Open Access Publisher. https://doi.org/10.5772/9632

Zhu WF (2007) Concepts and techniques in software watermarking and obfuscation, PhD thesis. ResearchSpace, Auckland

Zhu W, Thomborson C (2005) A provable scheme for homomorphic obfuscation in software security. In: The IASTED International Conference on Communication, Network and Information Security

Zhu W, Thomborson C, Wang F-Y (2006) Applications of homomorphic functions to software obfuscation. In: Intelligence and security informatics. Springer. https://doi.org/10.1007/11734628_18

Zimmerman J (2015) How to obfuscate programs directly. In: Annual international conference on the theory and applications of cryptographic techniques. Springer. https://doi.org/10.1007/978-3-662-46803-6_15

The manufacturer's authorised representative in the EU is Springer Nature Customer Service Centre GmbH, Europaplatz 3, 69115 Heidelberg, Germany. If you have any concerns regarding our products, please contact ProductSafety@springernature.com

Printed and bound by CPI Group (UK) Ltd, Croydon, CR0 4YY
28/09/2026
02224088-0008